INDULGE
100 PERFECT DESSERTS

For my family: Mum, Dad, Vincent and Kirsten,
without whom my life would be incomplete.
Stephen Clark, for many years of love and
tolerance. Pam Bullockflint, my godmother,
for being an inspiration.

INDULGE

100 PERFECT DESSERTS

CLAIRE CLARK

HEAD PASTRY CHEF AT
THE FRENCH LAUNDRY

FOREWORD
THOMAS KELLER

Published in Canada and the United States in 2007 by
Whitecap Books Ltd.

For more information, contact:
Whitecap Books Ltd.
351 Lynn Avenue, North Vancouver
British Columbia, Canada V7J 2C4.
Visit our website at **www.whitecap.ca**.

First published in Great Britain in 2007 by
Absolute Press, Scarborough House
29 James Street West, Bath BA1 2BT, England
Phone 44 (0) 1225 316013 / Fax 44 (0) 1225 445836
E-mail info@absolutepress.co.uk
Website www.absolutepress.co.uk

Publisher Jon Croft
Commissioning Editor Meg Avent
Designer Matt Inwood
Publishing Assistant Meg Devenish
Editor Jane Middleton
Photographer Jean Cazals
Props Stylist Sue Rowlands
All food styling Claire Clark

ISBN 10: 1-55285-909-6
ISBN 13: 978-1-55285-909-4

**Library and Archives Canada Cataloguing
in Publication**
Clark, Claire
  Indulge : 100 perfect desserts / Claire Clark.
Includes index.
ISBN 978-1-55285-909-4

  1. Desserts. I. Title.
TX773.C349 2007   641.8'6
C2007-904551-0

A note about the text
This book was set using Helvetica Neue, Sabon MT
and Blair. Helvetica was designed in 1957 by Max
Miedinger of the Swiss-based Haas foundry. In the
early 1980s, Linotype redrew the entire Helvetica
family. The result was Helvetica Neue. Sabon was
designed by Jan Tschichold in 1964. The roman design
is based on type by Claude Garamond, whereas the
italic design is based on types by Robert Granjon.
Blair was designed in 1997 by Jim Spiece, reflecting
some of the basic forms of early twentieth-century
sans-serif typefaces.

Printed and bound by 1010 Printing International

CONTENTS

6   FOREWORD
     BY THOMAS KELLER
8   INTRODUCTION
9   NOTES FOR AMERICAN
     READERS

10   BISCUITS AND COOKIES
30   CAKES
56   PASTRY
96   MERINGUES
116 CUSTARDS AND CREAMS
134 DESSERTS, MOUSSES
      AND JELLIES
172 PUDDINGS
190 ICES
210 PETITS FOURS

234 SUPPLIERS
236 INDEX
239 ACKNOWLEDGEMENTS

FOREWORD

Claire and I met at my hotel lobby one afternoon. She had been hoping to introduce herself for a pastry chef position we had recently posted in the papers. I was so struck by her personality and energy that I made it a point to visit her restaurant that evening and sample her desserts at the Wolseley, where she was working at the time. Needless to say, I left very impressed by the quality and breadth of her execution and I immediately invited her to join us at The French Laundry. It remains one of my best-ever decisions!

I was concerned about Claire coming to our small quiet town of Yountville after having worked all her life in a bustling city. Her move to the Napa Valley uprooted her from all she had known and would separate her from her tightly knit family and friends. Her challenges were compounded by her inexperience of working with American products, having to convert all her recipes, adapting to our changing seasons and, more importantly, understanding our philosophy about desserts. To say that it was an adjustment for her is an understatement. I am really proud to say that through hard work and determination she has earned the respect of her peers not just in her native country, but all over the world. She has also come to embrace her new surroundings and now considers herself a Yountville local.

No one would know from her modest demeanor that Claire has built a distinguished career for herself. Prior to coming to The French Laundry, Claire was named 'Best Pastry Chef' by *Restaurant* magazine while working at the Wolseley. Even more significantly, she is a recipient of the 'Meilleur Ouvrier de Grande Bretagne' award, also known as the MOGB – the highest honour given to a craftsperson in Great Britain on the grounds of professional excellence. Her accomplishments are extraordinary but she will be the first to shyly change the subject and focus the limelight elsewhere.

Claire's greatest strength is her ability to lead and teach her staff, so that there is always a continuous evolution to their work and an aspiration to reach higher standards. The French Laundry has continued to grow, mature and receive more recognition through the years – a large part of the credit is due to Claire and her staff in the pastry department. As a pastry chef, Claire is as exacting as they come. The quality of her execution is always beautiful and spot on; her talent in chocolate production and pulled sugars is exceptional. Her expertise touches on all the dish's components, so the end result is a deceptively simple, elegant dessert matched with a flavour profile that is both complex and satisfying. Claire's constant striving for perfection brings her as close to it as can possibly be.

People often ask me what is my favourite dessert that she makes. Everything I have had so far has been amazing, but I must say that I cannot get enough of her shortbread recipe! It is something I always look forward to after travelling. Her shortbread is so beloved that it has become a signature dessert at both The French Laundry and Bouchon Bakery. I highly recommend that you take the time to make this at home whenever you can.

It is with tremendous pride, gratitude and pleasure that I introduce you to Claire Clark – an integral member of The French Laundry family. Each page within this book is a testament to her passion and dedication to her craft. Claire has been creating wonderful dining memories for our restaurant guests ever since she first started working with us. Now it is your turn to be warmly welcomed into her world of delicious and unforgettable desserts.

Thomas A. Keller
The French Laundry, Yountville
July 2007

INTRODUCTION

I love to bake. I find baking immensely rewarding and comforting: it is an indulgent pleasure that brings a warmth and rosiness and a sense of peace and contentment.

I have wonderfully fond memories of baking with my mother as a child. I would sit, or sometimes stand precariously, on a rickety wooden chair at our large wooden kitchen table which was positioned right in the middle of the room. We would mix and roll, spoon and chop in a gentle and meandering way. Food was never hurried or hastily prepared; baking was a labour of love, something to be enjoyed and savoured.

I grew up in a large old Victorian Vicarage that cost too much to heat and the only room that was warm was the kitchen, the heat provided by a solid fuel stove – an ancient cast-iron Aga. The kitchen was the heart and hub of our home. I would rush through the long draughty uncarpeted corridors, arriving at the kitchen with a crash and on flinging open the door would be met with cries of, 'Close the door Claire, you'll let the heat out!'. Once the door was open, aromas of vanilla and spice or caramel and chocolate would slap you in the face, along with a rush of welcome warmth. Cooling wires were placed in the centre of the kitchen table laden with baking trays full of the sweet temptations of the day. The table was often multi-functional; on school nights my mother would bake at one end of the table and my brother and I would sit at the other doing our homework, the trays of baked goodies looking like trophies enticing us to hurry up and finish our studies while they were still warm.

Perhaps at this point I should tell briefly the story of how someone so immersed in the quintessential English way of life should come to find herself cooking in one of the world's top three restaurants, just outside San Francisco in the American state of California.

How does a woman get into and survive the environment of a Michelin-starred restaurant, an environment that is so often saturated with male egotism? Well, more often than not it starts as a baptism of fire. As a female you are always going to be one of the few girls in the brigade. Many female chefs have a fantastic career when they are young, they then marry and have families and the demanding world of the restaurant kitchen is a thing of the past, left far behind.

My first job was as a grill chef, and at just 17 and straight out of college it was a severe shock to the system of this impressionable young girl. My father was a country parson and so the guys were quick to nickname me 'Vicar's Knickers'. It seemed that, regardless of your sex, everyone slapped each other on the bottom and on the back and generally got friendly in a physical way. I was left wondering if this was something that males did to bond, or was it just the way of crazy chefs? In most other professions you would have been sent straight to Human Resources if you called the new girl Vicar's Knickers and slapped her on the bum in her first week. On one occasion, upon meeting a new chef for the first time, he took his knife and slashed all the buttons off my chef's coat. A handshake would have done – but then chefs do those sorts of things!

Once the initial shock of the swear words contained within almost every sentence, and the slaps on the bottom and back had worn off, I was left wondering if catering was really going to be the right profession for me. I thought long and hard, took a deep breath, looked deep inside, and decided it was, and that to properly fit in I would need to adapt quickly to my surroundings. I would have to do as the men did – I would have to work extremely hard and expect no special treatment just because I was a woman, and, most importantly, 'give as good as I got'. When I thought I was right, I stood up for myself and made myself heard. I proved myself by showing that I could cook as well as them and showed that I wanted to be one of them. Life is stressful in the kitchen, tempers are lost, names are called, but at the end of a very long day it is all forgotten and we are still 'the Team' – all striving for the same thing: excellence.

Of course, there were times in those early days when it all seemed too much and I ended up in the changing rooms having a good cry. I always tell the girls I work with now that if you are going to cry, go do it in private, wash your face and come back with a clear positive perspective on why and what you want from your work and why you are where you are. Develop a defiant attitude and get on with being part of the kitchen.

My career has spanned three incredible decades, through positions at The Ritz Hotel, The Intercontinental at Hyde Park Corner, a teaching job at Le Cordon Bleu, Head Pastry Chef at Sir Terence Conran's Bluebird Restaurant on the Kings Road, then on to Claridges and a brief spell planning and setting up the Pastry Department at The House of Commons (with other stops in between). Prior to moving to California I helped open the Wolseley, the famous and impossibly glamorous restaurant on Piccadilly, with Chris Galvin, now of the Michelin-starred Galvin's Bistrot de Luxe in Baker Street.

It was at the Wolseley that I first met Thomas Keller, the most amazing and incredible chef I have ever come across. His passion and personality just blew me away and I knew immediately that I had to work for him in his restaurant in California. I quickly learnt that he expects nothing less than excellence 24/7 in everything you do: he is the most exceptional chef, a creative genius and a true inspiration, quite simply one of the most wonderful and amazing people I know.

In order to succeed and then excel as a woman you have to really want to be in the kitchen with the boys, sometimes suffering, sometimes elated, but always driven by the desire to be the best and to be exceptional in all that you do. That is very much the philosophy of the 'The French Laundry' – every person there, from the dish washer to the gardener to the food runner to myself, is driven by the same desire and passion. And we are all at The French Laundry because we are the best. It is the best family in the world.

As much as I love The French Laundry, nothing will come between me and my first love – baking. For me, baking is a way to relax and to have fun. It does not have to be difficult or a trial; with a little forward planning it can be delightful and rewarding. Just treat it like a day at the Spa and it will reward you many times over. Pamper yourself, allow yourself the whole day to bake the most sumptuous, decadent, rich, luxurious cake you have ever made, and then invite your friends over to marvel at your magnificent masterpiece. Even better, cook with your friends or family and make it fun.

Successful baking is easier than you think – really, it is. Break your recipe down into steps and treat each step like a building block with which to construct your masterpiece. Take your time over each individual step.

Pay attention to small detail. Weighing ingredients correctly is vital to success. Precision and accuracy in all that you do will ensure good results. Don't cut corners or rush tasks – there are no compromises in baking.

Baking is essentially about a few core ingredients – butter, sugar, flour, eggs, cream, milk, nuts, chocolate, fruit and vanilla – so be sure to select the best. The quality of the ingredients will inevitably affect the overall taste and flavour of the finished dessert. How your ingredients are amalgamated to form various cakes, doughs, biscuits, pastes and petit fours is, of course, a skill, but one that can be learnt if you have the right information to hand. The *Secrets of Success* sections in this book provide some key information to help you with any pastry wizardry that might have previously put you off baking. Some recipes have as little as three or four ingredients and the results are still mouthwatering.

The recipes in *Indulge* are my favourites, taken from my last 25 years as a pastry cook, some from my childhood passed down from family, some from 5-star hotels and one-, two- and three-star Michelin restaurants. Some recipes are as simple as the shortbread, which we make on a daily basis at The French Laundry. Others are rather more complicated but absolutely possible and completely wonderful when cooked correctly. All of them are easily achieved if you follow the guidelines and allow yourself enough time. Even if the finished result does not look quite as exquisite as the photograph that accompanies the recipe, just remember that practice makes perfect, and it is still going to taste better than a commercially-made, E-number-laden offering from your local supermarket.

Dessert is to be enjoyed. Everyone loves to be a little naughty once in a while, and allow themselves a little taste of heaven in eating and enjoying a calorie-laden frivolity. So go on: live a little and enjoy baking. Indulge yourself.

Claire Clark
The French Laundry, Yountville
July 2007

NOTES FOR NORTH AMERICAN READERS

The quantities in this book are listed in metric and Imperial measures but not in cups. That is because baking is about precision and accuracy, and cups as a measurement give neither. The cup system is essentially a way of measuring liquid volume, not dry weight, and there is no reliable method of converting from one to the other. Furthermore, cup measures will alter from one person to another, depending on how accurately they level the contents.

As successful baking depends on exact measures, I recommend you invest in some weighing scales before starting to cook from this book. They are not expensive and it could be one of the best investments of your life, allowing you to produce the most amazing desserts and pastries consistently time after time.

GLOSSARY

Opposite are the American terms for some of the ingredients and equipment used in this book.

baking parchment = parchment paper
baking sheet = cookie sheet
baking tin = baking pan
bicarbonate of soda = baking soda
black cherries = dark sweet cherries
black treacle = use molasses
Bramley apples = use Golden Delicious
cake tin = cake pan
candied peel = confited peel
caster sugar = superfine sugar
cling film = plastic wrap
cocktail stick = wooden toothpick
cornflour = cornstarch
dark chocolate = semisweet chocolate
demerara sugar = brown granulated sugar
desiccated coconut = shredded coconut
digestive biscuits = use graham crackers
double cream = heavy cream
flaked almonds = slivered almonds
flan case = tart shell
glacé cherries = candied cherries
ground almonds = almond flour
icing sugar = powdered sugar
liquid glucose = glucose syrup
loaf tin = loaf pan
marzipan = almond paste
muscovado sugar = dark brown sugar
muslin = cheesecloth
nibbed sugar = pearl sugar
palette knife = metal spatula
piping bag (with piping nozzle) = pastry bag (with piping tip)
plain flour = all-purpose flour
roasting tin = roasting pan
sea salt = coarse salt
self-raising flour = self-rising flour
sieve = strainer
spray oil = spray grease
strong white flour = bread flour
sugar thermometer = candy thermometer
sultanas = golden raisins
Swiss roll tin = jelly roll pan
tart tin = tart pan
vanilla pod = vanilla bean
wholemeal flour = whole wheat flour

BISCUITS
AND COOKIES

SHORTBREAD

225g/8oz plain flour
75g/2³/₄oz caster sugar
1 vanilla pod
150g/5¹/₂oz unsalted butter, at
   room temperature
50g/1³/₄oz granulated sugar, for
   dusting

**MAKES
15 BISCUITS**

This Scottish favourite has a wonderful buttery taste and firm but light crumb – an irresistible combination. If you happen to be in Yountville, California, at approximately 2pm you will see members of my pastry team from the French Laundry kitchen briskly walking up the road on their way to Bouchon Bakery, where their daily routine of mixing, rolling, cutting, baking and bagging 9 kilos of shortbread is about to begin. This winner of a recipe is my mother's. She is amazed that even to this day I choose to use her recipe over any others.

Preheat the oven to 180°C/350°F/Gas Mark 4. Sift the flour into a large mixing bowl and add the caster sugar. Using a sharp knife, slit the vanilla pod open lengthways and scrape out the seeds with the tip of the knife. Add the seeds to the bowl, along with the butter. Using your fingertips, rub the butter into the dry ingredients. As the mixture begins to come together, use your hand to help it form a dough (alternatively, you could use an electric mixer with the paddle attachment on a low speed to make the dough).

Shape the dough into a ball and flatten it slightly. Roll out on a lightly floured surface to about 1cm/¹/₂ inch thick. Cut into 15 oblongs and place them on a baking sheet lined with baking parchment.

Bake for 15 minutes, then turn the baking sheet around and continue baking for 10 minutes, until the shortbread is golden brown. Remove from the oven and dust with an even coating of granulated sugar. Leave on the baking sheet to cool.

Claire's Notes
• Cutting the biscuits into oblongs (or squares) will give you a higher yield and prevent wastage and unnecessary trimmings.
• For a perfectly even finish, use a tea strainer to dust the biscuits with sugar when they come out of the oven.

OATMEAL, PECAN AND RAISIN COOKIES

110g/3³/₄oz soft dark brown sugar
200g/7oz caster sugar
225g/8oz rolled oats
75g/2³/₄oz dried cherries
75g/2³/₄oz raisins
200g/7oz pecan nuts, chopped
1 capful of vanilla extract
225g/8oz unsalted butter
1 medium egg, lightly beaten
225g/8oz plain flour
1 teaspoon bicarbonate of soda
1 teaspoon ground cinnamon (if
  you have a spice grinder, grind
  your own)

MAKES 20

I try to kid myself that these cookies are a healthy option compared to, say, chocolate cookies, but in my heart I know they are laden with butter and sugar. But hey, there are oats, nuts and raisins too, and those are good for us. My three-year-old twin nephews, Sam and Alex, enjoy these in the afternoon with a glass of milk, and it is fun to have them in the kitchen to help with the baking. Of course the clearing up takes longer than if I had been baking alone but the pleasure is the peace and quiet when they sit down to watch children's TV with their cookies and milk.

The cookies will keep if stored in an airtight container but they are best eaten on the day they are made. If you need to make them in advance, prepare the cookie dough, put it on the lined baking sheets and store in the fridge. Bake the next day, anything up to 2 hours before you need them.

Preheat the oven to 180°C/350°F/Gas Mark 4. Mix the two sugars with the oats, dried cherries, raisins, chopped pecans and vanilla extract. Melt the butter in a small saucepan. Add the melted butter and the egg to the sugar mix and stir well to combine.

Sift the flour with the bicarbonate of soda and ground cinnamon, then sift again and add to the other ingredients. It is best to use your hand to mix the ingredients together. Pinch them together to form a workable dough. Divide the dough in half and shape 10 balls from each piece. Place 5cm/2 inches apart on baking sheets lined with baking parchment. They do spread a little, but not as much as some cookie doughs. Flatten them a little with the back of a damp spoon if you prefer them not to be so rounded.

Bake in the centre of the oven for 12–15 minutes, until golden brown. Leave on the baking sheets to cool.

Claire's Notes
• I find most ovens cook a little unevenly. Turn the baking sheets half way through cooking to help colour the cookies evenly. They can remain a little clumplike, so even cooking is important.
• Chopped semi-dried apricots are a great addition to these cookies if you are not keen on cherries, or you could mix the two.

GOOBER COOKIES

240g/8$\frac{1}{2}$oz unsalted butter, at
   room temperature
180g/6oz caster sugar
180g/6oz soft light brown sugar
1 small egg, lightly beaten
1 teaspoon vanilla extract
100g/3$\frac{1}{2}$oz crunchy peanut butter
180g/6oz plain flour
2 teaspoons bicarbonate of soda
1 teaspoon baking powder
$\frac{1}{4}$ teaspoon salt
120g/4$\frac{1}{4}$oz large rolled oats

For the filling
100g/3$\frac{1}{2}$oz salted butter
100g/3$\frac{1}{2}$oz icing sugar, sifted
250g/9oz smooth peanut butter

MAKES 15

My love affair with peanuts goes back to my childhood and days of hot buttered toast spread thick with Marmite and lashings of crunchy peanut butter. Peanuts are big here in the States. The American Peanut Board states that Americans eat an average of three pounds of peanut butter per person every year. That is an annual total of 700 million pounds of peanut butter – enough, they claim, to coat the floor of the Grand Canyon.

This recipe was given to me by an American colleague. No names mentioned for fear of passing on trade secrets but you know who you are, 'Mosko', and I have to say I love it. The cookies have a lovely balance of crunchiness, lightness and extreme peanut pleasure, since there's a double hit from the cookies themselves and from the smooth peanut butter filling that sandwiches them together. Best of all, the recipe is simple and foolproof – child's play in fact.

Preheat the oven to 170°C/325°F/Gas Mark 3. Cream the butter with both the sugars until pale and fluffy. Mix in the egg a little at a time and continue to cream the mixture until it is smooth. Stir in the vanilla extract and peanut butter until thoroughly combined.

Sift the flour, bicarbonate of soda, baking powder and salt together twice. Mix in the oats, then tip all the dry ingredients into the creamed mixture. Stir well to form a soft dough (if you are using an electric mixer, do this by hand, with a wooden spoon).

Scoop 30 cookies on to baking sheets lined with baking parchment, spacing them 7.5cm/3 inches apart, as they spread during baking. Bake in the centre of the oven for about 15 minutes, until golden brown and firm to the touch. Leave to cool on the baking sheets.

Meanwhile, make the peanut filling. Cream together the butter and icing sugar until pale and fluffy; if using an electric mixer, do this with the whisk attachment. Add the peanut butter and mix just enough to combine all the ingredients.

When the cookies are completely cold, pipe or spoon a generous amount of the filling on to the flat side of 15 of them, then sandwich them together in pairs with the remaining cookies. There should be enough filling for it to show between the cookies. They are best eaten on the day they are made but they can be stored in an airtight container.

Claire's Notes
• To make chocolate and peanut cookies, add 50g/1$\frac{3}{4}$ small chocolate chips to the mixture.
• The raw mixture will keep in the freezer for a week. Scoop the cookies and freeze them on the baking sheets. Once they are frozen, transfer them to a plastic container, stacked between sheets of baking parchment, and seal tightly. Make sure they are thoroughly defrosted before baking.

CHOCOLATE CHIP COOKIES

185g/6¹/₂oz plain flour
¹/₄ teaspoon bicarbonate of soda
a pinch of salt
125g/4¹/₂oz softened unsalted
 butter
165g/5³/₄oz soft dark brown sugar
¹/₂ teaspoon vanilla extract
1 medium egg, lightly beaten
225g/8oz dark chocolate (55–70
 per cent cocoa solids), chopped

MAKES 20

There are some things Americans simply do better than anyone else and making chocolate chip cookies is one of them. It's not just the ingredients, the proportions differ too, and that makes all the difference.

We make these cookies at The French Laundry for staff meals and they are really good, especially when you eat them warm. The trick is to underbake them and let them complete the cooking while they are cooling on the baking tray. This recipe came from my chef de partie, Courtney Schmidig, but it is normally Milton Able, my demi-chef, who makes them and I think he has the baking down to perfection – exactly what you would expect at The French Laundry.

Preheat the oven to 180°C/350°F/Gas Mark 4. Sift the flour, bicarbonate of soda and salt on to a piece of baking parchment, then sift again and set aside.

Cream the butter and sugar together until pale and fluffy. If doing this by hand, use a wooden spoon. Add the vanilla extract and mix well. Add the egg a little at a time, beating well between each addition. Add the dry ingredients. If doing this with an electric mixer, use a very low speed and bring the ingredients together just enough to form a soft, slightly sticky dough. Do not over work. If making by hand, incorporate the dry ingredients using your hand to bring the dough together. Gently mix in the chocolate.

Scoop out the mix on to a baking sheet lined with baking parchment, leaving at least 5cm/2 inches between each scoop. In America they use an ice cream scoop for this – a medium-sized one works well. At home I use a tablespoon and round the mixture a little in my hand before placing it on the baking sheet. Bake in the centre of the oven for 10–12 minutes, until golden brown and slightly puffed. Remove and leave to cool on the baking sheets. Although the cookies will continue to cook a little whilst cooling, they should remain soft and gooey in the centre.

Claire's Notes
• If you want a sweeter cookie for children, use milk or white chocolate chips.
• If you do not like your cookies soft in the centre, cook for 5–8 minutes longer to give a crisper texture.
• If you find the dough a little too sticky or soft to scoop without making a mess, chill it for 20–30 minutes to firm up.

FRASCATI BISCUITS

150g/5^{1}/$_{2}$oz ground almonds
10g/^{1}/$_{4}$oz plain flour
10g/^{1}/$_{4}$oz cornflour
5 large egg whites
150g/5^{1}/$_{2}$oz caster sugar
250–300g/9–10^{1}/$_{2}$oz nibbed
  almonds

To finish
300g/10^{1}/$_{2}$oz tempered dark
  chocolate for dipping (see pages
  212–213)
10–15 crystallised violets, crushed
  into small pieces

MAKES 50

There's a long story behind these biscuits from the Italian town of Frascati, involving pregnant women from the local town, who bathed in nearby Lake Nemi to improve their chances of successful childbirth. Interestingly, recent studies have confirmed notable levels of magnesium in the water, which is beneficial to pregnant mothers. Later in the same area, St Anna, who was apparently three breasted, developed quite a following. A local baker invented a biscuit in the shape of a female form with three breasts, in recognition of St Anna and the magical powers of Lake Nemi.

I have never seen the original version of the biscuit but I believe it is still produced in Frascati and neighbouring areas. I pipe mine in straight lines, so there is not much resemblance to the female form, but they still taste fantastic. They are best eaten whilst still crisp, and make a wonderful accompaniment to ice cream, panna cotta and custard dishes in general. I always dip mine in tempered chocolate and finish them with tiny pieces of crystallised violet.

Preheat the oven to 170°C/325°F/Gas Mark 3. Sift the ground almonds with both types of flour and then sift again so they are well mixed.

Put the egg whites and sugar in a large bowl and whisk with an electric beater on medium speed for 2–3 minutes, then finishing on high speed, to make a firm-peak meringue. Fold in the dry ingredients with a large metal spoon, taking extreme care not to lose any volume. Be as gentle as possible, turning the bowl as you fold in the dry ingredients.

Line a baking sheet with baking parchment and, using a piping bag fitted with a 5mm/^{1}/$_{4}$ inch plain nozzle, pipe sticks of the mixture at a slight slant about 7.5cm/3 inches in length. When you need to stop piping, bring the tip of the bag down on to the paper and press gently to cut off the mix, giving a clean, neat finish to your biscuit. Pipe them in staged rows. Next sprinkle the nibbed almonds over the biscuits so they are as evenly covered as possible.

The next step is a little tricky, so think it over before starting. You will need a clean, empty baking sheet before you start. Pick up the 2 far corners of the baking parchment, firmly grasping them in each hand. Lift the paper quickly so the excess nuts fall from around the piped biscuits on to the baking sheet. Lay the paper back down on the empty tray. The nuts should be stuck to the piped biscuits and all the excess nuts on the other tray – it's important to get rid of the excess, otherwise the frascati will not bake properly. The secret to this manoeuvre is to do it with composure and in one smooth, controlled motion rather than as a jerky, rushed operation.

Bake in the centre of the oven for 15–18 minutes, until the biscuits are golden brown and firm to the touch. Leave to cool on the baking sheet. They should be firm and crisp enough to peel away from the paper once cool.

Dip the smooth, flat underside of each biscuit in the tempered chocolate and sprinkle with the crushed crystallised violets. Leave in a cool place for the chocolate to harden. The biscuits will keep for a few days in an airtight tin but are best eaten within 48 hours.

WEDDING FINGERS

250g/9oz softened unsalted butter
195g/6³/₄oz caster sugar
1 capful of vanilla extract
310g/11oz plain flour
125g/4¹/₂oz ground almonds
125g/4¹/₂oz walnuts, finely
   chopped
icing sugar, for coating

MAKES 50

These biscuits are traditionally served at Australian weddings but also make a great addition to the biscuit tin. They are similar to a sablé biscuit, with a rich, buttery taste, but are lighter and sweeter. Children always seem to love them.

Preheat the oven to 180°C/350°F/Gas Mark 4. Lightly cream the butter, sugar and vanilla together. Sift the flour and almonds into a bowl and combine with the walnuts. Beat the dry ingredients into the butter and sugar mixture until a dough is formed, being careful not to overmix.

   Turn out the dough and shape it into a log 2.5cm/1 inch in diameter. Cut it into discs 1cm/¹/₂ inch thick. Roll each disc into a sausage shape about 12cm/5 inches long and place on a baking sheet lined with baking parchment, arranging them about 2.5cm/1 inch apart. Bake for 20–25 minutes, until golden brown. Cool slightly, then roll them in icing sugar while still warm. Leave to cool completely. These biscuits keep quite well but are at their best when fresh.

Claire's Notes
• If the dough seems soft or sticky, roll it in a little flour to form the log, then chill before shaping the fingers.
• You could substitute pecans or hazelnuts for the walnuts.

CHOCOLATE-DIPPED GINGERNUTS

230g/8¼oz softened unsalted butter
100g/3½oz soft dark brown sugar
1 medium egg
85g/3oz black treacle
250g/9oz plain flour
2 teaspoons bicarbonate of soda
½ teaspoon salt
2 teaspoons ground ginger
1 teaspoon freshly grated nutmeg
1 teaspoon ground cinnamon
caster sugar for dusting
300g/10½oz tempered dark chocolate for dipping (see pages 212–213)

MAKES ABOUT 60

I so enjoy a gingernut with my cup of tea. I often have Ed Keller, Thomas Keller's father, over for a cup of tea in the afternoon on my day off but sadly I have been barred from serving gingernuts, as he's not keen. However, I can assure you that this is a fantastic, very grown-up version of the humble biscuit, with a wonderful molasses flavour from the black treacle and dark brown sugar. I like to dip them in dark 70 per cent chocolate for that luxurious taste and decadent finish.

Cream together the butter and sugar. You are making dough, so don't over beat; just mix long enough to combine the ingredients thoroughly. Beat in the egg and then mix in the treacle.

Sift the flour, bicarbonate of soda, salt and spices together, then sift them again, 3 times in total. It is vital to make sure all the dry ingredients are well combined to eliminate pockets of bicarbonate of soda or spices. Add the sifted ingredients to the butter and sugar mixture and gently fold them in to make a dough (do this by hand if you are making the mixture in a machine). Turn the dough out on to a piece of parchment paper and, with lightly floured hands, flatten to approximately 1cm/½ inch thick. Wrap in cling film and chill for at least 2 hours.

Preheat the oven to 170°C/325°F/Gas Mark 3. Roll the dough out on a floured work surface to 5mm/¼ inch thick, keeping it in an oblong shape. Cut it into oblongs about 7.5 x 2.5cm/3 x 1 inch (or use a biscuit cutter to cut it into rounds, if you prefer) and place them on a baking sheet lined with baking parchment, spacing them about 2.5cm/1 inch apart so they do not join together during baking. Sprinkle with caster sugar and bake for 20–25 minutes, until you can lift the biscuits easily from the baking sheet. Remove from the oven and leave to cool completely.

Dip the gingernuts in the tempered chocolate and decorate with a little piped tempered chocolate, if you like. Set them on a tray lined with baking parchment to dry. Stored in a tin in a cool place, they will keep for weeks.

Claire's Notes
• You could make the dough the day before you bake the biscuits, to give it plenty of time to chill and firm. It will make rolling and cutting an easy task.
• You can use the same recipe for gingerbread men if you include an extra 60g/2¼oz flour. If the gingerbread men are for children, you might like to cut back on the spices and use half caster sugar and half soft light brown sugar. You could also substitute golden syrup for some of the treacle to make them lighter in colour and taste.
• These make great Christmas presents for ginger lovers. Box or bag them to give as a gift.

FOUR-NUT FLORENTINES

140g/5oz flaked almonds

50g/1³/₄oz hazelnuts, roughly
chopped

50g/1³/₄oz baton almonds (or
whole blanched almonds,
roughly chopped)

50g/1³/₄oz shelled peeled
pistachio nuts

65g/2¹/₄oz unsalted butter, diced

90g/3¹/₄oz caster sugar

125ml/4fl oz double cream

30ml/2 tablespoons honey

300g/10¹/₂oz tempered dark
chocolate (see pages 212–213)
or 125g/4¹/₂oz dark chocolate
(70 per cent cocoa solids)

MAKES 32

Florentines were created in the kitchens of the Château de Versailles during the rein of Louis XIV, in honour of the visiting Médicos (doctors) of Florence. Traditionally they are made from almonds, honey and orange, although the version found in England usually contains angelica and glacé cherries. This recipe is a little less complicated than most but does need a sugar thermometer. It is very useful if you can find a silicone Florentine mat, which has individual wells for each biscuit, about 5cm/2 inches in diameter. Alternatively use an ordinary nonstick baking mat.

I adapted this recipe for my mother, who has a passion for nuts, but you can replace some of the nuts with glacé cherries, angelica, candied orange peel or sultanas, if you prefer. Classically the back of the Florentine is dipped in chocolate and combed to create wavy lines. You can buy special comb scrapers from catering equipment suppliers. However, it is quite acceptable – and easier – to dip the backs of the Florentines in chocolate and sit them down flat on baking parchment to set.

Preheat the oven to 170°C/325°F/Gas Mark 3. Spread the nuts evenly over a baking tray lined with baking parchment and bake for 10–15 minutes, until golden brown, turning them occasionally with a palette knife to help them brown evenly. Remove from the oven and keep warm.

Put the butter, sugar, cream and honey in a medium, heavy-based saucepan and stir over a low heat until dissolved. Turn up the heat and place a sugar thermometer in the pan. Let the mixture boil, without stirring, until it reaches the soft-ball stage (118°C/245°F) on the thermometer. Remove the thermometer and place it in a jug of warm water to soak. Turn off the heat and add the warm roasted nuts to the pan. Mix well to combine all the ingredients.

Be careful, as the pan and mix will be very hot. Sit the Florentine mat on a baking sheet, spoon in the mix and flatten it with the back of a wet dessertspoon so it covers the base of the mould and is no thicker than the nuts themselves.

Place near the top of the oven and bake for 15–18 minutes, until the mixture in each well begins to bubble and boil and turns golden brown. Remove from the oven and leave the biscuits to cool in the mats. They will pop out of the mats easily when they are cold. Dip the backs into tempered dark chocolate and comb them if desired (if you don't have a comb scraper, you can use a fork). Sit them combed-side up on baking parchment until they are set or, if you are not going to comb them, chocolate-side down. If you are using ordinary chocolate, simply melt it in a bowl placed over a pan of simmering water and dip the Florentines into it, then leave on parchment to cool and set.

FRENCH MACAROONS

125g/4^{1}/$_{2}$oz ground almonds
225g/8oz icing sugar
4 medium egg whites
a pinch of cream of tartar
25g/1oz caster sugar

For the flavourings
Vanilla ^{1}/$_{2}$ teaspoon vanilla extract
Chocolate 1 tablespoon cocoa
  powder
Raspberry ^{1}/$_{2}$ teaspoon raspberry
  essence, plus a couple of drops
  of red food colouring
Coconut substitute desiccated
  coconut for 50g/1^{3}/$_{4}$oz of the
  ground almonds
Lemon zest of ^{1}/$_{2}$ lemon

For the fillings
Vanilla vanilla butter cream (follow
  the recipe on page 42,
  substituting a few drops of
  vanilla extract for the ground
  ginger)
Chocolate ganache (see page
  158), made with 100ml/3^{1}/$_{2}$fl oz
  double cream and 180g/6oz
  dark chocolate
Raspberry 100g/3^{1}/$_{2}$oz raspberry
  jam
Coconut banana ganache (see
  Notes below)
Lemon lemon curd (see page 101)

MAKES 40

The story of the macaroon goes back to eighteenth-century Venice, but it was made famous by Louis Ladurée, who opened a pâtisserie and tea salon in Paris in the 1870s. To this day, the grand windows of Ladurée boast beautiful displays of macaroons in 20 or more different colours and flavours. Classics such as chocolate and praline sit next to new creations like icy mint, blackcurrant, violet and salted butter caramel. The 40 pastry chefs and 45 chefs that work at Ladurée still have to find time in their busy baking day to create seasonal varieties, such as chestnut, lime and basil.

My recipe can be adapted to different flavours as long as you choose pastes and essences to flavour the macaroon itself, and purées, pastes and extracts for the fillings, which will give a more intense flavour. The baking is an important part of the cooking procedure to ensure a crisp outside in contrast to the creamy filling.

Preheat the oven to 180°C/350°F/Gas Mark 4. Sift the ground almonds and icing sugar together on to a piece of baking parchment, then sift again. (If you are making chocolate macaroons, sift the cocoa powder with the ground almonds and icing sugar.)

Using a freestanding electric mixer, whisk the egg whites until they are just foamy, then add the cream of tartar and whisk to soft peaks. Reduce the speed and add the caster sugar, then return to a high speed and whisk until the meringue is firm. Remove the bowl from the machine and add your chosen flavouring by hand. Using a large metal spoon, fold in the dry ingredients. The mix should be smooth and shiny.

Using a piping bag fitted with a 1cm/^{1}/$_{2}$ inch nozzle, pipe the mixture on to a baking sheet lined with baking parchment. The macaroons should be about 2cm/^{3}/$_{4}$ inch in diameter, with 2.5cm/1 inch between each one. Tap the tray from underneath to flatten the mixture slightly. Leave the macaroons for 15 minutes to form a skin, then bake in the centre of the oven for 10 minutes, with the oven door very slightly ajar to let the steam escape. They should rise from the bases a little and be crisp and firm on top. As soon as you remove them from the oven, run a little cold water between the baking parchment and the baking tray. This will make it easier to remove them from the paper. Allow 2–3 minutes for them to cool before lifting them off the baking parchment. Leave until completely cold, then sandwich with the filling. Make sure you use a good amount of filling, as it is always desirable to see a little of it.

Claire's Notes
• Although these are fragile once filled, if you stack them carefully in a plastic container between layers of baking parchment they will keep really well in the freezer for up to 3 months.
• To make banana ganache, bring 100ml/3^{1}/$_{2}$fl oz double cream to the boil and pour it over half a mashed banana and 100g/3^{1}/$_{2}$oz chopped white chocolate. Stir well and cool completely before using.

AMARETTI

500g/1lb 2oz white marzipan
150g/5^1/$_2$oz caster sugar
50ml/2fl oz Amaretto liqueur
400g/14oz icing sugar for rolling

MAKES 20

Claire's Notes

• Amaretti biscuits can be used in so many dishes – trifles, cheesecake bases, apple strudel – or crushed and sprinkled over orange-flavoured mascarpone cheese with a little Amaretto poured over the top. They are great with ice cream, or you could make smaller versions and serve them with an after-dinner brandy or Amaretto.

• For an unusual treat, add chopped dried figs and cranberries to the mix. They look and taste wonderful and make lovely gifts for friends and family at Easter and Christmas.

I went to Italy in my late twenties and was fortunate enough to visit a small factory where they still made these historic biscuits by hand. The oven room was filled with a heavenly, sweet almond and apricot aroma that made you want to stay in Italy for ever. While I was working at the Bluebird restaurant on London's King's Road many years later, the buyer imported amaretti from the very same factory, and happy memories of my time in Italy came flooding back. It's worth baking these for the aroma in your kitchen alone.

I recommend you enjoy amaretti with a small glass of Amaretto liqueur. I love the story of Bernardino Luini, a student of Da Vinci who was commissioned to paint a fresco of the Madonna for the church in Saronna. A young widow became his model and, it is said, his lover. She steeped apricot kernels in brandy as a gift for the painter and Amaretto was created.

Amaretti biscuits come from the same town in Italy. A local couple baked them on the spur of the moment to honour a visiting bishop, and the original recipe has remained a secret over many generations.

Cut the marzipan into 8 pieces and place them in a large mixing bowl. Add the caster sugar and knead it into the marzipan just enough to work it in (don't do this in an electric mixer, as it makes the paste too soft). Pour in half the Amaretto and work it into the paste. Add the rest and bring the paste together to form a ball. It should be soft but not sticky; if necessary, work in a tablespoon of icing sugar to achieve the right consistency.

Sift half the icing sugar on to a work surface in an even layer, covering an area of 20–25cm/8–10 inches. Use a scraper to transfer the mix from the bowl to the well-dusted work surface. Now roll it into a log about 5cm/2 inches in diameter, using the sifted sugar to prevent it sticking to the work surface. The soft roll of mix should be coated in the icing sugar and look white on the outside. Using a small, sharp knife, cut pieces from the log about 1cm/^{1}/$_2$ inch thick, dipping the knife into a jug of warm water and then drying it to keep it clean between each cut.

Sift the remaining icing sugar into a small bowl. Place one piece of the dough in the icing sugar at a time and roll it into a neat ball. Make sure each ball is well covered in the icing sugar and looks completely white.

Place the balls on a baking sheet lined with baking parchment, spacing them 5cm/2 inches apart. Leave for 20 minutes to form a crust. Meanwhile, preheat the oven to 200°C/400°F/Gas Mark 6.

Cup your hand, fingers facing downwards, over each biscuit and pinch it with your fingers and thumb so it has 5 marks on the side. Place in the centre of the oven and bake for about 10 minutes, until golden on the outside but still soft in the centre. Do not over bake the amaretti or they will collapse and be flat on the tray; stay close to the oven and check them after 8 minutes. Allow to cool on the baking tray, then store in an airtight container.

ARLETTES

200g/7oz puff pastry – either homemade (see pages 58–60) or bought
a little plain flour for dusting
spray oil
500g/1lb 2oz icing sugar

MAKES 20

These crisp, wafer-thin, sugared biscuits are a combination of wonderful caramel crunch and buttery puff pastry. They are so addictive that once you start eating them it is hard to know when to stop. They are an excellent way of using up scraps of leftover puff pastry; if you use bought pastry I promise you no one will ever know the difference.

These biscuits are traditionally leaf-shaped and there is such a thing as an arlette cutter but they are hard to find. I suggest you use an oval or round fluted cutter instead.

I sometimes use the biscuits to sandwich strawberries and cream together to make a kind of arlette sandwich, as petits fours, and also as accompaniments to custard-based desserts, where they add interest and texture.

If you are using puff pastry trimmings, shape them into a flat, square block. On a lightly floured surface, roll the pastry into a sheet about 20 x 40cm/ 8 x 16 inches, approximately 5mm/¼ inch thick. Trim the edges so you have a neat rectangle. Roll the pastry into a tight, coiled log. I start by pinching the pastry over to make the centre of the coil and then roll it away from me, keeping the coil as tight as possible. There should be no gaps in it. Wrap the rolled-up tube of pastry in baking parchment and place on a baking tray. Leave in the freezer for 30–40 minutes, until it is firm but not frozen solid. Preheat the oven to 200°C/400°F/Gas Mark 6.

Slice the pastry into discs about 3mm/⅛ inch thick; it should be firm enough to cut without the rolls squashing down. Arrange the cut discs on a baking sheet lined with baking parchment and place in the fridge to prevent them going soft.

Line a separate baking sheet with parchment and coat it very lightly with spray oil. Sift half the icing sugar into a mound directly on a clean cold work surface and flatten the mound to about 5mm/¼ inch think. Sift the other half on to a piece of baking parchment, then tip it into a small bowl.

Take one disc of cut paste and toss it in the icing sugar in the bowl until it is heavily coated in sugar on both sides. Place the disc on the mound of sifted sugar on the work surface and roll a little one way and a little the other to make it into a round or oval about 7.5–10cm/3–4 inches long and 5–7.5cm/2–3 inches wide, depending on the shape of the cutter you are using. As you roll them, turn the discs over and over to prevent them sticking and to make sure they get lots of icing sugar on both sides. The discs should be fractionally larger than your cutter and wafer thin. Cut with the cutter and place on the prepared baking sheet. Repeat the process until all the discs have been rolled and cut.

Bake at the top of the oven for 5–6 minutes, until the arlettes are golden brown and the sugar has caramelised. It caramelises quickly, so do not leave the oven unattended, not even for a minute. Remove the tray from the oven and, using a palette knife, flip the arlettes over. Return them to the oven to colour the other side and finish baking. The caramelised sugar will make the arlettes look shiny. Leave to cool on the tray before serving. They are best eaten within a few hours of baking.

Claire's Notes
• You can leave the rolled tube of pastry in the freezer for up to a month. When you want to cook it, defrost the roll in the fridge to keep it firm enough to cut into discs.
• The arlettes do tend to stick to the rolling pin. I use a small plastic rolling pin, 15cm/6 inches long and 2.5cm/1 inch wide. I keep it coated in icing sugar the whole time and wipe it frequently to remove bits of pastry
• If the arlettes are not brown and caramelised, you have not used enough sugar during rolling. If you are unsure, roll one and bake it first to see how it caramelises.

CAKES

THE SECRETS OF SUCCESS

The three major cake-making methods are creaming, whisking and the all-in-one. In all of them, incorporating air into the batter is of critical importance – this is what gives the cake its lift and lightness. Once the air has been incorporated, pay attention to your folding technique when mixing in the dry ingredients, as this is where people tend to lose a great deal of volume.

THE CREAMING METHOD

Creaming is used for butter- and sugar-based cakes, such as the Battenburg Cake on page 47. The butter and sugar are beaten together until they form a light, fluffy mass and become paler in colour. You can do this in an electric mixer fitted with the paddle attachment, or with a wooden spoon or a handheld electric beater.

The creaming of the fat and sugar is a critical point in the cake-making process, as it establishes the foundation for raising the batter, thus ensuring a light cake. The sharp edges of the sugar crystals create small pockets of air in the fat as they are beaten together. The butter should therefore be soft enough to beat but not so soft that it will melt. If it does begin to melt, it will not be able to trap the air effectively and the cake will be heavy. The ideal temperature is 18°C/65°F, or average room temperature.

Adding the eggs

Ideally the eggs should be at the same temperature as the butter, so if you store them in the fridge, take them out well in advance. Beat them together lightly, just to combine, then add them to the creamed mixture about a third of an egg at a time, beating well between each addition. Adding the egg a little at a time helps prevent curdling. If the batter begins to look slightly curdled when you've incorporated nearly all the egg, add a tablespoonful of the sifted flour to bring the ingredients back together, then continue to add the egg as before.

Folding in the flour

The flour acts as a stabiliser for the cake and will hold the air you have created in suspension. Always sift the flour first to remove any lumps and to aerate it. Chemical raising agents, such as baking powder, may react when mixed into batters and create carbon dioxide bubbles but their primary role is to expand the bubbles created by the creaming. Be sure to sift any chemical leaveners with the flour to help distribute them evenly throughout the batter. Many people sift the flour twice if combining it with baking powder. This is entirely up to you.

If you are adding liquid, such as milk or wine, to the cake batter, add a little of the flour first. The flour coats the fat particles and this will help minimise gluten formation, which can give cakes a heavy, dough-like texture. Adding liquid too fast can cause the batter to curdle. When the remaining flour is added, the batter will become smooth again.

Even if you are making the cake in an electric mixer, always fold in the flour and other dry ingredients by hand to prevent over mixing – otherwise the batter can become tight, which will affect the overall lightness of the cake. Sift about a third of the flour over the cake batter and, using a large metal spoon, gently scoop up the mixture and turn it over to mix in the flour without losing any air. Repeat with the remaining flour in two batches.

THE WHISKED METHOD

This is the classic Continental way of making sponges, as opposed to the English, butter-rich Victoria sponge. Cakes are made by the whisked method when you require a particularly light and airy texture – for example, in the Swiss roll for the Charlotte Royal on page 162. As a general rule the cake should rise to twice the height of the batter when baked.

The eggs and sugar are whisked together until they form a thick, pale foam and increase greatly in volume. It is easier to do this with an electric mixer but you can do it successfully by hand, using a balloon whisk or a rotary whisk, as long as you set the bowl of eggs and sugar over a pan of hot water. The gentle heat will help them thicken. Whisk until the mixture trebles in volume and reaches the 'ribbon' stage – i.e. until it is thick enough to hold a ribbon trail on the surface for 3-4 seconds when drizzled from the whisk. Use eggs at room temperature for maximum volume.

The flour should be sifted and folded in as for The Creaming Method, above. Again, use a large metal spoon and avoid overmixing, as this will tighten the batter and knock out the air.

Some whisked sponges don't contain any butter, while others include a small amount for flavour. Fat improves the keeping qualities of the cake. Sponges made without butter should ideally be eaten on the day they are made. If using butter, melt it and let it cool, then trickle it down the side of the bowl after adding the flour and fold it in very gently so as not to knock the air out.

THE ALL-IN-ONE METHOD

This relies on chemical raising agents, such as baking powder, rather than creaming or whisking for aeration. It generally produces cakes with less volume and a denser texture. However, they will be beautifully moist, as long as they are not overbaked. They can be made with vegetable oil instead of butter – for example, the Carrot Cake on page 34 and the Frosted Banana Cake on page 40. Use a whisk to mix oil-based cakes and a paddle attachment (or a wooden spoon, if mixing by hand) for butter-based ones.

In some recipes, such as Lemon Cake (page 46), all the ingredients are put in the bowl together and beaten until combined. In others, the fat, sugar and eggs are whisked together, then the flour is folded in separately. If you are making an oil-based cake, the whisked ingredients will be quite liquid and I recommend sifting a little of the flour at a time over the entire surface of the batter, then using a large metal spoon to lift and fold it in. Lifting the flour first helps disperse it rather than pushing it down into the mix in a clump, thus making it less likely to lump together.

LINING CAKE TINS

Lining the cake tin prevents the cake sticking and makes it easier to turn out of the tin. It also gives the sides and bottom of the cake some protection from the heat of the oven.

Grease the entire tin first with butter or a little spray oil, as this will help to prevent the baking parchment sliding around. Greasing and flouring tins not only assists in releasing the finished cake but ensures good volume, by helping the cake to 'climb' up the sides of the tin.

When using small, individual tins, there is no need to line them at all, just grease them and then flour them very lightly.

LOAF TINS

When lining loaf tins, I only ever cut an oblong of baking parchment and place it in the greased tin so it covers the base and two long sides, leaving the shorter sides completely free of parchment. The cake will turn out easily if you run a knife along the short sides first. Make sure the paper does not come past the top of the tin. If the cake is not expected to rise above a certain height, cut the paper and line the tin accordingly.

ROUND CAKE TINS

Be precise and cut a circle of parchment exactly the same size as the base of your cake tin. Draw around the base of the tin as a guide and then cut out the disc with scissors. Grease the base and sides of the tin first, then lay the parchment paper on the base. If making a fruitcake, or any cake that needs to bake for more than an hour, you will need to line the sides of the tin too, using a long strip of baking parchment cut to size.

SHALLOW OBLONG BAKING TINS

Cut out an oblong of baking parchment about 2.5cm/1 inch bigger all round than your tin and snip in about 4cm/1^{1}/$_{2}$ inches towards the centre of the paper at each corner. The corners will overlap neatly when you fit the paper into the tin.

CARROT CAKE

250g/9oz wholemeal flour
25g/1oz baking powder
1$^1/_2$ teaspoons ground cinnamon
1 teaspoon freshly grated nutmeg
125g/4$^1/_2$oz desiccated coconut
5 medium eggs
250g/9oz muscovado sugar
185ml/6$^1/_2$fl oz vegetable oil or
    canola oil
500g/1lb 2oz carrots, grated
125g/4$^1/_2$oz Californian raisins

For the cream cheese frosting
125g/4$^1/_2$oz cream cheese
375g/13oz icing sugar, sifted
250g/9oz unsalted butter, at room
    temperature
a capful of vanilla extract

For the marzipan carrots
250g/9oz white marzipan
orange food colouring
green food colouring
a little icing sugar for dusting

Claire's Notes
• To add colouring to marzipan, you can dip a cocktail stick into the food colouring and wipe it on the marzipan – this way there's no risk of adding too much.
• If you want to make individual carrot cakes like the ones in the photo, bake the mixture in 30 mini muffin tins. They will take 10–12 minutes. You will need only half the quantity of frosting.

The versatility of this recipe never ceases to amaze me. A few years ago I ran my own catering company, and was hired by Anton Mosimann's famous party service, which carries the Royal Warrant. Miniature versions of this moist, frosted cake were paraded across the lawns of Buckingham Palace on silver trays at summer garden parties. Topped with miniature marzipan carrots, they looked so whimsical. It worked just as well as part of a 'family meal' to celebrate the twelfth anniversary of The French Laundry. In and Out burgers and fries were delivered to the copper-plated back door of the restaurant, where staff washed them down with vast quantities of fizzy drinks, then tucked into my triple-layer 'go-large, all-American' version of the humble carrot cake. Packed with moist Californian raisins and sweet coconut, each layer was a couple of inches thick, with half an inch of frosting between them and more on the top. It was soon devoured while everyone recalled happy memories of past years and debated whose grandmother had made the best carrot cake.

Preheat the oven to 180°C/350°F/Gas Mark 4. Grease a 25cm/10 inch deep, round springform cake tin and line the base with baking parchment.

Sift the flour, baking powder, cinnamon and nutmeg together, then stir in the coconut so it does not clump together. Using an electric mixer, whisk the eggs, sugar and oil together until the mixture becomes pale and has doubled in volume. Gently fold in the dry ingredients, being careful not to overmix and lose volume. Finally fold in the carrots and raisins. Spoon the mixture into the prepared tin and bake in the centre of the oven for about 40 minutes, until a skewer inserted in the centre comes out clean. Leave to cool in the tin.

Meanwhile, to make the frosting, simply beat all the ingredients together until pale and fluffy. Cover and set aside.

To make the carrots, you need to colour two-thirds of the marzipan orange and the remaining third green. Add the colouring to the marzipan a drop at a time and knead it in well. If the marzipan becomes sticky, knead in a little icing sugar. Keep the marzipan wrapped in cling film to prevent it drying out while you are making the carrots. Roll a small ball of orange marzipan between the palms of your hands to make an elongated cone. Mark this with a knife to give the impression of a carrot. With a very small amount of green marzipan, make a thin, tapering line. Lay this piece over the top of the cone and press down firmly in the middle to give you 2 green pieces standing upright (see picture). Repeat to make 10 carrots (or enough for the number of people you want the cake to serve).

Turn the cake out of the tin and, using a long serrated knife, slice it into 3 layers. Sandwich them together with the cream cheese frosting and spread a third of it over the top. Decorate with the marzipan carrots.

APPLE AND POPPY SEED CAKE

1 tangy dessert apple, such as
    Cox's
juice and grated zest of $1/4$ lemon
55g/2oz ground almonds
15g/$1/2$oz plain flour
a pinch of salt
55g/2oz poppy seeds
60g/$2^1/4$oz unsalted butter, at
    room temperature
60g/$2^1/4$oz icing sugar, sifted, plus
    extra for dusting
1 large egg, separated
25g/1oz caster sugar

I use icing sugar in this recipe as it gives the cake a soft texture. The sharpness of the apples complements the crunch of the poppy seeds very well. I normally bake this cake in a loaf tin but don't be afraid to use it as a base for other cakes – for example, I once baked it in a rectangular tin, layered it with lemon curd and topped it with a lemon mousse to make a celebration cake. It is just as good plain with a dollop of crème fraîche, though. Just be creative.

Preheat the oven to 170°C/325°C/Gas Mark 3. Grease a 500g/1lb 2oz loaf tin and line it with baking parchment. Peel and core the apple, then grate it into a mixing bowl, using the widest option on a box cheese grater – the one you would use for grating Cheddar cheese. Add the lemon juice and zest.

Sift the ground almonds and flour together with the salt, then mix in the poppy seeds.

Cream the butter and icing sugar together until pale and thick, then beat in the egg yolk. In a separate bowl, whisk the egg white with the caster sugar until it forms stiff peaks.

Fold half the beaten egg white into the egg yolk mixture, followed by half the sifted dry ingredients. Repeat the process. Gently fold in the grated apple and lemon, making sure all the ingredients are well combined. Transfer the mixture to the prepared tin and bake in the centre of the oven for 35–40 minutes, until the top is golden brown and a skewer inserted in the centre comes out clean. Leave to cool in the tin.

When the cake is completely cold, turn it out of the tin, dust the top with a little icing sugar and serve with crème fraîche.

Claire's Notes
• Do not be tempted to make the cake mix fill the loaf tin. The cake is not normally more than 5cm/2 inches high when baked. A higher cake tends to dry too much on the edges before it cooks in the centre.

ORANGE PISTACHIO CAKES

2 small navel oranges
125g/4$\frac{1}{2}$oz unsalted butter
145g/5oz caster sugar
2 medium eggs, lightly beaten
60g/2$\frac{1}{4}$oz rice flour
100g/3$\frac{1}{2}$oz ground almonds
1 teaspoon baking powder
45g/1$\frac{1}{2}$oz semolina
75g/2$\frac{3}{4}$oz shelled peeled
    pistachio nuts

For the orange syrup
250ml/9fl oz orange juice (from
    about 4–5 oranges)
juice of 1 lemon
125g/4$\frac{1}{2}$oz caster sugar
2 tablespoons Cointreau or other
    orange liqueur

To decorate
4 tablespoons apricot preserve
2 tablespoons water
2–3 strips of candied orange peel,
    sliced
12 pistachio nuts

MAKES 12

Claire's Notes
• Take care when soaking the
cakes. If they do not feel soft
enough when you turn them out
of the moulds, you can brush
more syrup on to them with a
small pastry brush.
• Most supermarkets now stock
fabulous soft strips or quarters of
candied peel, which you can use
for the decoration.
• You can make these with
passionfruit juice instead of orange.
• If you are going to make the
cakes in advance, freeze them
without soaking them, defrost
thoroughly and then soak and
finish them. They will taste as if
you just made them that day.

These delightful little cakes are suitable for anyone with an intolerance to wheat. They are made with semolina and rice flour, then drenched in an intoxicating orange syrup. The texture is a little coarser than that of a sponge made with ordinary flour.

The recipe came about when I worked at the Wolseley, in London. My sous-chef, Emma Williamson, and I liked to feature at least one wheat-free cake on the menu for afternoon tea. It is surprising how good a wheat-free cake can be – especially when it is still warm, crammed with pistachio nuts and dunked in fresh orange juice. Of course, you don't have to have a wheat intolerance to enjoy it.

Preheat the oven to 170°C/325°F/Gas Mark 3. Grease and flour 12 dariole moulds or muffin tins.

Peel the oranges and chop the flesh into a pulp, reserving any juice that comes out. Place the pulp and juice in a small pan, add a tablespoon of water and bring to the boil. Turn down the heat and simmer for 8–10 minutes, until the fruit is soft and almost all the liquid has evaporated. Place in a blender or food processor and process until smooth, then leave to cool.

Cream together the butter and sugar until light and fluffy. Add the beaten egg a little at a time, mixing well between each addition. Sift the rice flour, ground almonds and baking powder together, then mix in the semolina. Using a large metal spoon, fold the dry ingredients into the creamed batter a third at a time, taking care to be as gentle as possible. Add the processed oranges and the pistachio nuts and gently fold them through the mixture. Spoon the mix into the prepared moulds and bake for 25–30 minutes, until a skewer inserted in the centre comes out clean. Leave the cakes in the moulds for about 10 minutes, until cool enough to handle, then gently remove them from the tins and leave on a wire rack to cool completely.

Meanwhile, wash and dry the moulds and make the syrup. Place the orange and lemon juice in a small pan with the sugar, stir to dissolve the sugar, then place over a medium heat and bring to the boil. Reduce the heat and simmer for 2–3 minutes, until the syrup thickens slightly. Remove from the heat and add the Cointreau.

Place a tablespoon of the syrup in each clean dariole mould and drop the cakes back in. Spoon more syrup over the top of the cakes. They should be moist but not falling apart when you turn them out of the moulds. Turn them out on to a small tray lined with baking parchment and let them cool slightly; they will be warm from the hot syrup.

To finish the cakes, bring the apricot preserve to the boil with 2 tablespoons of water to make a glaze. Brush the hot preserve over the cakes so they are completely covered and look shiny. Finish with a little candied orange peel and a pistachio nut. Serve warm or cold. The cakes are very good with Vanilla Ice Cream (see page 192) and a glass of chilled Cointreau.

FROSTED BANANA CAKE

180g/6oz plain flour, sifted
2¹/₂ teaspoons baking powder
180g/6oz soft dark brown sugar
2 medium eggs
4 tablespoons vegetable oil
180g/6oz ripe bananas (peeled
  weight), mashed to a pulp
50g/1³/₄oz pecan nuts

For the frosting
65g/2¹/₄oz cream cheese
190g/6³/₄oz icing sugar, sifted,
  plus extra for dusting
125g/4¹/₂oz unsalted butter,
  at room temperature
1 teaspoon vanilla extract
50g/1³/₄oz pecan nuts, chopped

This is a teatime favourite of mine but it has to be frosted for me to enjoy it properly. Ripe bananas make the best cake. Use ones that are turning black on the outside. I love the caramel flavour from the dark sugar and I have always favoured pecans rather than walnuts, although both work well.

This particular recipe was served for afternoon tea at the Hilton London Metropole Hotel, where Mandy, my sous-chef, and I would bake enough for 600 portions at a time. We would sit illicitly on the marble table at the end of a long shift and scoff warm banana bread, spreading it with frosting straight from the tub while planning our schedule for the next day. If frosting is not your thing, bake the cake in a loaf tin, cut thick slices when cold, and toast them, spreading them with butter whilst still warm.

Preheat the oven to 170°C/325°F/Gas Mark 3. Grease a round 20cm/8 inch springform cake tin and line the base with baking parchment, or grease 10–12 muffin tins.

Sift the flour and baking powder together. Place the sugar, eggs and oil in a large bowl and whisk with an electric mixer on medium speed for about 4 minutes, until pale and fluffy. Add the sifted flour mixture and the bananas and mix on a low speed for 30 seconds. Stir in the pecan nuts. Pour the mixture into the prepared tin or muffin tins and bake for about 40 minutes for a large cake, 20 minutes for muffins, until the top springs back when pressed gently and a skewer inserted in the centre comes out clean. Leave in the tin to cool completely before frosting.

For the frosting, combine all the ingredients except the pecan nuts in a bowl and beat until pale and fluffy. Spread the frosting over the cake with a palette knife and sprinkle with the chopped pecans. Finally, dust with icing sugar.

Claire's Notes
• If you are making the cake by hand, use a wooden spoon and mix all the ingredients except the pecans together in one go. Beat for 8–10 minutes and then add the nuts.
• Try baking the mixture in mini muffin tins (they will take only about 10–12 minutes) and pipe on the frosting with a plain 1cm/¹/₂ inch nozzle for a cupcake effect.
• If the flavour of dark brown sugar is too strong for you, substitute soft light brown sugar.
• To give a crunchy texture, sprinkle the top of the cake with demerara sugar before baking.

FRUITCAKE

375g/13oz raisins

180g/6oz sultanas

50g/1³/₄oz natural-coloured glacé
   cherries

50g/1³/₄oz candied orange peel,
   finely chopped

25g/1oz whole unblanched
   almonds

50ml/2fl oz brandy, plus 75ml/2
   ¹/₂fl oz for soaking the cake

50ml/2fl oz rum

juice of ¹/₂ orange

125g/4¹/₂oz unsalted butter,
   at room temperature

110g/3³/₄oz soft dark brown sugar

4 small eggs

25g/1oz chocolate hazelnut
   spread, such as Green & Black's
   or Nutella

1 teaspoon black treacle

150g/5¹/₂oz plain flour

25g/1oz ground almonds

¹/₄ teaspoon baking powder

¹/₂ teaspoon ground mixed spice

Claire's Notes

• Use the candied orange peel
that comes in large pieces and
chop it yourself; it is better quality
than the pre-cut product.

• Use Tia Maria and Cointreau
instead of brandy and rum for an
interesting flavour.

I guarantee that this recipe will stay in your favourites file for years to come. It is so delicious and keeps for ages if you store it correctly, wrapped in waxed paper or foil in an airtight tin. Fruitcake improves with age, so try to make it at least a week before you need it. If you are able to plan, make it up to a month in advance. If you need the cake in a hurry for that next-day wedding-cake order – believe me, it has happened – then my tip is to freeze the cake as soon as it is cold, even if it is just overnight. As the cake defrosts, it will take on extra moisture, which improves the eating quality.

This recipe is packed full of fruit, with one or two secret ingredients that make it special. If you like a particular spice more than another, create your own combination to use instead of commercial mixed spice. I like to include ground ginger, cinnamon and nutmeg in mine.

Put the raisins, sultanas, cherries, candied orange peel and almonds in a bowl. Gently warm the brandy and rum with the orange juice. Do not let it boil or the alcohol will evaporate. Pour this mixture over the fruit and nuts and leave to soak overnight.

Preheat the oven to 150°C/300°F/Gas Mark 2. Grease a deep, round 20cm/8 inch springform cake tin and line the base and sides with a double layer of baking parchment.

With an electric mixer, cream the butter and sugar together until pale and fluffy. Add the eggs one at a time, beating well between each addition. Once all the eggs have been incorporated, beat the mixture for another 1–2 minutes on high speed, then mix in the chocolate hazelnut spread and black treacle. Sift the flour and baking powder and fold them in with the ground almonds and mixed spice. Add the soaked fruits and mix in well. Be sure to add any liquid that has not been absorbed by the fruit.

Transfer the mixture to the prepared tin. Make a well, about 2.5cm/1 inch deep and 7.5cm/3 inches wide, in the centre of the mixture to prevent the cake doming. Take some old newspaper and fold it into a triple-thickness strip as high as the cake tin. Tie it around the tin with string. This will help prevent the cake drying on the sides while it is baking. Place in the centre of the oven and bake for 45 minutes. Reduce the heat to 140°C/275°F/Gas Mark 1 and continue to bake for 30–45 minutes, until the cake is a dark golden colour and a skewer inserted in the centre comes out clean. Take care not to overbake the cake or it will become dry.

Leave the cake to cool in the tin. Pierce the cake in several places with a skewer, going almost all the way through to the bottom, and brush with the extra brandy. It will not absorb all the brandy in one go but continue to brush daily for about a week until you have used all the brandy. You can leave the cake in its tin while you do this and store it in a cool place such as a pantry.

GINGERBREAD

60g/2¼oz unsalted butter, at
   room temperature
60g/2¼oz soft dark brown sugar
110g/3¾oz black treacle
1 medium egg, lightly beaten
110g/3¾oz self-raising flour, sifted
a pinch of salt
1 tablespoon ground ginger
1½ teaspoons ground allspice
¼ teaspoon bicarbonate of soda
chopped candied ginger in syrup,
   to decorate

For the crystallised rose petals
1 large, open pink rose
1 egg white
100g/3½oz caster sugar

For the syrup
100g/3½oz caster sugar
a piece of fresh root ginger,
   weighing about 5g/⅕oz
100ml/3½fl oz water

For the butter cream
100g/3½oz icing sugar, plus extra
   for dusting
100g/3½oz softened unsalted
   butter
ground ginger, to taste

MAKES 1 LARGE CAKE OR 12 INDIVIDUAL ONES

Claire's Notes
• Make the rose petals the day before, if you have time; they will dry better and be more stable.
• If you cannot get a comb scraper from a cake decorating specialist, you should be able to find a small comb scraper at a hardware store, in the plaster and paint area. They are used for texturing walls.

This wonderful recipe was given to me by Rosalind Batty, who worked with me at Bluebird and later at Claridge's. She is a great baker and a truly gifted cake maker. This cake includes all three types of ginger: fresh, ground and candied. I garnish it with crystallised rose petals, as they contrast well with the darkness of the cake for a stunning presentation. It also makes a delicious dessert, teamed with spiced poached pears and honey ice cream.

The cake works well if cooked in a shallow baking tray, cut into squares and finished with butter cream. Alternatively you could make little individual cakes, as in the picture. For these I use flexible silicone baking moulds.

Start by crystallising the rose petals, as they take a while to dry. Remove the petals from the rose. Using a small, fine paintbrush, brush both sides of each petal carefully and evenly with the egg white. Toss the petals one at a time in the caster sugar until completely covered. Gently lift out the petals and leave to dry on a tray lined with baking parchment, until they're firm enough to pick up. A warm place is best, near a radiator or on top of the stove if the oven is on.

Preheat the oven to 170°C/325°F/Gas Mark 3. Grease a Swiss roll tin and line it with baking parchment, or grease 12 individual moulds. Cream the butter, dark brown sugar and treacle together until fluffy and slightly paler in colour. Add the egg a little at a time, beating well between each addition. Sift the flour, salt, spices and bicarbonate of soda and fold them in well. Transfer the mixture to the Swiss roll tin or individual moulds and bake until the top springs back when pressed gently – 30–35 minutes for one large cake, 18 minutes for small ones. Because of the depth of the individual moulds, the centres will sink a little. This is fine, as it provides a well for the butter cream and does not affect the taste.

While the cake is baking, put all the ingredients for the syrup in a pan and bring to the boil, stirring to dissolve the sugar. Boil for 4–5 minutes, until it forms a light syrup. As soon as the cake comes out of the oven, pour the syrup evenly over the top. Leave to cool in the tin.

For the butter cream, beat the butter and sugar together until light and fluffy, then add ground ginger to taste.

Turn the cake out of the tin on to a board and, using a palette knife, spread evenly with the butter cream. Comb the top with a comb scraper to make wavy lines. Cut into neat squares and decorate with chopped candied ginger, a dusting of icing sugar and the crystallised rose petals. If you have made the cake in individual moulds, simply pipe the butter cream into the wells on the top of the cakes, using a piping bag fitted with a 1cm/½ inch plain nozzle, then finished with a dusting of icing sugar and the rose petals.

SACHERTORTE

125g/4^1/$_2$oz unsalted butter, at
    room temperature
125g/4^1/$_2$oz caster sugar
6 medium eggs, separated
125g/4^1/$_2$oz dark chocolate
    (70 per cent cocoa solids), melted
125g/4^1/$_2$oz plain flour
a pinch of salt
200g/7oz apricot preserve

For the glaze
115g/4oz caster sugar
6 tablespoons water
115g/4oz dark chocolate (70 per
    cent cocoa solids), finely
    chopped

Claire's Notes
• Before cutting the cake in half,
make a small incision down the
side of the cake just big enough to
leave a mark that you can see.
When you come to sandwich the
cake together, line up the 2 marks
so you know that the torte has
been put together correctly.
• The original Sachertorte had the
name Sacher piped on top. If you
are feeling adventurous, scoop up
the excess cold glaze and, using a
small piping bag and a no. 1 nozzle,
pipe the word Sacher on top of the
torte once the glaze has firmed.

The long legal battle between the Sacher family and Demel's pâtisserie in Vienna has made the Sachertorte legendary around the world. The original recipe is thought to be the earliest written record of a recipe based on chocolate. The dispute over ownership lasted for some 200 years, until the Sacher family finally won a lawsuit in the 1950s that had ended up in Austria's Supreme Court. A single chocolate plaque on top of each torte was to be the indication of the 'genuine' article.

Both Sacher and Demel still produce their versions of this classic chocolate cake. Here is my version, which during my time as head pastry chef at the Wolseley in London's Piccadilly stood proud on its elevated glass cakestand in the popular, bustling tea salon.

Preheat the oven to 180°C/350°F/Gas Mark 4. Butter a deep 20cm/8 inch cake tin and line the base with baking parchment. Butter the paper, then dust the paper and the sides of the tin with flour.

Cream the butter and three-quarters of the sugar together until light and fluffy. Beat in the egg yolks one at a time, then stir in the melted chocolate. Sift the flour and gently fold it in, using a large metal spoon.

In a separate bowl, whisk the egg whites with the remaining sugar and the salt until they form stiff peaks. Fold the egg whites into the cake batter 2 tablespoons at a time, using the same metal spoon. Be careful not to overmix, as this will make the cake heavy.

Transfer the mixture to the prepared tin and bake for 45 minutes–1 hour, until a skewer inserted in the centre comes out clean. Leave the cake to cool in the tin for 15 minutes before turning it out upside down on to a wire rack to cool completely. Leave the cake overnight if at all possible; this will make it easier to handle when filling and decorating.

Cut the cake in half horizontally and place the bottom half on a 20cm/8 inch cake card. Bring the apricot preserve to the boil in a small pan and strain it through a fine sieve. Brush a layer of preserve over the bottom half of the cake. Sandwich the top and bottom half together and press down gently to level the top. Place the cake, still on its cake card, on a wire rack with a baking sheet beneath it. Brush the top and sides of the cake with the remaining strained preserve.

To make the glaze, put the sugar and water in a pan and stir well to dissolve the sugar, then bring to the boil over a medium–high heat. Remove from the heat and immediately add the chocolate. Stir gently to form a smooth, bubble-free glaze. Fast or heavy mixing will create too many air bubbles and give an unpleasant finish to your torte. Immediately pour the glaze over the cake and, working quickly, use a palette knife to push the glaze from the centre of the cake over the sides. To give a smooth finish, try to do this with as few movements of the palette knife as possible. Remove the cake from the wire rack and clean any excess drips of glaze from the card. Leave the glaze to set before cutting and serving the cake.

LEMON CAKE

170g/6oz unsalted butter, at room
    temperature
170g/6oz caster sugar
170g/6oz self-raising flour, sifted
a pinch of salt
2 large eggs
grated zest of 2 lemons

For the syrup
juice of 2 lemons
90g/3^1/$_4$oz icing sugar, sifted

For the adult lemon trifle
100g/3^1/$_2$oz Lemon Curd (see
    page 101)
Limoncello liqueur
10 amaretti biscuits, crushed
1 quantity of freshly made Lemon
    Posset (see page 120)
250ml/9fl oz double cream
50g/1^3/$_4$oz flaked almonds,
    toasted
icing sugar, for dusting
white chocolate curls (see pages
    213–214), to decorate

Besides the basic lemon cake recipe, I have included a version of a seriously adult dinner-party trifle here, which can be made very quickly once you have the cake. It looks classy and is so much less work than it actually appears. The cake, of course, is great served plain with a cup of tea at any time of day – Earl Grey works well. I am very particular about my tea, as my colleagues would tell you. It has to be Earl Grey, preferably Fortnum & Mason's, made in a silver teapot and served in a china cup with a saucer – with or without lemon cake is acceptable, but preferably with.

Preheat the oven to 170°C/325°F/Gas Mark 3. Grease a 17.5 x 25cm/ 7 x 10 inch baking tin (or a round 15cm/6 inch cake tin) and line it with baking parchment.

You can mix the cake by the all-in-one method if you use an electric mixer. Put the butter, sugar, flour, salt, eggs and lemon zest in the bowl of an electric mixer and beat them together for about 3 minutes. Transfer the mixture to the lined tin and bake in the centre of the oven for about 35 minutes, until the cake is golden and a skewer inserted in the centre comes out clean. Meanwhile, for the syrup, boil together the lemon juice and icing sugar for a minute. Pour the syrup over the cake immediately it comes out of the oven, then leave in the tin to cool. Cut into squares to serve.

If you are making the lemon trifle, this is how to assemble it. Cut the lemon cake horizontally in half and sandwich it together with the lemon curd. Cut the cake into 2.5cm/1 inch cubes and place 2 or 3 cubes into each of 6 martini glasses or pretty glass dishes. Soak the sponge well with plenty of Limoncello liqueur, then sprinkle with the crushed amaretti biscuits. Pour the lemon posset over the sponge to cover it and come two-thirds of the way up the sides of the glasses – the posset should still be slightly warm, not set. Leave to cool, then chill.

Whip the cream until it forms firm peaks and pipe it on to the posset using a piping bag fitted with a plain 1cm/^{1}/$_2$ inch nozzle. Sprinkle with the toasted almonds and dust with icing sugar. Finally, add one or two white chocolate curls to each trifle.

Claire's Notes
• Serve the cake with a scoop of hazelnut ice cream and a couple of hazelnut biscotti for a simple lunchtime dessert.
• If you really want to dress up the trifle, use a little gold leaf too and a touch of candied lemon peel.

BATTENBURG CAKE

480g/1lb 1oz softened unsalted
    butter
480g/1lb 1oz caster sugar
8 medium eggs
1 capful of vanilla extract
480g/1lb 1oz plain flour
20g/³/₄oz baking powder
red food colouring
yellow food colouring

For finishing
1 jar of apricot preserve
100g/3¹/₂oz icing sugar
750g/1lb 10oz yellow marzipan

MAKES 2 CAKES

*This lovely chequered cake was supposedly named in honour of the marriage
of Queen Victoria's granddaughter to Prince Louis of Battenberg in 1884.
The four quarters of the sponge are in honour of the four Battenberg princes.
During the First World War, the family decided it should anglicise its name
and Battenberg became Mountbatten. The cake, however, kept its original
name, albeit with an optional spelling variation (Battenburg).*

  *I, for one, am glad this cake has stayed with us over the years. An immense
amount of skill and precision is needed to shape it properly. When I was
teaching at Le Cordon Bleu, I would get the second-year students to make,
bake and assemble Battenburg for their end-of-term exam. It weeded out the
cooks from the perfectionists. The art of pastry is like building a house.
You need solid foundations on which to create the masterpiece of your
dreams. Without the foundations, there will be no real success.*

  *Thankfully Silverwood Ltd (see page 234) now makes a Battenburg tin,
which eliminates the judgment and skill needed to cut the sponge. For those
of you who aspire to be pastry perfectionists, be as nit-picking as possible
over every step of this recipe and use a baking tray, at least 2.5cm/1 inch
deep, with a piece of waxed card (available from craft shops) as a divide.*

Preheat the oven to 170°C/325°F/Gas Mark 3. Take a 25 x30cm/10 x 12 inch
baking tin, at least 2.5cm/1 inch deep, and line the base with a piece of
baking parchment. Lightly grease the parchment and the sides of the tray.
If you are using a Battenburg tin, prepare it according to the manufacturer's
instructions.

  Cream the butter and sugar together until pale and fluffy. Beat the eggs
lightly with the vanilla extract and add to the creamed mixture a little at a
time, beating well between each addition. Sift the flour and baking powder
on to a piece of baking parchment and then sift again. Fold the dry ingredients
into the creamed mix with a large metal spoon; do this in 3 stages, being
careful not to overmix and tighten the batter.

  Divide the batter evenly between 2 bowls – the best way to make sure you've
divided it accurately is to use weighing scales. Add a drop of red colouring
to one bowl and a drop of yellow colouring to the other; pale pink and
yellow are more attractive than bright colours, which look too synthetic.
Gently fold the colouring in, being particularly careful not to handle the
mixture too heavily.

  If using a baking tray, place one of the mixes on one side of the tray and
spread it over half the tray widthways as evenly as you can, making sure it
is level. Place the waxed divider in the tin, then add the second mix on the
empty side of the tray and level it with a palette knife as evenly as possible.
If using a Battenburg tin, spoon in the mix as per the maker's instructions.
Bake in the centre of the oven for 40–45 minutes, until the cake is golden
brown and springs back when gently pressed, or a knife comes out clean

(continued on page 49)

(continued from page 47)

when inserted in the centre. Leave the cake to cool in the tin. If you have used a baking tin, it will be easier to cut the cake when it is completely cold. Once the cake has cooled, refrigerate it for at least an hour, until it feels firm enough to cut. If possible, leave it in the fridge for 24 hours, then it will be easier to handle and assemble it.

Remove the card by cutting either side of it with a sharp knife and then pulling it away. Place a piece of baking parchment on top of the cake and cover it with a clean tray, flat-side to the cake. Flip the cake over on to the clean tray. Slide the cake from the tray on to a clean, level work surface and remove the baking paper from the top of the cake.

Bring the apricot preserve to the boil in a small pan and pass it through a fine sieve to remove the pieces of fruit. Take the yellow piece of cake and make sure the side that was on the base of the baking tray is facing up. Brush the surface with the hot apricot preserve. Place the pink section of cake, with the side that was on the base of the baking tray down, on top of the apricot-brushed yellow cake. Using a sharp serrated bread knife, cut the cake into equal strips approximately 2.5cm/1 inch wide. As you do this, flip each strip over so the cut side is up and the sides that were the top and bottom of the cake are either side of the cut section, which will be yellow and pink. Lay the pieces next to each other so they touch. They should all be equal heights and widths at this stage. Using the same knife, cut the skin (the brown layer that was the top and bottom of the cake) from each strip. This can be done easily if you flipped the strips as you were cutting them. They will be on either side of the joined strips. You need to keep the knife as close to the skin as possible so you do not cut away too much cake. Your cake strips should now be lying pink, yellow, pink, yellow next to each other, still touching, and still be equal in width and height.

Brush hot apricot preserve over the entire surface of the laid-out strips. Now flip one section over on to the next to create the 4 squares. Do this twice to make 2 sets of 4 squares (there will be a couple of strips left over, which you can use to make half a cake, if you like). Trim off either end of the sandwiched blocks so they are neat and tidy.

Dust a work surface with the sifted icing sugar and roll out the marzipan so it is the same length as your cakes but 4 times as wide as each sandwiched block of 4 squares. Do not roll the marzipan too thinly; it should be about 3–4mm/$\frac{1}{8}$ inch thick. Brush the marzipan with the hot apricot preserve. Place a sandwiched block of squares on the marzipan with the edge on the left-hand side of the marzipan. Now roll the block up in the marzipan, turning the block over to your right. Trim away the excess marzipan so there is a nice clean join. Take a clean, dry pastry brush and brush off any icing sugar from the marzipan-wrapped cake, then use a pair of cake crimpers to crimp the top of the marzipan at the edges. Roll up the second cake in the remaining marzipan in the same way.

Claire's Notes

• The wrapped cake keeps very well in a tin but if you want to freeze a section, freeze the sandwiched blocks unwrapped in marzipan.

• The top of the marzipan can be marked with the back of a knife in a criss-cross fashion and browned with a blowtorch for a different look. Allow to cool before attempting to cut the cake.

CHOCOLATE RED WINE CAKE

125g/4¹/₂oz softened unsalted
   butter
125g/4¹/₂oz caster sugar
2 medium eggs, lightly beaten
150ml/5fl oz red wine, at room
   temperature
125g/4¹/₂oz plain flour
1 teaspoon ground cinnamon
¹/₄ teaspoon ground cloves
1 teaspoon cocoa powder
1 teaspoon baking powder
65g/2¹/₄oz dark chocolate (55–70
   per cent cocoa solids), grated

For soaking
50ml/2fl oz water
30g/1oz caster sugar
125ml/4fl oz red wine

For finishing
1 jar of redcurrant jelly
about 300g/10¹/₂oz tempered dark
   chocolate (see pages 212–213)

When I needed a birthday cake for a local Californian winemaker, I immediately thought of this recipe. I met Eric Sterling at his winery, Everett Ridge, near Healdsburg and discovered that he doubles up as a local ER doctor, making wine in his spare time. After enjoying a glass or two of his award-winning Pinot Noir, which came from his family-run winery Esterlina, over in Philo, I modified this recipe so it would soak up large quantities of red wine, making it a rather alcoholic but very yummy cake. I suggest you use a good, inexpensive Cabernet Sauvignon or Merlot.

Despite the amount of wine in this cake, it cuts really well and is suitable for serving as a dessert. Try making individual ones to serve with raspberry sorbet and hot Chocolate Sauce (see pages 148–149). I have used a bundt tin here but a plain round or square tin will work just as well.

Preheat the oven to 170°C/325°F/Gas Mark 3. Grease and flour a 25cm/10 inch bundt tin.

Cream together the butter and sugar until pale and fluffy, then add the beaten eggs a little at a time, beating well between each addition. Add the wine and mix well.

Sift the flour, cinnamon, cloves, cocoa powder and baking powder together. Sift again to make sure the ingredients are well mixed. Fold the dry ingredients a tablespoon at a time into the creamed cake mixture. Lastly fold in the grated chocolate. Transfer the mixture to the prepared tin and level the top. Bake in the centre of the oven for 35 minutes, until the cake is well risen and a skewer inserted in the centre comes out clean.

Let the cake cool in the tin for 20 minutes and then place a thin cake card over the top and invert the tin. Lift off the tin so the cake sits on the card. It will still be warm, so do not try to move it at this stage. Cool the cake completely.

To soak the cake, bring the water and sugar to the boil in a small pan and stir in the red wine. Fill the cleaned bundt tin with the red wine syrup and place the cooled cake back in the tin. It will quickly absorb the hot liquid. Once the liquid has been absorbed, reverse the cake on to the cake card as before. Remove the tin, being careful not to damage the cake.

Leave the cake to cool before glazing. Bring the redcurrant jelly to a rolling boil in a small pan, then remove from the heat and, with a small, flat brush, quickly brush the hot jelly over the cake using large strokes. Let the jelly set, then repeat the process for a beautiful glossy finish.

To finish the cake, you need to make little discs of tempered chocolate. Spoon 10–15 small blobs of the chocolate, about 1cm/¹/₂ inch wide, on to a sheet of acetate, spacing them 5cm/2 inches apart. Place a second sheet of acetate on top of the chocolate and press down to flatten each blob to a smooth circle. They do not have to be completely round – that is half the fun. Place the chocolate discs, still sandwiched in the acetate, on a

(continued on page 52)

(continued from page 50)

baking sheet, put another baking sheet on top of it and leave in the fridge for 10–15 minutes to set.

Remove the top sheet of acetate and peel away the chocolate circles. Using a hot knife, cut the base off each circle so they sit flat at the bottom of the cake. Push them one at a time on to the sides of the cake round the base; they will stick to the jelly.

Claire's Notes
• Make the chocolate decorations the day before you make the cake, to take the hassle out of finishing it. If you do not feel up to tempering chocolate, look in your local supermarket for chocolate decorations – they can be fun.
• The cake will keep for a week in a sealed container in the fridge.
• Sheets of acetate can be bought in boxes from most stationery stores.

CHOCOLATE FUDGE BROWNIES

280g/10oz dark chocolate (70 per cent cocoa solids)
3 large eggs
2 teaspoons vanilla extract
280g/10oz soft dark brown sugar
80g/2³/₄oz plain flour
1¹/₂ teaspoons baking powder
a pinch of salt
200g/7oz unsalted butter, melted
200g/7oz pecan nuts

MAKES 20

I thought hard about which brownie recipe to include in this book, as I have several I use when compiling different dishes. However, the one I have chosen is the one I actually like to eat the best, simply as a brownie. It is also versatile enough to double up as a base for a dessert, if you so wish. One of my favourite brownie desserts consists of chocolate brownie cubes, Butterscotch Sauce (see page 130), velvety White Chocolate Mousse (page 130) and lots of dark chocolate shavings and whipped cream, with possibly a little hot Chocolate Sauce (pages 148–149) too.

Preheat the oven to 170°C/325°F/Gas Mark 3. Break up half the chocolate and place it in a bowl set over a pan of simmering water to melt, making sure the water isn't touching the base of the bowl. As soon as it has melted, remove the bowl from over the pan and leave on the stove top to keep warm. Chop the remaining chocolate into small pieces.

Whisk the eggs, vanilla and sugar with an electric mixer until pale and doubled in volume. Sift the flour, baking powder and salt and fold them in. Combine the warm melted chocolate and melted butter and fold them in too. Lastly add the chopped chocolate and pecan nuts, and mix well.

Transfer to a lined 20 x 30cm/8 x12 inch baking tin, about 2.5cm/1 inch deep, and bake for 20–22 minutes, until a skewer inserted in the centre comes out clean. Do not overbake the brownies, as they are best soft and chewy. Cool slightly in the tin, then cut into squares. Serve the brownies warm, with Vanilla Ice Cream (see page 192).

SCONES

440g/15³/₄oz plain flour
50g/1³/₄oz baking powder
a pinch of salt
80g/2³/₄oz unsalted butter, diced
40g1¹/₂oz sultanas
150ml/5fl oz double cream
150ml/5fl oz milk
80g/2³/₄oz caster sugar

For the egg wash
1 egg
1 egg yolk
a good pinch of salt

MAKES 16

I began my career as a pastry chef in 1984, working in the basement of the Ritz Hotel on Piccadilly. In many ways this was a baptism of fire. We would start at 8am and finish at some ungodly hour the following morning, working flat out in the old and worn-out confines of a kitchen that could have told many a story about its past. I dreaded the run-up to the weekend, when the hotel held its famous tea dances. We would slave away all week constructing the intricate, delicate and elegant pastries to give ourselves time to make, roll, cut and bake the vast quantity of scones on the day. I still visit the kitchens of the Ritz to see my good friend, John Williams, who is now head chef there. The kitchen has transformed to become modern and spanking new, but afternoon tea has remained as popular as ever – so popular that at weekends they start serving it at 11am!

Sift the flour, baking powder and salt into a bowl. Using just your fingertips, rub the butter into the flour until it is no longer visible. Add the sultanas.

Mix the cream and milk together. Add them to the flour mixture and mix well. Once it starts to come together, turn out on to a lightly floured surface and knead gently just until it forms a smooth, soft dough. Wrap in cling film and chill for 1 hour.

Preheat the oven to 200°C/400°F/Gas Mark 6. Roll the dough out on a lightly floured surface to 2.5cm/1 inch thick and cut it into rounds with a 5cm/2 inch cutter. Place on a baking tray lined with baking parchment.

For the egg wash, beat all the ingredients together and pass through a fine sieve. Brush the tops of the scones with the egg wash. Bake for 10 minutes, until golden brown. Do not overbake them or they will be dry.

Claire's Notes
• Turn the scones over before placing them on the baking sheet, so that the top becomes the bottom. This makes them rise more evenly.
• To check if the scones are cooked, pull one apart and see if the centre is done.

PASTRY

THE SECRETS
OF SUCCESS

In its most basic form, pastry is a combination of flour, fat and liquid, with a little sugar or salt. It can then be flavoured and enriched with eggs, ground nuts, cocoa powder, spices and herbs, etc. It is quite amazing that if you take the four primary ingredients – flour, fat, water and salt – you can make puff pastry, shortcrust and choux paste, all of which are completely different in taste and appearance. For the recipes in this chapter, I have used the pastry that I think suits each tart best, but there is no reason why you cannot substitute shortcrust for sweet pastry, if you prefer.

SHORTCRUST PASTRY

Shortcrust is the quickest and easiest pastry to make. When baked, it is flakier and more crumbly than sweet pastry and not quite so rich.

The method relies on working the fat into small particles throughout the flour. When the water or other liquid is added, it coats the particles of fat. During baking, the water creates steam and pockets of air, resulting in a light, crisp pastry.

It is therefore important that the butter is cold when you rub it into the flour. If it is too soft, it will not form as many particles and the pastry will not be as light and crisp. Use your fingertips to rub it in: pick up a little of the flour and butter mixture, lift it up to aerate it and then lightly rub it over your fingertips with your thumbs so it drops back into the bowl. Shake the bowl occasionally so any remaining lumps come to the surface. The mixture should resemble fine breadcrumbs when the butter has been rubbed in sufficiently. Always handle it as lightly as possible to keep the butter cool. If you have hot hands, run them under cold water before you start the mixing process.

Use chilled water to keep the overall temperature of the pastry low. This will help prevent the dough being too soft and squashing all the fat into a mass when you bring the ingredients together into a dough. Add the water slowly and bring the dough together gently so it is soft but not sticky. It should form a ball. You may need a little more or a little less water than the amount specified in the recipe.

Never overhandle the dough so it becomes greasy and grey. Always handle it as quickly and lightly as possible. Let the pastry rest in the fridge before rolling. This relaxes the gluten and prevents shrinkage.

SWEET PASTRY

Sweet pastry relies on creaming butter and sugar together to make a soft, light pastry. There is no need to beat them until they are light and fluffy, as you would for cakes (see page 32). In fact, if you overmix the butter and sugar, the pastry will be very difficult to roll out and handle. The butter should be at room temperature, so it blends with the sugar easily. Once the two are combined, you can start to add the eggs or egg yolks a little at a time. The eggs enrich the dough and add flavour and colour. Make sure they are at room temperature, otherwise the mixture might curdle. Once the sifted flour has been added, the dough should be brought together as quickly as possible, without overhandling.

You can make sweet pastry very easily in a food processor. All the ingredients can be added at the beginning, as the mixing is so quick.

A creamed pastry will always be harder to handle and roll than one that has been made by rubbing the fat into the flour. Letting it rest in the fridge for several hours before rolling will help to overcome this. If possible, always make the pastry the day before and rolling and handling will be a problem of the past. If the pastry is too firm to roll after a night in the fridge, you can soften it slightly by kneading it gently on a lightly floured work surface.

PUFF PASTRY

Puff pastry consists of lots of very fine, light and airy layers, the success of which depends on rolling and folding the rich, buttery dough in a series of 'turns'. Even experienced cooks can be daunted by the thought of making puff at home. I have tried to simplify the recipes below to make them as easy as possible for home cooks to tackle.

If you have a marble slab, do use it for making your puff pastry, as it will really make a difference. Marble remains colder than other worktops and is also slightly porous, which will make rolling a little easier.

The Three-quarters Puff below is a super-fast pastry that gives perfect lift and is easier to make than a full puff. The name refers to the type of fold that is made during production. You can use Three-quarters Puff any time you would use full puff where a good rise and lift is required, as in the Tutti Frutti Vol-au-Vents on page 90.

The Quick Puff Pastry has 30 per cent less rise than the Three-quarters Puff. It is suitable for pies, flan shells and mille-feuille, where the rise is not paramount but flakiness is.

Here are some important points to remember when making puff:

- Always work in a cool environment.
- Use strong bread flour rather than ordinary plain flour. It has a higher gluten content, which allows the pastry to hold its shape during baking.
- Contrary to popular belief, the water does not have to be chilled. Cold water from the tap is fine.
- Dust the work surface evenly and lightly with flour and move the pastry regularly as you roll, so you can check that it is not sticking to the work surface. Keep dusting the surface to prevent sticking.
- When enclosing the butter in the dough for Three-quarters Puff, make sure the pastry edges are firmly pressed down around the butter to seal it in. This will prevent it leaking later on during the turning process.
- Roll right to the edges of the dough or you will form what we in the trade call 'pig's ears' in the corners. These will spoil the even rising of the dough.
- Never squeeze or press down the dough, as this will break the layers.
- Always bake puff pastry in a hot oven (200°C/400°F/Gas Mark 6) to ensure maximum rise.

THREE-QUARTERS PUFF PASTRY

No one said making puff pastry was easy, and there is a fair amount of rolling and folding to be done. However, it is well worth the effort. This recipe makes a large amount of pastry, which can be divided into five 500g/1lb 2oz blocks, to be stored in the freezer. By all means halve the quantities if you prefer.

600g/1lb 5oz unsalted butter, plus 125g/4$\frac{1}{2}$oz unsalted butter cut into small cubes
1kg/2$\frac{1}{4}$lb strong white flour
500ml/18fl oz cold water
20g/$\frac{3}{4}$oz salt
1 teaspoon lemon juice

The 600g/1lb 5oz butter should be lightly chilled but just pliable. Shape it into a square 2cm/$\frac{3}{4}$ inch thick and set aside.

Sift the flour into a bowl and rub in the diced butter with your fingertips. Combine the water, salt and lemon juice, then mix them into the flour, using your fingers. Knead the dough lightly for a minute, until it is firm but elastic.

On a lightly floured work surface (preferably a marble slab), roll out the dough to form a rectangle twice as long as it is broad. It should be about 2cm/$\frac{3}{4}$ inch thick. Place the square of butter at one end of the dough, then fold the dough back over to enclose it. Seal the edges with your fingers; you should have a neat square in which 2 layers of dough sandwich a single layer of butter.

Turn the pastry so the sealed, round, bookend edge of the block is on your right, then roll it out in a length towards and away from you until it is 1cm/$\frac{1}{2}$ inch thick, dusting the work surface regularly with flour and picking up the pastry to make sure it is not sticking; it should be 4 times as long as it is broad and form a neat, precise rectangle. Fold one short edge of the pastry to a point roughly two-thirds of the way along the rolled-out length, then fold back the other short edge to meet it. Align the 2 edges and fold the dough in half to form a square. This is your first 'turn'. Wrap the pastry in cling film and leave to rest in the fridge for half an hour. Repeat the rolling and folding process, making sure you begin with the sealed edge on your right, and then rest the dough in the fridge for half an hour again, wrapped in cling film.

Repeat 2 more turns, making 4 in total. Wrap the pastry well in cling film and chill for 1 hour before using. You can store it in the fridge for a couple of days or in the freezer for 3 months.

QUICK PUFF PASTRY

Like the Three-quarters Puff, this makes a large quantity of pastry, which can be cut up and stored in the freezer in five 500g/1lb 2oz blocks. Halve the quantities if you prefer to make a smaller amount.

When making this pastry in the States, I have found that I only need about half the amount of water, because of the different absorbency rate of the flour. I would recommend that readers in the US add the water gradually, using just enough to form a dough.

MAKES 2.5KG/5LB 10OZ

1kg/2^1/$_4$lb strong white flour
20g/^{3}/$_4$oz salt
1kg/2^1/$_4$lb unsalted butter (it should be firm, but not hard),
   cut into 2.5cm/1 inch cubes
500ml/18fl oz cold water

Sift the flour and salt on to a cool work surface (preferably a marble slab) and make a large well in the centre. The well should be wide and shallow rather than tall and deep. Place the cubes of butter in the well and, using your fingertips, lightly work the ingredients together, gradually drawing in the flour. When the cubes of butter have become very small and half squashed, add the water to the well and gradually mix all the ingredients together. Do not knead it, and stop working the pastry as soon as it becomes homogeneous. It should still contain flakes of butter.

Clean the marble slab and flour it lightly. Roll out the dough into a rectangle 3 times as long as it is wide. Fold in one third of the dough, then fold the remaining third on top to make 3 layers. Make sure the block is neat and precise, with square edges. Give it a quarter turn so the sealed, bookend edge is on your right. This is your first 'turn'. Now roll the pastry out in a length towards and away from you until it is 1cm/^{1}/$_2$ inch thick, dusting the work surface regularly with flour and picking up the pastry to make sure it is not sticking. When it is 3 times as long as it is wide again, fold it as before. Wrap in cling film and leave to rest in the fridge for 20 minutes.

Repeat the rolling and folding process twice more, to make 4 turns in total. Wrap the pastry well in cling film and chill for 1 hour before using. You can store it in the fridge for a couple of days or in the freezer for 3 months.

ROLLING OUT PASTRY AND LINING A TART TIN

All pastry dough should be rested in the fridge before rolling so the gluten (the protein in the flour, which is only formed once the liquid is added) relaxes, thereby preventing shrinkage. Chilling the pastry also helps enormously to make it firm enough to roll and handle easily.

Whatever type of pastry you are rolling out, the same basic rules apply:

• Use a lightly floured work surface. A cool surface, such as a chilled marble slab, is an advantage. Besides flouring the work surface, you can lightly flour the top of the pastry too, to prevent it sticking to the rolling pin.
• Don't be tempted to turn the pastry over when rolling, as this would incorporate too much flour and can make it dry and hard. However, do keep giving the pastry a quarter turn to your right or left, to make sure it isn't sticking to the work surface and to keep it in shape.
• Try to use only roughly the amount of pastry you need to line your tart tin. A smaller amount is easier to roll and handle than a large one. Ideally you need enough pastry to be able to roll into a circle about 5cm/2 inches bigger than the diameter of your tin.
• Once you have rolled the pastry, if you find it too soft to work with, roll it loosely around the rolling pin and then unroll it on to a baking sheet lined with baking parchment. Chill in the fridge until it is firm enough for you to be able to handle it easily.
• To line the tart tin or flan ring, lightly dust the surface of the pastry with flour to prevent it sticking and then roll it loosely around the rolling pin to lift it up and transport it easily to the tin (if you're nervous about doing this, you can slide a flat, thin cake card under the rolled pastry, then lift the pastry on the card and slide it off over your tin). Unroll it over the tart tin or flan ring, easing it into the edges and making sure it sits well in the base of the ring. Never stretch the pastry. You can use a small piece of dough made into a ball to push the pastry into the base and up the sides.
• Trim off the excess pastry either with a small, sharp knife or by rolling the rolling pin over the top of the tart tin. Always leave to rest in the fridge before baking blind.

BAKING BLIND

A pastry case needs to be baked blind whenever the filling takes less time to cook than the pastry, or if the filling is liquid and likely to soften the pastry, preventing it cooking properly – a good example of this is the Lemon Tart on page 74. The pastry case is lined with cling film or baking parchment (I prefer cling film) and then filled with baking beans to prevent the pastry slipping down the sides of the tin as it cooks.

Line the pastry case with enough cling film to overhang the sides by about 15cm/6 inches. Fill the case to the top with baking beans – you can buy special ceramic ones but ordinary dried beans or rice will do the job just as well and can be kept and reused. Bring in the excess cling film to make a sealed parcel. Be careful not to pull the cling film away from the edge of the tin; the beans need to be touching the side of the lined ring to prevent the pastry collapsing during baking. Bake in the centre of the oven on a preheated baking sheet for the time specified in the recipe, then remove the parcel of beans; the pastry on the base should be set but not fully cooked. Continue baking, without the beans and cling film, until the pastry is firm and lightly coloured.

CHOUX PASTRY

Choux pastry is a cross between a batter and a dough. The water and butter are heated together, the flour is tipped in and beaten to form a dough, then the eggs are gradually added. The eggs transform the mixture into a softer batter that can be piped into shapes. Choux pastry is used to make finger-shaped cases for éclairs and round buns for profiteroles and petits fours. Here are some tips for successful choux pastry:

• Once the flour has been added to the boiling water and butter, remember to cook the dough until it forms a ball in the centre of the pan.
• The paste should be stirred or mixed lightly to let some, but not all of the heat out before adding the eggs; this prevents them cooking.

• Always beat the eggs together before adding them to the batter. Mix them in a little at a time; this will help ensure they are distributed evenly. The batter can go lumpy if the eggs are added too quickly.
• The oven temperature is very important. Choux pastry should be baked in a hot oven (200°C/400°F/Gas Mark 6). If the oven is too cool, the water in the dough will not evaporate quickly enough and the buns will not form a well-risen bubble. As the heat evaporates the water and pushes the dough upwards, the surface sets quickly while the interior stays nearly liquid. It is therefore very important to lower the temperature after about 20 minutes, to dry out the interior of the bun.

BAKEWELL TART

150g/5^1/$_2$oz raspberry jam
30g/1oz flaked almonds

For the pastry
125g/4^1/$_2$oz unsalted butter, at
room temperature
50g/1^3/$_4$oz caster sugar
1 medium egg, lightly beaten
200g/7oz plain flour
a pinch of salt

For the frangipane
230g/8oz unsalted butter, at room
temperature
230g/8oz caster sugar
2 medium eggs, lightly beaten
grated zest of 1 lemon
6 drops of vanilla extract
230g/8oz ground almonds
60g//2^1/$_4$oz plain flour

To decorate
50g/1^3/$_4$oz icing sugar
a little kirsch or Amaretto liqueur
3 tablespoons apricot preserve

SERVES 8

This is best eaten still warm. However, the wonderful thing about this classic tart is that, because of the large proportion of almonds and the natural fat they contain, it stays moist for days and can be baked a day or two ahead, then reheated for that 'just out of the oven' freshness. My little secret is to finish the top with some water icing but replace the water with kirsch or Amaretto liqueur.

First make the pastry. Lightly cream the butter and sugar together, then mix in the beaten egg. Sift the flour and salt into the bowl and bring the mixture together to form a dough. Do not overwork it, making it too soft, or it will become difficult to handle later on. Wrap in cling film and chill for at least 2 hours.

Roll out the pastry on a lightly floured work surface and use to line a 25cm/10 inch tart tin, pushing it down well into the base of the tin and trimming off the excess. Chill for 30 minutes.

Meanwhile, for the frangipane, beat together the butter and sugar until light and fluffy. Gradually add the beaten eggs, mixing well between each addition. Mix in the lemon zest and vanilla. Sift the almonds with the flour and add to the batter in one go. Fold through the mix gently until all the dry ingredients are incorporated.

Preheat the oven to 180°C/350°F/Gas Mark 4. Spread the raspberry jam evenly over the base of the prepared pastry case. Fill with the frangipane and level the surface with a palette knife so it comes flush with the top of the tin. Scatter the flaked almonds over the top. Bake for 40 minutes or until the surface is golden brown and the top springs back when pressed gently. If you are unsure, test with a skewer; it should come out clean.

Leave the tart in the tin to cool slightly before serving. Meanwhile, mix the icing sugar with enough kirsch or Amaretto to make a thin, translucent icing. Bring the apricot preserve to the boil with a tablespoon of water, then pass through a fine sieve. Bring to the boil again in a clean pan. Brush the top of the tart with the boiled apricot preserve and then brush with the icing.

Claire's Notes
• If you prefer not to use alcohol, make the icing with water. It makes the tart shine and adds a sweet, soft finish.
• Instead of one large tart, you could make 8 individual ones, using little tartlet tins. To give them a restaurant finish like the one in the photo, omit the glaze and the water icing and instead use the fondant icing on page 94 to decorate it, omitting the chocolate.

TREACLE TART

320g/11½oz golden syrup
250g/9oz fresh white breadcrumbs
1 teaspoon ground ginger
juice and grated zest of 1 lemon

For the shortcrust pastry
200g/7oz plain flour
a pinch of salt
50g/1¾oz lard or vegetable
  shortening, diced
50g/1¾oz unsalted butter, diced
about 2 tablespoons iced water

SERVES 6–8

I am convinced that the British have more desserts using stale bread than any other country, and every one of them is tasty and wholesome. For some, treacle conjures up images of black treacle but golden syrup is in fact also treacle. Treacle is the collective name for any syrup made during the refining of cane sugar. No one can dispute that Tate & Lyle made treacle, or golden syrup as they named it, famous by canning it in their distinctive green and gold tins crested with the lion emblem. They also, of course, can molasses in the same fashion and call it treacle. I can see why a non-native might get confused.

Enjoy this tart with Crème Anglaise (see page 118) and/or Vanilla Ice Cream (page 192).

To make the pastry, sift the flour and salt into a large mixing bowl and add the lard or shortening and the butter. Using only your fingertips, rub the fat into the flour until the mixture resembles fine breadcrumbs. Add the iced water a little at a time, lightly kneading the pastry together to form a soft but not sticky dough. Form the dough into a ball and flatten slightly with your hand; this will make it easier to roll later. Wrap in cling film and chill for 30 minutes.

Preheat the oven to 190°C/375°F/Gas Mark 5. On a lightly floured work surface, roll out the dough to about 5mm/¼ inch thick and use to line a 20cm/8 inch loose-bottomed tart tin. Trim off the excess and then chill the pastry case while you make the filling.

Put the golden syrup in a saucepan and heat it almost to boiling point, then mix with the breadcrumbs, ginger and lemon juice and zest. Pour the filling into the pastry case and bake near the top of the oven for 25–30 minutes, until the mix is just softly set and the pastry is golden. Remember, the treacle is extremely hot, so take care when removing the tart from the oven and let it cool slightly before removing the ring.

Claire's Notes
• If you like your treacle tart to have more texture, substitute oats for a quarter of the breadcrumbs.
• You can make the pastry case ahead of time and freeze it in the tart tin. It will keep for up to 6 weeks in the freezer. Defrost before filling and baking.

GOOSEBERRY, BROWN SUGAR AND MASCARPONE TART

500g/1lb 2oz mascarpone cheese
juice of 1 orange and grated zest
    of $^3/_4$ orange
2–3 tablespoons soft light brown
    sugar
400–600g/14oz–1lb 5oz fresh
    gooseberries, topped and tailed
1 tablespoon demerara sugar

For the pastry
110g/3$^3/_4$oz softened unsalted
    butter
50g/1$^3/_4$oz caster sugar
1 medium egg
grated zest of $^1/_4$ orange (taken
    from the orange for the filling)
$^1/_2$ capful of vanilla extract
210g/7$^1/_2$oz plain flour
a pinch of salt

SERVES 8

Claire's Notes
• The unbaked pastry case can be
frozen ahead of time. The finished
tart will keep in a sealed container
in the fridge for 2–3 days.
• If you like more of a caramel
taste, use soft dark brown sugar,
which gives a molasses flavour to
the tart.
• Use a selection of different-
coloured gooseberries – this gives
a variation in sweetness and also a
pretty effect.

I have fond memories of picking gooseberries with my father as a child. We would make a crumble while my mother was out shopping and were always very pleased with our trophy pudding when she came home.

Gooseberries will stay fresh in the fridge for up to two weeks. Depending on the variety, the colour varies from a golden colour to anything from pale pink to dark purple. The darker they are, the less tart they will be. Avoid bright green gooseberries unless making jam, as they are not ripe. When making your selection, choose hard, dry berries with a high sheen.

Make the pastry in a food processor, if you have one, by placing all the ingredients in the machine and pulsing gently until they form a soft but not sticky dough. If you are making the pastry by hand, lightly cream the butter and sugar together with a wooden or plastic spoon. Beat the egg with the orange zest and vanilla extract and add to the creamed mixture a little at a time, beating well between each addition. Sift the flour and salt on to a piece of baking parchment and add to the creamed mixture all in one go. Bring together with your hand to form a ball of soft but not sticky dough.

Flatten the dough to about 1cm/$^1/_2$ inch thick, wrap in cling film and leave in the fridge for 30 minutes. Then roll it out to about 5mm/$^1/_4$ inch thick on a lightly floured work surface and use to line a 25cm/10 inch loose-bottomed tart tin, pushing it well down into the rim at the bottom. Trim off any dough overhanging the edges with a small knife, place the tin on a baking tray and leave in the fridge to rest for 30 minutes. Preheat the oven to 180°C/350°F/Gas Mark 4.

To bake the pastry case blind, line with cling film and fill with baking beans (see page 61). Bake in the centre of the oven for 15 minutes, then remove the parcel of beans; the pastry on the base should be set but not fully cooked. Continue baking, without the beans and cling film, for about 10 minutes to finish cooking the pastry. Remove from the oven and leave to cool.

Meanwhile, mix the mascarpone cheese with the orange juice and zest. Add the soft brown sugar and mix well.

When the pastry case is completely cold, fill it two-thirds full with the flavoured mascarpone cheese and level it with a palette knife or spatula. Place the gooseberries on top of the mascarpone cheese in a circular fashion, starting at the edge of the tart tin and working to the centre. Make sure as much of the mascarpone is covered as possible.

Sprinkle with the demerara sugar and bake in the centre of the oven for 20–25 minutes, until the gooseberries are soft. Leave to cool in the tin before attempting to remove the tart. The mascarpone will firm as it cools.

WARM CHOCOLATE AND RASPBERRY TARTS

300g/10$\frac{1}{2}$oz dark chocolate
(70 per cent cocoa solids)
200g/7oz unsalted butter
3 medium eggs
4 medium egg yolks
50g/1$\frac{3}{4}$oz caster sugar
about 450g/1lb raspberries, plus
extra to serve
crème fraîche, to serve

For the chocolate pastry
100g/3$\frac{1}{2}$oz softened unsalted
butter
100g/3$\frac{1}{2}$oz icing sugar, sifted
1 large egg
$\frac{1}{2}$ capful of vanilla extract
225g/8oz plain flour
25g/1oz cocoa powder
a pinch of salt

To finish (optional)
3–4 tablespoons apricot preserve
chocolate curls, to decorate (see
pages 213–214)
a little icing sugar for dusting

SERVES 8

Crammed full of ripe raspberries cloaked in warm, molten chocolate, these tarts scream decadence. They are a great choice for a dinner party. If you want to serve them warm they do need to be baked just before serving to be soft in the centre but the good news is that you can prepare them in advance, right up to the point where you put the chocolate filling in, then store them in the fridge. They take only 8 minutes to bake, and I can assure you your guests will think it worth the short wait. If you want to serve the tarts barely warm or within an hour or two of baking, they have a lovely, fudgy texture and you can decorate them with chocolate curls and raspberries as shown in the picture. Either way they will both look and taste good.

Make the pastry in a food processor, if you have one, by putting all the ingredients in the machine and pulsing to form a soft but not sticky dough. If you're making the pastry by hand, lightly cream together the soft butter and icing sugar just enough to bring them together. Beat the egg with the vanilla extract and mix into the creamed mixture a little at a time, beating well between each addition. Sift the flour, cocoa powder and salt together on to a piece of baking parchment. Add them all in one go and bring together with your hand to form a soft but not sticky dough.

Flatten the dough to about 1cm/$\frac{1}{2}$ inch thick, wrap in cling film and leave to rest in the fridge for 30 minutes. Roll it out on a lightly floured work surface to about 5mm/$\frac{1}{4}$ inch thick and cut out 8 discs with a 15cm/6 inch cutter. Use the discs of pastry to line 8 loose-bottomed tart tins, 10cm/4 inches in diameter, making sure they are well pressed into the rim of the tins at the base. Trim off any excess with a small, sharp knife. Lightly prick the bases with a fork and return to the fridge for 15 minutes to rest. Preheat the oven to 180°C/350°F/Gas Mark 4.

To bake the pastry cases blind, line with cling film and fill with baking beans (see page 61). Place on a baking sheet in the centre of the oven and bake for 15 minutes, then remove the parcels of beans; the pastry on the base should be set but not fully cooked. Continue baking, without the beans and cling film, for about 10 minutes to finish cooking the pastry.

Meanwhile, put the chocolate and butter in a bowl set over a pan of simmering water, making sure the water doesn't touch the base of the bowl, and leave to melt. Using an electric mixer, whisk the eggs, egg yolks and sugar until pale, fluffy and tripled in volume. Fold in the melted butter and chocolate with a large metal spoon. The chocolate and butter mixture should be warm when you add it.

Place 6–8 raspberries in each pastry case and squash them a little so they are no higher than the top of the tart. Spoon or pipe the chocolate filling into each tart and level with a palette knife. Place them on a baking sheet and bake near the top of the oven for 8 minutes. The centre should look damp and not quite cooked. Serve immediately, with lots of fresh raspberries and a spoonful of crème fraîche.

If you do not mind a more fudgy texture, let the tarts cool and then dress them up a little. They can be just warm, but not so hot they melt the chocolate decoration. Cover the centre of the tarts with fresh raspberries and brush with a little sieved boiled apricot preserve. Decorate the outside rim with the chocolate curls and dust lightly with icing sugar.

Claire's Notes
• The tarts will keep for 2–3 days in a sealed container in the fridge and are great eaten cold with crème fraîche or plain yoghurt.
• This recipe works well without the raspberries. I just add a little orange zest and a couple of drops of orange flower water to the filling with the melted butter and chocolate, if I want a change. Fresh cherries and strawberries also work well.

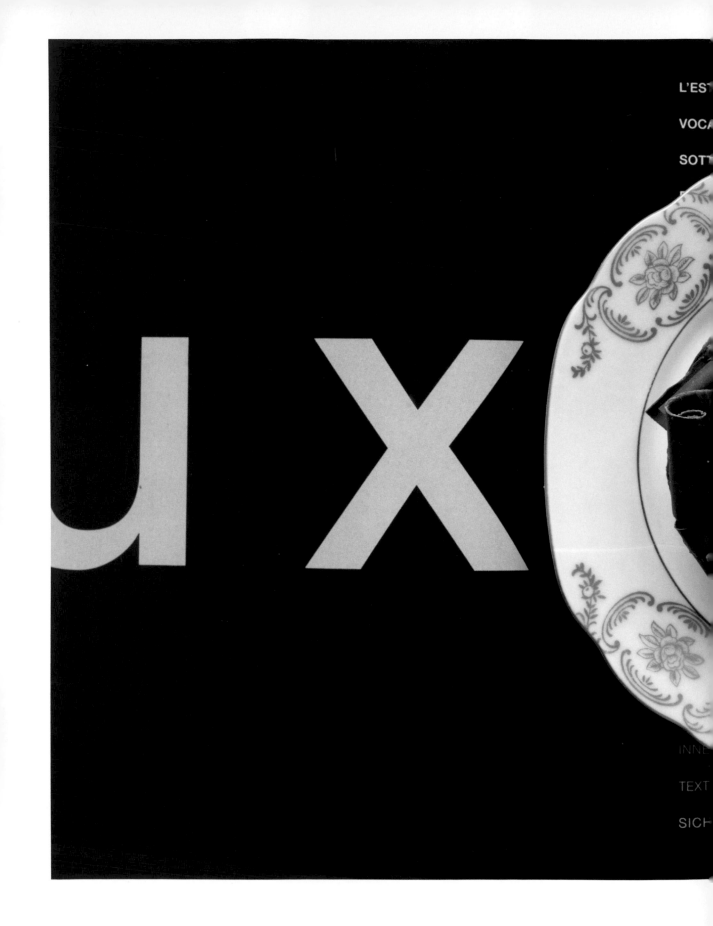

L'EST

VOCA

SOTT

INNE

TEXT

SICH

IN LEGNO HA LO CHARME DI CERTE CASE DI CAMPAGNA, QUI RILETTE CON UN

RIO ARCHITETTONICO CONTEMPORANEO. IL GRANDE PRATO CHE LA CIRCONDA

LOGO CON LA NATURA. L'INTERNO NON RINUNCIA AD

E FINITURE, DELLE PARETI, DEI TESSUTI.

CCEZIONE PIÙ DISCRETA E, PER

CALLS A CHARMING COUNTRY

ESSION. A LARGE LAWN

TH NATURE. INTERNALLY,

WALLS AND FABRICS.

OIS A LE CHARME DE

RAVERS UNE VISION

OURE SOULIGNE LA

IT NE RENONCE PAS À

ES MURS, DES TISSUS,

QUE PLUS SOPHISTIQUÉ.

LANDHÄUSERN, DER SICH HIER

ERFINDET. DER WEITE, DAS HAUS

CH EINEM DIALOG MIT DER NATUR. DIE

WAHL IHRER AUSFÜHRUNG, DER WÄNDE, DER

INE RAFFINIERTERE AUSDRUCKSFORM. EINE INTERPRETATION VON LUXUS, WIE ER

INER DISKRETESTEN UND DAHER IN SEINER EDELSTEN FORM DARSTELLT.

APPLE AND BLACKBERRY BANDE AUX FRUITS

100g/3^1/$_2$oz blackberries

3–4 apples

3–4 tablespoons apricot preserve

2–3 tablespoons icing sugar

1 tablespoon Calvados or cider

For the sweet pastry

110g/3^3/$_4$oz softened unsalted
   butter

50g/1^3/$_4$oz caster sugar

1 medium egg

^{1}/$_2$ capful of vanilla extract

210g/7^1/$_2$oz plain flour

a pinch of salt

For the almond cream

125g/4^1/$_2$oz softened unsalted
   butter

125g/4^1/$_2$oz caster sugar

2 large eggs, at room temperature,
   lightly beaten

grated zest of ^{1}/$_2$ lemon

^{1}/$_2$ teaspoon vanilla extract

40g/1^1/$_2$oz plain flour

125g/4^1/$_2$oz ground almonds

SERVES 6–8

I was fortunate enough to spend some of my life on a farm, and spring was definitely my favourite time of year, when the daffodils would surround the pond in a crown of glory and the lambs would skip across the green fields. Come autumn, the hay was cut and everywhere looked a little brown, but the hedgerows, laden with ripe, plump blackberries, cheered up the mile-long driveway. There were so many berries you could not pick them fast enough. I used to freeze as many as I could and make a variety of blackberry desserts in the winter months.

I would always recommend you pick your own blackberries if you can, but frozen ones can be pretty good too. I use Cox's Orange Pippin apples here, but Braeburn, Pink Lady and the American variety, Washington Red Skin, all make good substitutes.

You will need an oblong tart tin for this recipe, about 25 x 10cm/ 10 x 4 inches.

Make the pastry in a food processor, if you have one, by placing all the ingredients in the machine and pulsing gently until they form a soft but not sticky dough. If you are making the pastry by hand, lightly cream the butter and sugar together with a wooden or plastic spoon. Beat the egg with the vanilla extract and add to the creamed mixture a little at a time, beating well between each addition. Sift the flour and salt on to a piece of baking parchment and add to the creamed mixture all in one go. Bring together with your hand to form a ball of soft but not sticky dough.

Flatten the dough with your hand to about 1cm/^{1}/$_2$ inch thick, wrap in cling film and leave to rest in the fridge for about 30 minutes.

Meanwhile, make the almond cream. Cream the butter and sugar together until pale and fluffy. Add the beaten eggs a little at a time, mixing well between each addition. Mix in the lemon zest and vanilla extract. Sift the flour and ground almonds together on to a piece of baking parchment and add to the creamed mix all in one go. Fold in the dry ingredients (if using an electric mixer, you can do this with the machine but use a lower speed).

Preheat the oven to 180°C/350°F/Gas Mark 4. Roll the pastry out on a lightly floured work surface into a rectangle about 30 x 15cm/12 x 6 inches; it should be about 5mm/^{1}/$_4$ inch thick. Use to line the oblong tart tin, pressing it well into the base and up the sides. Lightly roll the pin over the top of the tin to remove the excess pastry. Spoon the almond cream into the lined tart tin so it is about two-thirds full and level with a spatula or palette knife. Set aside in a cool place, but not the fridge, while you prepare the apples.

(continued on page 72)

(continued from page 70)

Peel and core the apples, cut them in half and then slice them thinly, keeping them together in a half shape. Place the apple halves on to the almond cream, pressing on them lightly so they fan out slightly. Dot the blackberries around the apples. Bake in the middle of the oven for about 25 minutes, until the pastry is golden brown and the almond cream springs back when pressed gently. Check to see if the almond cream is cooked by inserting a small knife into the centre of the flan; it should come out clean.

Bring the apricot preserve to the boil with a tablespoon of water and pass through a fine sieve. Bring to the boil again in a clean pan. Using a pastry brush, brush the apricot glaze over the tart to seal in the moisture and give it a shine. Now combine the icing sugar and Calvados or cider in a small bowl until smooth and clear; it should be runny. Brush the mixture on top of the apricot glaze. Serve the tart warm, with lashings of hot Crème Anglaise (see page 118).

Claire's Notes

• If you have plenty of blackberries, make a compote to serve with the flan. Boil equal parts of sugar and water together to make a syrup and pour it over the washed and dried blackberries to poach them. Blitz half the poached blackberries in a blender with a little icing sugar to sweeten. Remove the remaining blackberries from the poaching syrup and mix with the puréed berries. Adjust the sweetness with a little lemon juice if needed, then serve with the tart.

TARTE TATIN

300g/10$\frac{1}{2}$oz Quick Puff Pastry
 (see page 60) or bought butter
 puff pastry
8 medium-sized dessert apples
150g/5$\frac{1}{2}$oz softened unsalted
 butter
300g/10$\frac{1}{2}$oz caster sugar

SERVES 6

This famous French tart was the creation of the Tatin sisters at the end of the nineteenth century. The winning combination of butter and sugar cooked to a caramel with the tartness of apples and the light, flaky butter puff pastry made it a good enough secret to steal. There seems to be some confusion as to how it became upside down. Did Stephanie Tatin drop the tart and bake it anyway? Was she having a bad hair day and taking shortcuts? Who knows? What I do know is that it has long been featured on the menu at Maxim's restaurant in Paris, which can really take the credit for making it so popular today. They wanted the recipe so much, apparently, that they were prepared to send a chef disguised as a gardener to spy on the Tatin sisters' restaurant.

You can use other fruits, such as bananas, mangoes and pears, with success but practise with apples first so you get the hang of the colour and the caramelisation. I like to use Braeburn apples, as they do not break up when cooking, but Cox's are also very good. You can use puff trimmings for the pastry, if you have any; they work just as well as the Quick Puff Pastry.

To bake the tart, you will need a 20–23cm/8–9 inch ovenproof frying pan or flameproof dish. Alternatively, you can use a special Tatin tin, if you have one.

Roll the puff pastry to a thickness of 4–5mm/$\frac{1}{4}$ inch on a lightly floured work surface. It should be about 5cm/2 inches bigger than the frying pan or dish you plan to use for the tart.

Peel, core and halve the apples. Spread the softened butter evenly over the base of your ovenproof frying pan, flameproof dish or Tatin tin. Sprinkle the sugar evenly over the butter. Arrange the apple halves neatly in the pan, round-side down, so they are just touching. They should cover the bottom of the pan. Lay the pastry over the apples and tuck the excess down the side of the pan around the apples. Leave to rest in the fridge for 30 minutes.

Preheat the oven to 220°C/425°F/Gas Mark 7. Place the pan or dish on the hob on a high heat and leave for about 15 minutes, until the butter and sugar are bubbling and turning a golden caramel colour; the pastry will shrink a little and the caramel will bubble up the sides. Make sure the golden colour is showing all round the pan, and not just in one place where the flame might be hotter. Do not leave it unattended, as the caramelisation can occur very quickly and it may burn.

Place the pan or dish at the top of the oven and bake for about 25–30 minutes, until the pastry is golden and the apples are soft but not broken. Remove from the oven and let the Tatin sit for about a minute. Put a plate or shallow dish on top, then invert it to turn out the tart. Take care not to burn yourself; the caramel syrup will be very hot. Serve hot, with ice cream or Crème Anglaise (see page 118).

Claire's Notes
• When inverting the pan to turn out the tart, use an oven glove or a thick cloth. Make sure the plate is pressed firmly on to the top of the pan and turn the tart over away from you, then lift off the pan.
• Serve immediately. Tarte Tatin is never as good when it is cold.

LEMON TART

8 large, unwaxed organic lemons
9 medium eggs
375g/13oz caster sugar, plus
    50–75g/1$\frac{3}{4}$–2 $\frac{3}{4}$oz to
    caramelise
300ml/10fl oz double cream

For the pastry
300g/10$\frac{1}{2}$oz softened unsalted
    butter
150g/5$\frac{1}{2}$oz icing sugar
3 medium egg yolks
a pinch of salt
grated zest of $\frac{1}{2}$ lemon
375g/13oz plain flour

SERVES 8

This must be one of the most popular tarts featured on British dessert menus. There is a fair bit of skill involved in making it well. This recipe is as simple and delicious as I can make it, but be sure to follow the guidelines closely, remembering to chill the pastry and rest it and paying attention to oven temperatures and cooking times.

I like to caramelise the top of the tart to add a little extra sweetness in the form of a thin layer of caramel, which cracks when tapped with a fork or spoon and adds texture to the smooth lemon custard beneath.

First make the pastry. Place the butter in a large mixing bowl and sift in the icing sugar. Mix them together without really creaming them, using a wooden or plastic spoon. As soon as they are combined, mix in the egg yolks, salt and lemon zest. Sift the flour into the bowl and, with your fingertips, combine it with the mixture to make a smooth, soft ball of dough. Do not overhandle it; it should be soft but not sticky. Place the dough on a large piece of cling film and press down to flatten it to about 1cm/$\frac{1}{2}$ inch thick, keeping it in a round shape. Wrap in the cling film and chill for 2 hours.

Meanwhile, make the lemon custard for the filling. Zest 3 of the lemons and then juice them all. Strain the juice into a small pan and simmer over a low heat until it has reduced by half. Remove from the heat and leave to cool. Break the eggs into a bowl and whisk in the sugar by hand. Add the cream and whisk gently to combine. Mix in the cooled lemon juice, then pass the mixture through a fine sieve. Stir in the lemon zest, cover and store in the fridge.

Roll the pastry out on a lightly floured work surface to about 5mm/$\frac{1}{4}$ inch thick. Place a 20cm/8 inch flan hoop, at least 4cm/1$\frac{1}{2}$ inches deep, on a baking tray lined with baking parchment. Wind the pastry loosely around the rolling pin and unwind it over the flan hoop. Making sure you do not stretch the pastry, push it into the bottom of the flan hoop and line the sides with it. It needs to overhang the flan hoop all the way round. Roll off the excess with the rolling pin. Push up the pastry from the inside of the hoop, using your thumb; a little will now be sitting above the ring. Place the lined ring in the fridge to rest for 30 minutes.

Preheat the oven to 190°C/375°F/Gas Mark 5. To bake the pastry case blind, line it with cling film and fill with baking beans (see page 61). Bake in the centre of the oven for 15 minutes, until the pastry has started to colour and is firm to the touch. Remove the cling film and baking beans, reduce the oven temperature to 180°C/350°F/Gas Mark 4 and put the pastry case back in the oven for 15 minutes, until it is an even golden brown and the base is well cooked. Reduce the oven temperature to 140°C/275°F/ Gas Mark 1.

(continued on page 76)

(continued from page 74)

Stir the lemon filling and pour it into the pastry case to just below the rim. Place in the oven and cook for 20 minutes, then turn the temperature down to 120°C/250°F/Gas Mark $1/2$. Cook for another 20 minutes, until the custard is set – if it isn't quite done by this time, continue to cook with the oven door slightly ajar. Do not let the tart filling boil and puff up at any point. Keep an eye on it and turn the oven down a little if you see the filling beginning to soufflé.

Remove the tart from the oven and leave to cool completely in the tin, then place it in the fridge, still in the tin, for 30 minutes. Remove from the fridge and cut away the excess pastry from the top by cutting it against the side of the metal hoop. Do this carefully, as the pastry will be fragile. Remove the hoop, letting the excess pastry fall away. Chill for another hour before caramelising the top with the sugar. Spread the sugar in a thin, even layer over the surface of the tart. Hold a blowtorch a few inches away from the surface and allow the sugar to caramelise over the entire surface. Let the sugar cool for 5 minutes before serving.

Claire's Notes
• It is easier to cut the lemon tart into portions with a clean sharp knife and then caramelise the top of each portion if you want the portions to look neat. If you caramelise the whole tart, it does look very good but will not cut as well.
• For some reason, this tart tastes much better the day after it is made. Caramelise the top when you are ready to serve it.
• The tart can be frozen for up to a week. Defrost well before caramelising the top.

MANGO AND KAFFIR LIME MIRLITON TART

300–400g/10^1/$_2$–14oz Quick Puff
   Pastry (see page 60)
2 large eggs
100g/3^1/$_2$oz caster sugar
grated zest of ^{1}/$_4$ kaffir lime
100g/3^1/$_2$oz ground almonds
15g/^{1}/$_2$oz unsalted butter
1 tablespoon sweet chilli sauce
   (optional)
1–2 mangoes, preferably Manila

SERVES 8

Claire's Notes
• Mangoes have a large, flat stone
that goes through the centre of the
fruit. Cut a little off the fruit from the
top and bottom so the mango sits
flat on the work surface. Peel with
a knife or vegetable peeler, then sit
the fruit back on the work surface.
Feel for the stone by putting your
knife on the top and pressing down
gently. As soon as you feel the fruit
and not the stone, cut downwards,
keeping the knife close to the stone.
Do the same on the other side of
the fruit to remove the stone. Lay
each piece flat and slice.
• The tart will keep in an airtight
container in the fridge for up to a
week.

This recipe is a favourite of my friend Susie Q B, who claims she once won a cookery class at a local horticultural show for her Bakewell tart. Susie, bless her, is not known for her baking or cooking abilities but I did give her this recipe when she asked for a simple dessert to make for a dinner party and I have to say she did a pretty good job.

I have been making this tart since my college days. The ground almonds make it moist and its keeping properties are superb. I added the mango and lime at a much later stage in my career, when I needed an almond tart with a little more interest. I really like the combination of mango and lime and, if you like things a little spicy, you could add some sweet chilli sauce for a kick. I use Manila mangoes from Mexico. They have a yellow skin when ripe and a floral flavour. The kaffir lime has very strong, aromatic zest, which should be used sparingly.

Roll the puff pastry out on a lightly floured work surface to about 5mm/ ^{1}/$_4$ inch thick, then use to line a 25cm/10 inch loose-bottomed tart tin. Do not trim off the excess pastry but leave it overhanging the tin. Place in the fridge to rest for 30 minutes.

Preheat the oven to 180°C/350°F/Gas Mark 4. Remove the tart tin from the fridge and trim off the excess pastry by rolling the pin over the top of the tin. To bake the pastry case blind, line it with cling film and fill with baking beans (see page 61). Bake in the centre of the oven for 15–20 minutes, until the pastry has started to colour and the base is firm to the touch; it should not be wet at this stage. Remove the package of beans and return the pastry case to the oven for about 10 minutes, until the pastry is golden brown. Leave to cool completely.

Using an electric mixer, whisk the eggs and sugar together until pale, fluffy and tripled in volume. Add the lime zest and mix in well. Sift the ground almonds and fold them into the mixture with a large metal spoon, taking care to keep the volume. Melt the butter and pour it down the side of the bowl so it does not drop to the bottom of the mixture. Fold it through gently.

If you are using the sweet chilli sauce, spread it over the base of the pastry case. Peel the mango and cut it into slices no more than 5mm/^{1}/$_4$ inch thick. Arrange them in the pastry case, then spoon the filling on top and level it with a spatula or palette knife.

Bake in the centre of the oven at 180°C/350°F/Gas Mark 4 for about 20 minutes, until the filling springs back when pressed gently. Cool in the tin a little, then turn out and place on a wire rack to cool completely. Serve with Mango Sorbet (see page 202).

RICH CHOCOLATE GANACHE TART WITH SALTED CARAMEL AND CANDIED PEANUTS

50ml/2fl oz Butterscotch Sauce
(see page 130)
2 level teaspoons Maldon sea salt
375ml/12^1/$_2$fl oz double cream
300g/10^1/$_2$oz chocolate (70 per
cent cocoa solids), finely
chopped
75g/2^3/$_4$oz chocolate (72 per cent
cocoa solids), finely chopped

For the sweet pastry
110g/3^3/$_4$oz softened unsalted
butter
80g/2^3/$_4$oz caster sugar
1 small egg
210g/7^1/$_2$oz plain flour
a pinch of salt

For the candied peanuts
100g/3^1/$_2$oz caster sugar
100ml/3^1/$_2$fl oz water
125g/4^1/$_2$oz shelled unsalted
peanuts
500ml/18fl oz canola or vegetable
oil for frying

SERVES 10

The Michelin Guide *came to San Francisco in 2006 and, of course, to The French Laundry. Chef Keller asked me to make a chocolate tart for the 'Michelin Man', who was to be dining with us that evening, specifying a plain, perfectly executed (what else?) rich chocolate ganache tart with no decoration or fuss, to be served with caramel ice cream. I was given a 35cm/14 inch plate and I had to cut a very thin, long wedge and serve it with the scoop of ice cream. With all my years of experience, and many a chocolate tart under my belt, I still made three tarts and hid them around the department just in case... in case I dropped one, in case one set too firm, in case I made a mess of cutting my one slice. There were bowls of cream and chocolate ready weighed in the storeroom, tucked away behind bags of sugar and flour, in case I needed to make another filling at the last minute. Everything was labelled MMO – Michelin Man Only. All staff members were briefed on the whereabouts of the various tarts and preparations in the event of a disaster. Eighteen courses later, Chef Keller at the pass – boy, did it seem a long night – I was up, dessert time. All had gone swimmingly well and all that remained was for me to cut the tart. The pressure was on.*

The chocolate tart was everything it should have been: the pastry a thin, even golden crust, the ganache smooth and shiny and cut to perfection, the ice cream scooped up beautifully. The only thing that was a mess was me, and all because of a chocolate tart for the MM!

This tart is the one I served that night but I have added salted caramel and candied peanuts to jazz it up a little.

Make the pastry in a food processor, if you have one, by placing all the ingredients in the machine and pulsing gently until they form a soft but not sticky dough. If you are making the pastry by hand, lightly cream the butter and sugar together with a wooden or plastic spoon. Beat the egg and add to the creamed mixture a little at a time, beating well between each addition. Sift the flour and salt on to a piece of baking parchment and add to the creamed mixture all in one go. Bring the paste together gently to form a soft but not sticky dough. Do not overhandle it.

Wrap the dough in cling film and chill for 2 hours. Then roll it out on a lightly floured work surface to about 5mm/^{1}/$_4$ inch thick and use to line a 25cm/10 inch loose-bottomed tart tin. Trim off excess pastry and leave the lined tart tin to rest in the fridge for 30 minutes.

Preheat the oven to 170°C/325°F/Gas Mark 3. To bake the pastry case blind, line it with cling film and fill with baking beans (see page 61). Bake in the centre of the oven for 15–20 minutes, until the pastry has started to colour and the base is firm to the touch; it should not be wet at this stage. Remove the package of beans and return the pastry case to the oven for about 10 minutes, until the pastry is golden brown. Leave to cool completely.

Mix the butterscotch sauce with 1 teaspoon of Maldon salt and spread it over the base of the pastry case. Put the tart tin on a baking sheet.

To make the tart filling, bring 250ml/9fl oz of the cream to the boil. Place the remaining cream in a large mixing bowl with all the finely chopped chocolate. Pour the boiled cream over the chocolate and leave for 30 seconds. Whisk very gently to make a smooth, shiny ganache. Do not whisk energetically or your ganache will have too many air bubbles, which will spoil the surface of the tart. Pour the ganache immediately into the centre of the pastry case and level it by gently shaking the baking sheet. Do not use a spatula or palette knife to level it, as this will dull the shiny surface. Leave to set and firm at room temperature. Do not refrigerate.

To make the candied peanuts, put the sugar and water in a pan and bring to the boil, stirring to dissolve the sugar. Add the peanuts and simmer for 10–15 minutes, until the sugar syrup thickens a little. Meanwhile, heat the oil in a deep saucepan to 180°C/350°F. Using a slotted spoon or a spider, remove the peanuts from the syrup and drop them into the hot oil. Cook for 4–5 minutes, until golden brown, then drain on kitchen paper. While they are cooling, use a fork to separate any that have stuck together. Once they are completely cold, sprinkle them over the top of the tart with the remaining teaspoon of Maldon salt. Serve with crème fraîche or Greek yoghurt.

Claire's Notes
• Make sure the pastry case is cold and has the butterscotch in the base before making the chocolate ganache. As soon as the filling is made, it needs to be poured quickly into the tart.
• Cut the tart using a hot bread knife. Have a large jug of hot water standing by and heat the knife in the water. Dry the knife before cutting the tart and warm again after each cut.

OLD-FASHIONED ECCLES CAKES

750g/1lb 10oz Quick Puff Pastry (see page 60) or bought butter puff pastry
100g/3¹/₂oz demerara sugar

For the filling
375g/13 oz sultanas
90g/3¹/₄oz currants
90g/3¹/₄oz candied mixed peel, finely chopped
juice and grated zest of ¹/₄ lemon
juice and grated zest of ¹/₄ orange
185g/6¹/₂oz dark soft brown sugar
1 teaspoon grated nutmeg
¹/₂ teaspoon ground cloves
¹/₂ teaspoon ground cinnamon
125g/4¹/₂oz unsalted butter
2 large eggs
250g/9oz dessert apples, peeled and grated

MAKES 12

Claire's Notes
• When shaping the parcels, try to fold the pastry into the middle tightly to make a neat, round cake. If you have an excess of pastry, you have not used enough filling. Try to avoid a thick lump of pastry on the base, as it won't cook through properly.
• If you do not like mixed peel or currants, replace them with the same weight of raisins or more sultanas.

The first published recipe for a kind of Eccles cakes was by Mrs Elizabeth Raffald, owner of a confectioner's shop in Arley Hall, Cheshire, who wrote a bestselling cookery book in 1769. Her recipe for 'sweet patties' included a filling rather like mincemeat, made of boiled calf's foot, apples, oranges, nutmeg, egg yolks, currants and French brandy, all wrapped in puff pastry. Somehow the recipe found its way to the town of Eccles, and it was James Birch's shop on the corner of Vicarage Road that made them famous. He could not make enough of them and they really did sell like hot cakes.

Of course, the mincemeat is now a mix of dried fruits and spices. Currants usually predominate but I prefer sultanas, as they make the filling moister. I include grated apple in my recipe and I always sprinkle the tops of the Eccles cakes with demerara sugar for extra crunch. They are quite irresistible, especially when served warm.

Roll the pastry out to 5mm/¹/₄ inch thick on a lightly floured work surface. Loosely roll the pastry around the rolling pin and unroll it on to a baking sheet lined with baking parchment. Place in the fridge to rest and relax for 30 minutes.

Meanwhile, mix the sultanas, currants and mixed peel in a bowl with the lemon and orange juice and zest. Add the soft brown sugar and spices and mix well. Melt the butter in a small pan and add to the fruit mix. Beat the eggs together just enough to combine the yolks with the whites. Weigh out 75g/2³/₄oz of the beaten egg and add to the mix (reserve the remaining egg for egg wash later). Add the grated apples and mix well.

Preheat the oven to 180°C/350°F/Gas Mark 4. Remove the pastry from the fridge and, using a 12.5cm/5 inch pastry cutter, cut out 12 discs. Put a large tablespoonful of the filling into the centre of each one, then bring the edges of the pastry into the centre, tucking them under each other to make sure the parcel is very firm and no filling is showing. The Eccles cakes should be round and firm. Place smooth-side up on a lined baking tray, 2.5cm/1 inch apart.

Brush the tops with the reserved beaten egg, then pick them up and dip them one at a time into the demerara sugar. Only the tops should be coated in the sugar. Make 2 slits about 1cm/¹/₂ inch long and 5mm/¹/₄ inch apart on the top of each cake for the steam to escape.

Place in the oven and bake for 20–25 minutes, until the cakes are golden brown. To check they are done, turn one of them over and make sure the pastry is cooked underneath. Leave to cool on a wire rack. They are really good when they are warm but do not serve straight from the oven, as the filling will be extremely hot.

FIG AND BLUEBERRY CRÈME FRAÎCHE TARTS

500g/1lb 2oz Three-quarters Puff
Pastry (see page 59) or bought
butter puff pastry
175ml/6fl oz crème fraîche
25g/1oz demerara sugar
85g/3oz blueberries
12–18 figs, depending on size
3–4 tablespoons honey

For the egg wash
1 egg
1 egg yolk
a large pinch of salt

MAKES 6

Claire's Notes
• Serve with ice cream or a fig and
blueberry sauce. To make the
sauce, cook any remaining pieces
of fig with any leftover blueberries
to a soft pulp. Sweeten with sugar
and adjust the flavour with a drop
of lemon juice.
• You can make the tart shells and
keep them unfilled in the freezer
for up to 8 weeks. There is no
need to defrost them before filling
and baking, but do increase the
cooking time by 12–15 minutes.
• These tarts will work well with all
figs. If you prefer, you can make
one large tart in a 20cm/8 inch tart
tin, rather than individual ones.

The French Laundry farm has at least ten varieties of fig trees, so I feel spoilt for choice. My favourites are the Mission fig – a large, purplish-black fig with a rich flavour – and the Violette de Bordeaux, a much smaller, jet-black fig. Peter Jacobson, who owns the farm, once showed me how important it is to pick the figs when they are perfectly ripe. It was pure indulgence, as I sampled the best-tasting figs I had ever had in my life.

Roll out the pastry to 5mm/¼ inch thick on a lightly floured work surface. The pastry sheet should be big enough to cut out twelve 7.5cm/3 inch discs after chilling. Roll the pastry loosely round the rolling pin and transfer it to a baking sheet. Dock half the pastry sheet (i.e. prick it lightly all over with a fork) and refrigerate for 1 hour, until firm; this helps prevent shrinkage.

Meanwhile, make the egg wash by beating together all the ingredients and passing them through a fine sieve. It will go a darker colour and look runnier but don't worry, this is how it should be.

After the pastry has rested for an hour, cut it in half and place the piece you haven't docked in the freezer on a baking tray lined with baking parchment. Using a 7.5cm/3 inch plain pastry cutter, cut 6 discs from the docked pastry and place on a baking tray lined with baking parchment. Brush them with egg wash.

Cut another 6 discs from the semi-frozen, non-docked piece of pastry. Using a 5cm/2 inch cutter, cut away the centres of each disc, giving you a hoop. Place one hoop on each egg-washed disc of pastry, lining them up neatly to make something resembling a vol-au-vent. If the pastry is too frozen, allow it to soften a little before cutting but do not let it defrost completely or the discs will be difficult to handle.

Scallop the edges using the back of a small knife and your thumb: place your thumb on the edge of the tart and, using the back of a knife, pull the pastry in towards the centre of the circle just enough to make a dent. Repeat all the way around each tart. Put the tray back in the fridge for 15 minutes so the pastry can firm up. Then brush the tops of the hoops with egg wash and mark with the back of a knife in a pretty pattern, as shown in the picture.

Preheat the oven to 200°C/400°F/Gas Mark 6. Mix the crème fraîche with a tablespoon of the demerara sugar and spread a little into the centre of each tart. Chop the blueberries roughly, reserving 6 for decoration. Place a teaspoon of the chopped blueberries over the crème fraîche in each tart, flattening them with the back of the spoon. Slice the figs and lay them, neatly overlapping, on top of the crème fraîche and blueberries. Sprinkle the remaining sugar over the figs and place one blueberry in the centre of each tart.

Bake at the top of the oven for 10–12 minutes, until the edges of the pastry are golden brown. Reduce the oven temperature to 180°C/350°F/Gas Mark 4 and continue baking until the pastry is golden and the figs begin to bubble. They may release some juice, but this will be soaked up by the crème fraîche when they are cooling. The sides of the pastry will rise a little and the base will remain weighted by the filling. To make sure the tarts are done, slide a palette knife under the base and check that the bottom of the pastry is golden brown.

Remove from the oven and cool on the tray a little, then transfer to a wire rack. Warm the honey and brush over each tart for a shiny finish. Serve warm.

APPLE, CINNAMON AND SULTANA STRUDEL

1.5kg/3lb 5oz apples, such as
   Cox's Orange Pippins or Golden
   Delicious
125g/4^1/$_2$oz soft breadcrumbs
225g/8oz unsalted butter
150g/5^1/$_2$oz caster sugar
2 teaspoons ground cinnamon
50g/1^3/$_4$oz sultanas
icing sugar for dusting

For the strudel dough
300g/10^1/$_2$oz strong white flour,
   sifted
1 teaspoon salt
125–150ml/4–5fl oz warm water
2 tablespoons vegetable oil
1 medium egg yolk

SERVES 10

Claire's Notes
• The melted butter should be no
more than lukewarm; this stops
the dough sticking to itself and
preserves its leaf-like quality.

This reminds me of my college days and my lecturer and mentor, Professor John Huber – an adorable Swiss man who swore that if he could not read his paper through the strudel dough, it was not thin enough. He came from Switzerland some 50 years ago to work in the then famous Lyons Corner House in London and found his way into teaching. There cannot be a famous – or not so famous, for that matter – pastry chef in the whole of England who has not passed through his hands or does not remember the Apfelstrudel lesson.

First make the dough, using an electric mixer fitted with the dough hook attachment. Place the sifted flour and salt in the bowl. Combine 125ml/4fl oz of the warm water with the oil and egg yolk and add to the flour, mixing on a low speed to make a smooth paste. If it seems dry, add a little more water. Keep mixing the dough in the machine until it becomes elastic and very smooth; this can take as long as 10–12 minutes. Now lightly dust the work surface and finish working the dough by hand, just until it is smooth and no longer sticky. Shape it into a ball, wrap in lightly oiled cling film and leave in the fridge for at least 30 minutes, longer if possible. As the dough relaxes, it becomes more elastic, which makes it easier to stretch without making any holes in it.

Core the apples but do not peel them. Slice them as thinly as possible, preferably on a mandoline. Place in a colander to drain off any liquid (the apples will discolour but it doesn't matter, as they will be brown after the strudel is cooked anyway).

Fry the breadcrumbs in 100g/3^1/$_2$oz of the butter until light brown, then cool thoroughly.

Preheat the oven to 220°C/425°F/Gas Mark 7. Cover a table with a cotton or linen cloth, such as a tea towel, and dust it lightly but evenly with flour. Lay the dough on the cloth at the same time as pulling it into a long strip. If the dough is relaxed enough, this should happen almost by itself, as it will hang due to its own weight. Roll out the dough with a rolling pin, both lengthwise and widthwise, until it is roughly 25cm/10 inches square. Now the fun begins. Take the dough from underneath with the flat of both hands and stretch it from the middle outwards. Continue this all around the table, until the pastry overlaps the whole cloth by about 1cm/^{1}/$_2$ inch, making sure it is thin enough to read a newspaper through (yes, it really has to be that thin). Any thick edges can be trimmed off.

Melt the remaining butter and use just under half of it to brush over the dough. Evenly sprinkle the fried breadcrumbs over two-thirds of the dough. Mix the sliced apples with the sugar, cinnamon and sultanas and spread these in an even layer over the breadcrumbs.

Now roll up the dough by lifting and moving the cloth, starting with the end that is covered in the filling. Keep the roll tight; it needs to be as compact as possible. Use the cloth to move the strudel on to a greased nonstick baking tray. Brush with the remaining melted butter and bake for about 30 minutes, until the dough is crisp and the apples tender. Dust with icing sugar and serve immediately, to enjoy the contrast between the crisp pastry and the soft apple.

STRAWBERRY MILLE-FEUILLES

350g/12oz Quick Puff Pastry (see page 60), puff pastry trimmings or bought butter puff pastry
500g/1lb 2oz strawberries, ideally all roughly the same size
2 tablespoons strawberry jam
icing sugar for dusting

For the Chantilly cream
500ml/18fl oz double cream
1 teaspoon vanilla extract
2 tablespoons icing sugar

SERVES 8

Claire's Notes
• If you haven't rolled the pastry thinly enough, it will probably have a core of raw paste in the middle after baking; this will look translucent and waxy. To avoid this, be sure to roll the pastry thinly and remember to lower the temperature after the pastry browns, so you can continue baking without burning the pastry.
• Make sure the strawberries are all the same size and height so the mille-feuille is level.
• Do not assemble the mille-feuille ahead of time, as the cream will make the pastry go soft. It will sit for an hour but will begin to soften as soon as you place it back in the fridge after cutting.

This is a great recipe for using up the puff pastry trimmings from lining tarts and making vol-au-vents (see page 90). Mille-feuille translates as 'a thousand leaves', referring to the crisp, thin layers of puff pastry. The pastry is baked in a sheet, then cut and sandwiched together with either Chantilly cream or crème pâtissière, also known as confectioner's custard or pastry cream. I like to use Chantilly cream but, if you prefer, you can substitute pastry cream – use one and a half times the amount in the Tutti Frutti Vol-au-Vents recipe on page 90.

In America, a mille-feuille is known as a Napoleon. The name is generally believed to have come from the French word napolitain, meaning Neapolitan, and then altered by association with the name of Emperor Napoleon I of France. Whatever you call it, the mille-feuille remains a favourite around the world.

Roll out the pastry on a lightly floured work surface to a rectangle that will cover a 35 x 25cm/14 x 10 inch baking tray. It should be about 3mm/^{1}/$_8$ inch thick; this will look quite thin. Roll evenly to keep the pastry in a neat, regular shape so it exactly fits your baking tray.

Line the baking tray with a sheet of baking parchment. Roll the pastry loosely around the rolling pin, then unroll it over the tray. Trim the pastry if necessary so it is exactly the same size as the baking tray. Prick the pastry very well with a fork and leave it to rest in the fridge for about half an hour. Preheat the oven to 220°C/425°F/Gas Mark 7.

Bake the pastry in the hot oven for 15–20 minutes, until puffed and light brown. Lower the temperature to 190°C/375°F/Gas Mark 5 and continue cooking until the pastry is golden brown and crisp. Make sure you lift it with a palette knife to check it is cooked underneath; there is nothing worse than a soft, uncooked mille-feuille sheet. Allow the pastry to cool slightly, then transfer it to a wire rack to cool completely.

Meanwhile, put all the ingredients for the Chantilly cream in a large bowl and whisk to firm peaks. Wash, hull and dry the strawberries, leaving them whole.

Carefully move the sheet of cooked pastry on to a board and cut it lengthwise into 3 equal pieces. Spread the jam over one of the pieces of pastry and place another piece on top. Cover the pastry with a layer of Chantilly cream about 5mm/^{1}/$_4$ inch thick and level it with a palette knife. Place the strawberries hull-side down on the cream, keeping them as close together as you can. Cover with the remaining cream and then place the last piece of pastry on top. Press the pastry down firmly on to the cream and, using a palette knife, level the cream on the sides a little to ensure it is smooth between the strawberries. Chill for 15 minutes before cutting.

Use a hot serrated knife to cut the mille-feuille into 8 pieces. Place the knife in hot water and dry it before cutting. Clean and warm the knife each time you make a cut. Trim off the edges first so the slices are neat and tidy. Dust the tops of the mille-feuilles with a little icing sugar before serving.

APRICOT AND ALMOND JALOUSIE

500g/1lb 2oz Three-quarters Puff
    Pastry (see page 59) or bought
    butter puff pastry
15–20 fresh apricots, halved and
    pitted (or canned apricots, well
    drained and dried)
3–4 tablespoons apricot preserve
2 tablespoons icing sugar
1 teaspoon kirsch or brandy

For the almond cream
125g/4$^{1}/_{2}$oz softened unsalted
    butter
125g/4$^{1}/_{2}$oz caster sugar
2 large eggs, at room temperature,
    lightly beaten
grated zest of $^{1}/_{2}$ lemon
$^{1}/_{2}$ teaspoon vanilla extract
40g/1$^{1}/_{2}$oz plain flour
125g/4$^{1}/_{2}$oz ground almonds

For the egg wash
1 egg
1 egg yolk
a good pinch of salt

SERVES 8

Jalousie is the French word not only for jealous but also for Venetian blinds, and this wonderful pastry consists of layers of crisp, buttery puff pastry, almond cream and juicy fruits, covered with a slatted lid like a Venetian blind. I like to think of a jealous lover spying from behind those slatted blinds.

You can use canned fruit with great success here. I have chosen apricots because their sharpness works well with the buttery pastry and almond cream. Other favourites are plum and greengage.

Roll out the puff pastry to 5mm/$^{1}/_{4}$ inch thick on a lightly floured work surface. It should be about 25cm/10 inches square. Loosely roll the pastry around the rolling pin and transfer it to a baking tray lined with baking parchment. Leave to rest in the fridge for 30 minutes.

Meanwhile, make the almond cream. Cream the butter and sugar together until pale and fluffy. Add the beaten eggs a little at a time, mixing well between each addition. Add the lemon zest and vanilla extract. Sift the flour and ground almonds together on to a piece of baking parchment and add to the creamed mix all in one go. Fold in the dry ingredients (if using an electric mixer, you can do this with the machine but use a lower speed). Place the almond cream in a piping bag fitted with a 1cm/$^{1}/_{2}$ inch plain nozzle.

Remove the sheet of puff pastry from the fridge. Working on the lined baking tray, cut the pastry lengthwise into 2 strips, one of them 25 x 15cm/ 10 x 6 inches, the other 25 x 10cm/10 x 4 inches. Lightly dust the larger piece with flour, then fold it lengthwise in half. The side with the folded seam is the side where you will make the incisions. Starting at the right-hand edge of the folded seam, make cuts into the pastry to within 2.5cm/1 inch of the open seam, leaving 3mm/$^{1}/_{8}$ inch between each cut. Carefully and very gently, without pressing the pastry down, fold the pastry widthways in half so it measures 12.5 x 7.5cm/5 x 3 inches. Pick up the pastry and lay it on another tray lined with baking parchment, then unfold it to how it was when you were cutting the slats; it should measure 25 x 7.5cm/10 x 3 inches. Place the tray in the fridge to prevent the pastry going soft.

Preheat the oven to 200°C/400°F/Gas Mark 6. Pipe the almond cream down the centre of the remaining piece of pastry, then pipe a line down either side, making sure it is 2.5cm/1 inch from the edge of the pastry. Pipe another line over the first line you piped in the centre. Arrange the apricot halves, flat-side down, on top so you have a row of them on top of the central line of almond cream and a row on either side; they should encase the cream. Make the egg wash by beating together all the ingredients and passing them through a fine sieve. Brush the edges of the pastry with the egg wash. You should have a 2.5cm/1 inch border of pastry on either side of the apricots.

Take the other piece of pastry from the fridge, place it over the apricots and unfold it. Line up the top with the bottom and pull it down gently so the edges meet. Press them down gently – the egg wash should seal them together. Pull the pastry over the short ends to seal in the apricots. Take a fork dipped in a little flour and press it around the border of the pastry to seal and mark it. Neaten the jalousie if necessary by cutting the pastry to form a neat oblong; do not cut away the pastry border. Brush the entire slice with egg wash and then bake near the top of the oven for 20 minutes, until golden brown. Lower the temperature to 180°C/350°F/Gas Mark 4 and continue to bake for about 25 minutes, until the filling is cooked and the apricots are soft when tested with a knife. Carefully lift the jalousie with a palette knife and check if the pastry is done underneath.

Bring the apricot preserve to the boil with a tablespoon of water and pass through a fine sieve. Bring to the boil again in a clean pan. Using a pastry brush, brush the apricot glaze over the jalousie to seal in the moisture and give it a shine. Now combine the icing sugar and kirsch or brandy in a small bowl until smooth and clear; it should be runny. Brush the mixture on top of the apricot glaze. It should be almost transparent, and not really visible, but it adds sweetness and a little punch.

TUTTI FRUTTI VOL-AU-VENTS

1kg/2¼lb Three-quarters Puff
    Pastry (see page 59) or bought
    butter puff pastry
a selection of fruits and berries
    (see above)
3 tablespoons apricot preserve

For the pastry cream
1 vanilla pod
500ml/18fl oz milk
6 medium egg yolks
125g/4½oz caster sugar
40g/1½oz plain flour, sifted
200ml/7fl oz double cream

For the egg wash
1 egg
1 egg yolk
a good pinch of salt

MAKES 8

I think these wonderful vol-au-vents look so impressive, with the vibrant colours of the fruit contrasting with the golden drum of crisp, flaky pastry. You can make one large tart (20cm/8 inches in diameter) instead of individual vol-au-vents, if you prefer, but it does mean that not everyone will get all the different kinds of fruit in their slice.

To make the tarts really colourful, you need to buy a lot of different fruits – there will probably be a little of each one left over. I like to use tropical fruits plus some seasonal berries – for example, one large mango, one papaya, three or four peaches, kiwi fruits and figs, plus a few berries such as cherries, raspberries, blueberries and strawberries. Pineapple, lychees, passionfruit, kiwi, orange, black grapes and lime zest (for flavour) make another good combination.

Cut the block of pastry in half and roll out on a lightly floured work surface to about 5mm/¼ inch thick. Each piece should be big enough to cut out eight 5cm/2 inch discs. Loosely roll each sheet of pastry round the rolling pin and unroll it on to a baking sheet lined with baking parchment. Leave in the fridge to rest for 30 minutes to prevent shrinkage, then transfer the pastry, still on the baking sheet, to the freezer for 30 minutes, or until it is firm enough for you to handle without it losing its shape and becoming soft.

Meanwhile, make the pastry cream for the filling. Slit the vanilla pod open lengthwise and scrape out the seeds with the back of a small knife. Place the pod and seeds in a small pan with the milk and bring to the boil. Beat the egg yolks and sugar together with a wooden spoon until they are pale and well mixed. Add the sifted flour and combine to make a smooth, thick paste. Pour in a little of the boiled milk and whisk until smooth. Add the rest of the milk and stir well. Remove the vanilla pod and return the mixture to the pan. Place over a medium heat and, using a small, flexible whisk, whisk continuously until the mixture comes to the boil. It will thicken as it reaches boiling point. Lower the heat and continue whisking for a minute or two to make sure the starch in the flour is cooked out. Transfer the pastry cream to a clean bowl, cover the surface with cling film to prevent a skin forming, then leave to cool.

Preheat the oven to 200°C/400°F/Gas Mark 6. Take one piece of puff pastry and cut out 8 discs with a 5cm/2 inch pastry cutter. Place them on a baking sheet lined with baking parchment. Make the egg wash by beating together all the ingredients and passing them through a fine sieve. Brush the pastry discs with the egg wash.

Take the second piece of pastry and cut out 8 more discs. This time, cut away the centre of each disc with a 4cm/1½ inch cutter. Place these pastry rings on top of the first discs you cut, lining them up exactly. Brush the tops of the second pastry discs with egg wash, being careful not to let it dribble down the inside or outside of the pastry, as this will prevent the vol-au-vents rising evenly.

(continued on page 92)

(continued from page 90)

Place in the centre of the oven and bake for 20 minutes, until the pastry cases are well risen and golden brown. Remove from the oven and transfer to a wire rack to cool. When the cases are cold, remove the centre pieces of pastry. Using a small knife, scrape out any uncooked pastry, leaving just the crisp shell.

Whisk the cold pastry cream until it is smooth. In a separate bowl, whip the double cream to firm peaks. Fold the whipped cream into the pastry cream and spoon it into the empty vol-au-vent cases to just below the surface. Level with the back of a spoon.

Wash, pit and prepare the fruits. Arrange the fruit on the vol-au-vents. Bring the apricot preserve to the boil in a small pan with a tablespoon of water, then strain it through a fine sieve. Bring back to the boil in a clean pan and brush it over the fruits to prevent them drying out.

Claire's Notes

• You can keep the unbaked vol-au-vents in the freezer for up to 8 weeks. Bake and fill them on the day you serve them.

• You could replace the vanilla in the pastry cream with about 75ml/2^1/$_2$fl oz fruit purée or passionfruit, stirring it in before you add the whipped cream. If it is a special occasion, add a tablespoon of Grand Marnier, Cointreau or framboise liqueur to the pastry cream as well as the vanilla, stirring it in at the end.

• If the apricot preserve is too thick, it will not brush on smoothly; add a drop or two more water if necessary.

• We in the trade have a trick for preventing the vol-au-vents toppling over in the oven. Find 4 moulds about 5–7.5cm/2–3 inches high and 4–5cm/1^1/$_2$–2 inches in diameter. Place them in the 4 corners of your baking tray with the vol-au-vents in the centre, then place a wire cooling rack over the tray, supported by the moulds. The vol-au-vents will rise only to the height of the rack, which will prevent them falling over.

• There will be a lot of puff pastry trimmings left over from making the vol-au-vents. You could use them to make Arlettes (see page 29) or Strawberry Mille-feuilles (page 86).

CRÈME PUFFS

For the choux pastry
75g/2³/₄oz plain flour
¹/₂ teaspoon caster sugar
125ml/4fl oz water
50g/1³/₄oz unsalted butter, cut into
    small pieces, plus a little melted
    butter for greasing
¹/₂ teaspoon salt
2 medium eggs, lightly beaten

For the egg wash
1 egg
1 egg yolk
a good pinch of salt

For the pastry cream
30g/1oz plain flour
30g/1oz cornflour
4 medium egg yolks
125g/4¹/₂oz caster sugar
500ml/18fl oz whole milk
1 vanilla pod

For the caramel topping
150g /5¹/₂oz caster sugar
75ml/2¹/₂fl oz water
nibbed sugar (or lightly crushed
    sugar cubes)

MAKES ABOUT 60 BITE-SIZED BUNS

Claire's Notes
• While the pastry cream is still hot, you could flavour it with melted chocolate, chocolate hazelnut spread, chopped pistachios or lemon zest. Colourfully decorate the buns with gold leaf, melted chocolate, chopped pistachios or hazelnuts.
• When making the caramel and dipping the buns, have a bowl of iced water nearby, in case you get hot sugar on your hand. Immerse your hand immediately in the water and the sugar will harden, so you can remove it, leaving your skin intact.

These sinful little mouthfuls are so versatile that they form the base of many a dessert and afternoon-tea fancy, from gâteau Saint Honoré all the way to that magnificent tower of caramel profiteroles, the croquembouche, traditionally served as a wedding cake in France.

First make the choux pastry. Sift the flour and sugar on to a sheet of baking parchment. Put the water, butter and salt in a pan and bring to the boil over a high heat. As soon as it comes to the boil, tip in the flour and sugar all in one go and stir constantly until it forms a ball in the centre of the pan. Keep stirring over a medium heat for about 1 minute to dry out the mixture. Be careful not too let it dry out too much or the buns will crack when cooked.

Immediately transfer the mixture to a bowl, stir briefly and then gradually work in the beaten eggs a little at a time, mixing well between each addition. Beat to a smooth paste with a wooden spoon; the mixture should be thick enough to drop from the spoon when gently shaken.

Preheat the oven to 200°C/400°F/Gas Mark 6. Grease 2 baking sheets lightly with melted butter and place them in the fridge so the butter hardens. This will allow you to pipe the buns without the paste sliding around on the butter. Place the choux paste in a piping bag fitted with a 1cm/¹/₂ inch plain nozzle and pipe it in 1cm/¹/₂ inch balls on the prepared baking sheets, leaving 2.5cm/1 inch between each one.

Beat together all the ingredients for the egg wash and strain through a fine sieve. Brush the buns with egg wash and press them down gently with the back of a fork. Place in the oven and bake for about 20 minutes, until firm on the outside and dry in the middle. You can check this by breaking one of the buns open and making sure there is no soft dough left inside. Place on a wire rack and leave to cool.

Next make the pastry cream. Sift the flour into a bowl, add the cornflour, then mix in the egg yolks and sugar to form a smooth paste. Put the milk into a pan. Slit the vanilla pod open lengthwise with a knife and scrape the seeds into the milk, then bring to the boil. Pour the boiling milk on to the egg mixture and stir well. Return the mixture to a clean pan and whisk continuously over a medium heat until it returns to the boil. Lower the heat and simmer gently for a minute or two to cook out the flavour of the starch. Remove from the heat, cover the surface with cling film to prevent a skin forming and leave to cool.

To fill the buns, make a small hole in the base of each one, using the end of a plain piping nozzle. Pipe the pastry cream into the buns using a piping bag fitted with a 5mm/¹/₄ inch nozzle.

To make the caramel, put the sugar and water in a small, heavy-based pan and bring to the boil, stirring to dissolve the sugar. Let it boil, without stirring, until it turns into a golden caramel (see page 137). Place the nibbed sugar in a small, shallow bowl. Dip the top of each bun in the caramel, being extremely careful not to touch the hot caramel. Dip them immediately into the nibbed sugar. They will set almost straight away. Eat on the day of making.

CHOCOLATE ÉCLAIRS

For the fondant icing
300g/10¹/2oz icing sugar
65ml/2¹/4fl oz water
1 tablespoon liquid glucose
100g/3¹/2oz dark chocolate
   (70 per cent cocoa solids),
   chopped

For the choux pastry
75g/2³/4oz plain flour
¹/2 teaspoon caster sugar
125ml/4fl oz water
50g/1³/4oz unsalted butter, cut into
   small pieces, plus a little melted
   butter for greasing
¹/2 teaspoon salt
2 medium eggs, lightly beaten

For the chocolate pastry cream
30g/1oz plain flour
30g/1oz cornflour
4 medium egg yolks
125g/4¹/2oz caster sugar
600ml/20fl oz whole milk
100g/3¹/2oz dark chocolate
   (70 per cent cocoa solids), finely
   chopped

MAKES 24

Even though my name sounds only slightly like éclair, I have had to endure a lifetime of chocolate éclairs/Claire jokes from culinary friends and colleagues. That aside, I do enjoy making them and even enjoy eating them if they are filled with chocolate pastry cream – a rich confectioner's custard flavoured with dark chocolate.

For the soft chocolate icing, I make a fondant. It is quite easy to do but refining the coating technique might take some practice. The French word, éclair, translates as 'a flash of lightening'. The fondant icing should be shiny when made correctly and some say it was the gleam from the fondant icing that looked like a flash of lightening, hence the name. I think this might be a little farfetched but no one seems to know for sure. Make the fondant the day before you need it, then warm it again slightly on the day; this gives the icing time to form and harden enough for you to work with it at its ideal temperature.

Start making the fondant icing the day before. Place the icing sugar, water and glucose in a medium pan and cook over a low heat, stirring constantly, until it reaches 33°C/92°F on a sugar thermometer. Remove from the heat and pour into a bowl. Cover the surface with cling film and leave to cool at room temperature.

To make the choux pastry, sift the flour and sugar on to a sheet of baking parchment. Put the water, butter and salt in a small pan and bring to the boil over a high heat. As soon as it comes to the boil, tip in the flour and sugar all in one go and stir constantly until it forms a ball in the centre of the pan. Keep stirring over a medium heat for about 1 minute to dry out the mixture. Be careful not too let it dry out too much or the éclairs will crack when cooked.

Immediately transfer the mixture to a bowl, stir briefly and then gradually work in the beaten eggs a little at a time, mixing well between each addition. Beat to a smooth paste with a wooden spoon; the mixture should be thick enough to drop from the spoon when gently shaken.

Preheat the oven to 200°C/400°F/Gas Mark 6. Grease 2 baking sheets lightly with melted butter and chill until hard. This will prevent the éclairs sliding around on the butter when you pipe them. Place the choux paste in a piping bag fitted with a 1cm/¹/2 inch plain nozzle and pipe it on the baking sheets in lines about 12cm/5 inches long, leaving at least 2.5cm/1 inch between each one, as they will puff outwards. Place on the top shelf of the oven and bake for about 20 minutes, until golden brown and firm to the touch; you should be able to pick them up from the tray. Turn the oven down to 180°C/350°F/Gas Mark 4 and continue to cook until the éclairs are firm and dry on the inside. You can check this by breaking one open and making sure there is no soft dough left inside the shells.

Transfer the éclairs to a wire rack to cool. Once they are cold, make 2 holes at either end of the base of each one. You can do this by pushing the tip of a 5mm/¹/4 inch plain piping nozzle into the éclair.

Next make the chocolate pastry cream. Sift the flour into a bowl, add the cornflour, then mix in the egg yolks and sugar to form a smooth paste.

Bring the milk to the boil in a pan. Pour the boiling milk on to the egg mixture and stir well. Return the mixture to a clean pan and whisk continuously over a medium heat until it returns to the boil. Lower the heat and simmer gently for a minute or two to cook out the flavour of the starch. Remove from the heat and add the chopped chocolate. Mix well until all the chocolate has melted, then transfer the mixture to a bowl and cover the surface with cling film to prevent it forming a skin. Leave to cool completely.

Whisk the cold pastry cream until it is smooth, then use to fill a piping bag fitted with a 5mm/$\frac{1}{4}$ inch plain nozzle. Pipe the cream into the éclairs from either end through the holes you made earlier. The mix will come out of the opposite hole when the éclair is full.

Finally, finish the fondant icing. Melt the chocolate in a bowl set over a pan of simmering water, making sure the water does not touch the base of the bowl. Place the fondant icing in a small pan that is big enough to dip the éclairs into and gently heat to blood temperature (about 32°C/90°F). Stir in the chocolate gradually; you can make it as dark as you like by adding more chocolate but take care not too add so much that the icing becomes too thick to use. It should still flow and coat the éclairs without running off, but it shouldn't be too thick and unsightly. Dip the top of each filled éclair into the warmed fondant, then hold the éclair at an angle pointed down towards the pan of icing and gently remove any excess fondant with your finger, so the top is neat and tidy. Place the éclairs on a tray lined with baking parchment and leave for a few minutes for the fondant to firm slightly.

Claire's Notes
• If making the fondant icing is too much work, simply melt some dark chocolate and dip the tops of the éclairs into it, then place them in the fridge. Take care not to overheat the chocolate. Stay with the pot while it is melting and stir it gently just until melted, no more.
• If you don't want to use chocolate pastry cream, you can fill the éclairs with whipped double cream.
• The unfilled éclairs will keep for 3 months in the freezer, stored in plastic bags. Defrost before filling. I suggest you place them in an oven heated to 180°C/350°F/Gas Mark 4 for 5 minutes once they are defrosted, as this freshens them up and makes them crisp again.

MERINGUES

THE SECRETS
OF SUCCESS

Although there are several different types of meringue, the recipes in this chapter all rely on a simple meringue, which involves just whisking egg whites and sugar together. Blackcurrant Spoom (see page 198), in the Ices chapter, uses the more complex Italian meringue, where a hot sugar syrup is beaten into the egg whites to create a foam. Sometimes the sugar is added in stages and sometimes it is all put in with the egg whites at the beginning. Follow the instructions in each individual recipe for the best results.

WHISKING EGG WHITES

I prefer to use older egg whites that are at room temperature, as they are thinner and therefore create a good volume. However, although fresh egg whites tend not to produce as much volume, they do provide a very stable foam. So it is completely up to you which you go for. Cold eggs can be used if you are whisking them in an electric mixer, as this warms them up.

The egg whites should be completely free of egg yolk, as the fat in the yolk will prevent them forming a meringue. For the same reason, always whisk the whites in a clean, grease-free bowl. Wiping the mixing bowl with a little white wine vinegar on clean kitchen paper before you add the whites and sugar will help to make the meringue firm.

Whisking egg whites in a freestanding electric mixer or with a handheld beater is easiest, as all the hard work is done for you. If you are beating egg whites by hand, use a balloon whisk for best results, or a rotary whisk.

You will need a metal, glass or ceramic bowl that is large enough to accommodate an eightfold expansion. Remember that the longer you beat the whites, the firmer they will become. Pay attention to the requirements of the recipe, as some require a stiffer meringue than others. You can tell if a meringue has reached the right stage by the kind of peaks it forms when the whisk is lifted, as follows:

SOFT PEAKS

The glossy foam retains some shape and does not droop. It does not cling to the bowl, and will quickly form a liquid at the bottom of the bowl if not folded into the other ingredients for its intended use straight away.

FIRM PEAKS

The glossy foam retains a full, well-defined shape. The foam will cling to the sides of the bowl and the whisk.

ADDING THE SUGAR

Sugar stabilises the egg white foam – the more sugar you add, the more stable and glossy the foam, and the crisper the meringue when baked. Certain recipes call for all the sugar to be added at the beginning, while others call for it to be added in stages. As a general rule, if you have less or the equivalent amount of sugar to egg whites it can be added at the beginning and still form a firm meringue; if you have more, it should be added in stages.

Adding sugar at different stages of the whisking process also produces different types of meringue. The Citrus Meringue Quiffs on pages 110–111, for example, are best if the sugar is added all at once, giving a thick, dense meringue that holds its shape but is not too firm. Bear in mind that if you add too much sugar at the end, the meringue will almost certainly go soft and lose its volume. Be careful not to overbeat with the final addition of sugar.

AVOIDING COMMON PROBLEMS

• Meringue that has been beaten for too long or not long enough may weep puddles of syrup around the base when baked. Keep an eye on the meringue as it forms, and check the consistency carefully.
• If the sugar doesn't dissolve completely in the egg whites, the meringue can have a gritty texture. If making the meringue in a machine, the heat generated during whisking is generally enough to dissolve the sugar. Granulated sugar does not dissolve properly, so always use caster.
• Beads of sugar syrup can form on the surface of baked meringues. This is caused by too high an oven temperature, which can also cause the meringue to rise and crack.
• A common problem with a meringue topping (for example, in lemon meringue pie) is that it weeps syrup on to the base. This is caused by undercooking the meringue.
• Humid weather and moisture cause meringues to go soft. Transfer cooled baked meringue shells to a sealed container directly after baking.

TROPICAL FRUIT PAVLOVA

4 large egg whites
200g/7oz caster sugar
1$\frac{1}{2}$ teaspoons cornflour, sifted
1 teaspoon white wine vinegar

For the decoration
1 ripe mango
3 kiwi fruit
3 ripe yellow or white peaches
250g/9oz strawberries
125g/4$\frac{1}{2}$oz raspberries

For the filling
250ml/9fl oz double cream
25g/1oz icing sugar
1 large, ripe passionfruit

SERVES 8

Claire's Notes
• You can make the pavlova shells several days in advance and store in an airtight container. Be sure to store them in a cool, dry place such as a larder.
• Fill the shells no more than 30 minutes before serving, as the cream softens the bases and they might collapse.
• Use papaya and blackberries for extra colour.
• I like to cut my fruit on the chunky side. It makes a better presentation, as the fruit does not lie flat. I slot the fruits into the cream at different angles for a funky look, then fill in the spaces with small berries.

This Australian speciality was created in honour of the famous Russian ballerina, Anna Pavlova, although it appears that versions of this meringue-based dessert had already been made in New Zealand for some time. Either way, it is fantastic served piled high with whipped cream and fresh fruit. I like to make individual ones and fill them with strawberries, kiwis, mango, peaches and raspberries, with a large spoonful of fresh passionfruit in the cream.

A low oven is recommended for pavlova so the meringue crisps on the outside but remains soft in the centre, like marshmallow. The inclusion of cornflour and a little acid, in the form of vinegar, helps to ensure a crisp shell. I always think a true pavlova should be slightly golden in colour.

Preheat the oven to 120°C/250°F/Gas Mark $\frac{1}{2}$. Place the egg whites in a bowl with a third of the sugar and whisk to firm peaks with an electric mixer – it is quite a task if you plan on making the meringue by hand. Add another third of the sugar, whisk for 1–2 minutes on medium speed, then add the rest of the sugar. Whisk just long enough to incorporate it. Using a large metal spoon, fold in the sifted cornflour and the white wine vinegar. Be careful not to overmix and lose volume.

Line 2 baking sheets with baking parchment and drop a large spoonful of the meringue in a mound on the paper. Using the back of the spoon, make a well in the centre of the mound for the cream and fresh fruit to sit in, trying to keep the meringue as round as possible. You can shape the mound with high sides, somewhat like a volcano. Repeat to make 8 volcano-shaped mounds in total, being sure to leave 5cm/2 inches between each one.

Bake in the centre of the oven for 1 hour or until the outside of the meringue is dry and golden and the inside is still soft. Leave to cool completely.

Peel the mango and cut all the flesh off the stone; peel the kiwis and remove the stones from the peaches. Cut the fruits into different-sized pieces – I leave the raspberries whole and halve or quarter the strawberries.

Whip the cream and icing sugar to soft peaks and fold in the pulp and seeds from the passionfruit. Whisk again to firm the cream slightly, until it forms medium peaks.

Pipe or spoon the passionfruit cream into the centre of the cooled pavlovas and decorate with an assortment of the prepared fruits. Pile the fruit high so you cover the cream completely.

LEMON MERINGUE

(continued on page 103)

For the pain de Gênes
150g/5^1/$_2$oz unsalted butter
120g/4^1/$_4$oz caster sugar
1 medium egg
150g/5^1/$_2$oz ground almonds
20g/^{3}/$_4$oz plain flour
20g/^{3}/$_4$oz cornflour
2 small eggs

For the lemon syrup and candied zest
2 lemons
100ml/3^1/$_2$fl oz water
100g/3^1/$_2$oz caster sugar

For the pavlova and meringue sticks
3 medium egg whites
90g/3^1/$_4$oz caster sugar
^{1}/$_4$ teaspoon white wine vinegar
a little spray oil or butter for greasing the tin
1 tablespoon icing sugar for dusting

For the lemon curd
180g/6oz unsalted butter, melted
150g/5^1/$_2$oz caster sugar
juice of 4 lemons
2 medium eggs
1 gelatine leaf

SERVES 15

If you like lemon meringue pie, you will love this version of it. The base is made not of pastry but a very soft almond sponge known as pain de Gênes (Genoa cake). The recipe for the pain de Gênes came from a friend and fellow pastry chef, Martin Docket. It is a little unusual, in that you add some of the eggs after the dry ingredients have been folded in, but it does work, I promise. The lemon curd sits on a soft layer of pavlova meringue and it is finished with crisp meringue logs. Use organic, unwaxed, leafy lemons, if possible, for an intense flavour.

You can make this dessert ahead of time as it freezes well.

Preheat the oven to 170°C/325°F/Gas Mark 3. Line the base of a 20 x 15cm/ 8 x 6 inch baking tin with baking parchment, making it long enough to overhang 2 sides of the tin.

Start by making the pain de Gênes. Cream together the butter and sugar till pale and fluffy. Lightly beat the medium egg, just to combine the yolk with the white, and add to the creamed mixture a little at a time, beating well between each addition. Sift the ground almonds, flour and cornflour together on to a piece of baking parchment, then fold them into the creamed mixture using a large metal spoon. Now break the 2 small eggs into a bowl and whisk just enough to combine them. Add them to the cake batter and mix in thoroughly. Transfer the mixture to the tin and level the top with a palette knife or spatula. Bake in the centre of the oven for 20–25 minutes, until the cake is well risen and light brown and the top springs back when gently pressed. A skewer inserted in the centre should come out clean. Leave to cool in the tin.

Make the syrup by zesting one of the lemons with a microplane or fine grater. Using a vegetable peeler, take 2–3 strips of zest from the other lemon, being careful not to remove the white pith as well, and reserve for candying. Remove the zest from the rest of the lemon with a microplane or fine grater. Put half the water and half the sugar in a small pan with all the finely grated lemon zest, stir well, then bring to the boil and simmer for 2–3 minutes. Pour this syrup over the cooled pain de Gênes, still in its tin.

For the candied zest, put the remaining sugar and water in a small pan, stir well and bring to the boil. Cut the large pieces of lemon zest into fine strips with a sharp knife. Place them in the hot syrup and simmer on a low heat for 5–10 minutes, until the zest softens and the syrup reduces a little and becomes more viscous. Remove from the heat and leave to cool.

Next make the pavlova. Using an electric mixer, whisk the egg whites with all the sugar and the white wine vinegar until they form medium-firm peaks. Line the base of a 20 x 15cm/8 x 6 inch baking tin with baking parchment and lightly grease the entire tin with spray oil or butter. Transfer two-thirds of the meringue to the tin and level the surface with a palette knife or spatula. Bake in the centre of the oven, still at 170°C/325°F/Gas Mark 3, for 15–18 minutes, until the meringue has puffed up and the top

(continued on page 103)

(continued from page 101)

is crisp. Test by inserting a knife to see if it comes out clean. Do not overbake, or the meringue will dry out too much and be hard; the base should remain white when it is turned out. Let the meringue cool a little in the tin and then loosen it around the edges with a small knife if needed.

Place the remaining meringue in a piping bag fitted with a 5mm/$\frac{1}{4}$ inch plain nozzle and pipe it in straight lines on a small baking sheet lined with baking parchment. Reduce the oven temperature very slightly and bake the meringue for 25–30 minutes, until it becomes firm and dry.

Now make the lemon curd. Put the melted butter, sugar, lemon juice and eggs into a large bowl and whisk until smooth. Place the bowl over a pan of gently simmering water, making sure the water does not touch the base of the bowl. Whisk continuously until the mixture thickens; it should leave a trail on the surface when drizzled from the whisk. Soak the gelatine leaf in a large bowl of cold water for about 5 minutes, until it is completely soft. Remove from the bowl, squeeze out excess water, then dissolve the gelatine in 1 tablespoon of boiling water. Add it to the hot curd and mix well. Pass the curd through a fine sieve and then blitz it in a liquidiser or food processor for 1–2 minutes, until it lightens slightly in colour and becomes aerated.

Pour 1–2 tablespoons of the lemon curd on to the soaked pain de Gênes, still in its tin, and spread it evenly over the top. Flip the pavlova over on to the cake and press down gently, then remove the baking parchment. The lemon curd should be sufficient to stick the pavlova to the base. Pour the remaining lemon curd over the pavlova and level with a spatula. Chill in the fridge for an hour, until the lemon curd is firm.

Remove the cake from the tin by running a small knife around the edges and then lifting it out using the overhanging baking parchment. Support it with both hands as you lift it from the tin on to a chopping board. Trim the edges off the cake to neaten it, then use a hot bread knife to cut it into slices (you can warm the knife by immersing it in hot water, then dry it before cutting the cake). Decorate each slice with pieces of the baked meringue strips, as in the picture, dust with the icing sugar and finish with the candied lemon zest.

Claire's Notes

• Make the cake and syrup a day in advance to take the stress out of preparing the dessert all on the same day. The pain de Gênes can even be frozen for up to 1 month if wrapped well in cling film. The pavlova and meringue logs can be made ahead of time if you freeze the pavlova once it is made and store the meringue logs in an airtight container. The pavlova will only keep for one day in the freezer; it needs to go in the freezer rather than the fridge otherwise it will weep.

• If you want to intensify the lemon flavour of the curd, use double the amount of lemon juice and boil it until reduced by half.

• The slice will keep a day or two in the fridge if you do not eat it all but the pavlova will begin to weep sugar after the second day and the meringue logs will soften.

VACHERIN MONT BLANC

3 medium egg whites
a pinch of cream of tartar
180g/6oz caster sugar

For the vanilla chestnut cream
350ml/12fl oz double cream
25g/1oz icing sugar
1 teaspoon vanilla extract
5 candied chestnuts in syrup, or
marrons glacés, chopped
1 tablespoon dark rum
3 tablespoons crème de marrons

For the chestnut vermicelli
1 large can of unsweetened
chestnut purée (about 450g/1lb)
100g/3^{1}/$_{2}$oz icing sugar
100g/3^{1}/$_{2}$oz softened unsalted
butter

To decorate
2 tablespoons icing sugar
2–3 candied chestnuts in syrup,
or marrons glacés, chopped

SERVES 10

Claire's Notes
• For a real treat, and I think the best way to enjoy a Mont Blanc, serve with hot black cherries in syrup. Canned cherries work really well. Empty the cherries and their juice into a pan and bring to the boil with a little lemon zest and a quarter of a cinnamon stick. Mix a tablespoon of cornflour with a little water to make a smooth, runny paste and add to the hot cherries. Bring back to the boil, stirring constantly, then spoon the cherries and their syrup over the Mont Blanc.

This dessert is named after the famous mountain in the Alps. In the 1800s Lord Byron described Mont Blanc as 'the monarch of mountains; They crowned him long ago. On a throne of rocks, in a robe of clouds, With a diadem of snow'. That pretty much describes this dessert to a T. A crisp shell of snow-white meringue holds a mountain of sweet vanilla chestnut cream studded with marrons glacés, which is covered in an avalanche of chestnut vermicelli, then topped with a single piece of marron glacé and a sprinkling of icing sugar.

This is one of those dishes where, if you keep a few meringue bases and a can of chestnut purée in your cupboard, you can whip up a stunning dessert on the spot. It really is as simple as that. Meringue shells will keep for months if you store them in a sealed container in a cool place. You should be able to find both the crème de marrons (sweetened chestnut cream) and the chestnut purée in good supermarkets, although they are more readily available at Christmas. You might try an Italian deli, as they seem to stock both the paste and the sweetened purée all year round.

Preheat the oven to 120°C/250°F/Gas Mark ^{1}/$_{2}$. Using an electric mixer, whisk the egg whites with the cream of tartar until they begin to foam. Add a third of the sugar and continue whisking until the meringue holds soft peaks. Add another third of the sugar and whisk on a high speed until the meringue holds firm peaks. Lower the speed, add the remaining sugar and whisk just long enough to combine. Spoon the meringue into a piping bag fitted with a 5mm/^{1}/$_{4}$ inch nozzle. Pipe 10 discs of meringue on to a baking sheet lined with baking parchment, starting each disc in the centre and piping in an increasing spiral to a diameter of 7.5cm/3 inches. Make sure the discs are spaced at least 2.5cm/1 inch apart. Then pipe 10 more discs, 5cm/2 inches in diameter.

Bake in the centre of the oven for 45–50 minutes, until the meringues are crisp and dry on the outside. When they are ready, they should peel away from the paper and still be soft and slightly gooey inside. Leave to cool completely on the baking sheet.

Make the vanilla chestnut cream by combining the double cream, icing sugar and vanilla in a bowl and whisking to firm peaks. Mix in the candied chestnuts. Mix the rum with the crème de marrons and fold it into the cream. Spoon or pipe about two thirds of the mixture in a large mound in the centre of each 7.5cm/3 inch meringue.

For the chestnut vermicelli, place the unsweetened chestnut purée in a large bowl and whisk it gently to make it smooth. Sift the icing sugar into the bowl and combine. Add the softened butter and whisk until smooth. Using a piping bag fitted with a 5mm/^{1}/$_{4}$ inch or smaller nozzle, pipe some of the vermicelli in a heap over the chestnut cream, then sit the smaller meringues on top. Spoon or pipe the remaining chestnut cream onto the smaller meringues, then cover with the remaining vermicelli. Finish with a dusting of icing sugar for a snow effect and top with a piece of marron glacé.

RED BERRY MERINGUE HEART TO SHARE

3 medium egg whites
1 teaspoon lemon juice
180g/6oz caster sugar

For the filling
150ml/5fl oz double cream
15g/$^1\!/_2$oz icing sugar
1 tablespoon crushed raspberries

To decorate
250–300g/9–10$^1\!/_2$oz fresh red
  berries
3 tablespoons redcurrant jelly
  (optional)

SERVES 2

Claire's Notes

• In winter I like to fill the centre of the heart with a blackberry cream, crowning it with poached winter fruits such as pears, rhubarb and apples. My special added ingredient is a little Stone's ginger wine in the poaching syrup.

• You can store the meringue heart in an airtight tin if you need to make it ahead of time.

• If you want to gild the lily, serve the meringue heart with Raspberry Sauce (see page 148) and Vanilla Ice Cream (page 192).

This is intended as a dessert for Valentine's Day, when it should be served on a single pretty plate with just one spoon. If it were me, I would want to be the one in possession of the spoon just to make sure I got my fair share of this wickedly tempting dessert.

You can, of course, make it for your loved one at any time of year. It is really good in June, when the berries are at their best. If you're not in the mood for romance, you can pipe the meringue in any shape, remembering to keep the sides higher than the base, then finish with fruit or berries that are in season.

Preheat the oven to 110°C/225°F/Gas Mark $^1\!/_4$. Using an electric mixer, whisk the egg whites with the lemon juice and a third of the sugar until they form firm peaks. Add another third of the sugar and continue to whisk for 2–3 minutes. Add the remaining sugar and mix just enough to incorporate it into the meringue.

Lightly oil a baking tray and then line it with baking parchment, pressing it down well. Using a piping bag fitted with a 5mm/$^1\!/_4$ inch plain nozzle, pipe out a heart shape about 15cm/6 inches long and 10–12cm/4–5 inches across. Fill in the centre by continuing to follow the shape of the heart until it is full. Starting on the outside rim of the heart, pipe another single line on top of the one you originally piped but pull the end away from the heart as shown in the picture, so it tapers away. Repeat the process a third time, making sure you pipe directly on top of the 2 lines you have already piped. You are building an outside edge that is higher than the middle of the heart. (You will probably have quite a lot of meringue left over after making the heart, but it's not practical to whisk up less than this quantity of meringue; make another heart with the surplus, if you like, as they store well.)

Bake the heart in the centre of the oven for 40–50 minutes, until the outside is set. You should be able to slide a palette knife under the heart and lift it up from the paper. Do not overbake the base or it will be totally dry in the centre. Leave to cool on the tray.

Whip the cream with the icing sugar and crushed raspberries until firm. Spoon or pipe the cream into the heart. Decorate the heart with the red berries, making sure all the cream is hidden.

If you want to glaze the berries, heat the redcurrant jelly in a small pan with a tablespoon of water and brush it over the berries to make them shine.

SUCCÈS

For the hazelnut butter cream
80g/2³/₄oz shelled hazelnuts
160g/5³/₄oz caster sugar
85ml/2¹/₂fl oz water
2 medium egg yolks
1 medium egg
250g/9oz unsalted butter, at room
    temperature

For the almond nougatine
50g/1³/₄oz blanched almonds
75g/2³/₄oz caster sugar

For the dacquoise
25g/1oz plain flour
125g/4¹/₂oz ground almonds
125g/4¹/₂oz icing sugar, plus
    2 tablespoons icing sugar to
    decorate
4 medium egg whites
50g/1³/₄oz caster sugar
a few drops of vanilla extract

MAKES 12

Succès is a classic French gâteau made from an almond meringue known as dacquoise. It consists of two layers of piped almond meringue encasing a rich hazelnut butter cream, the outside of which is rolled in almond nougatine. The result is a rich, decadent dessert. This recipe is for individual ones, as I always find a large one hard to cut neatly. They are perfect for afternoon tea, as they look pretty and dainty and can be eaten with a dessert fork. An electric mixer will help make the preparation almost effortless.

Preheat the oven to 180°C/350°F/Gas Mark 4. Place the hazelnuts on a baking tray lined with baking parchment and bake for about 10 minutes, until golden. While they are still warm, transfer them to a food processor and process to a paste. The heat should help them form a paste. Bake the almonds for the nougatine in the same way on a separate tray and set aside for later. Do not process them.

To make the butter cream, place the sugar and water in a small, heavy-based saucepan and bring to the boil, stirring to dissolve the sugar. Put a sugar thermometer in the pan and cook on a high heat, without stirring, until the sugar reaches soft-ball stage (118°C/245°F). While the syrup is boiling, brush down the sides of the pan occasionally with a clean pastry brush dipped in a little cold water to prevent crystallisation.

Meanwhile, place the egg yolks and whole egg into a freestanding electric mixer and whisk until they begin to pale and thicken slightly. Once the sugar syrup reaches soft-ball stage, remove it from the heat and, with the electric mixer running at low speed, pour it in a steady stream on to the eggs. Make sure you pour the sugar syrup down the side of the bowl, away from the whisk, so as not to spin the hot sugar around the edge of the bowl. You could do all this using a handheld electric beater but you will have to ask someone to pour the syrup in for you while you whisk. In both cases, whisk until the eggs and sugar are pale, thick and just warm, not hot. Add the butter a tablespoonful at a time, still whisking. The cream should hold its shape and be smooth and shiny when all the butter has been added. If the butter is too cold and the eggs are not warm, it will be lumpy. If the eggs and sugar are too hot when you add the butter, they will melt the butter and the cream will be too runny. If this happens, you can chill the butter cream in the bowl until it firms and then whisk it until it is smooth, shiny and firm. Add the hazelnut paste and mix well to combine. Transfer to a clean bowl and set aside.

Next make the nougatine. Place a nonstick baking mat on a baking sheet. Put the sugar in a medium, heavy-based pan and stir continuously over a medium to high heat until it dissolves and turns a golden caramel colour (see page 137). Add the cooked whole almonds and mix them together. Pour the almonds and sugar on to the nonstick baking mat and leave to cool completely. Once the nougatine is cold, place it in a food processor and process until it is reduced to pieces the size of couscous.

Finally prepare the dacquoise. Preheat the oven to 170°C/325°F/Gas Mark 3. Line 2 baking sheets with baking parchment and draw around a 5cm/2 inch cutter on it 24 times, leaving a 1cm/$^1/_2$ inch gap between each circle. Turn the parchment over. You need to be able to see the circles, as this is going to be your template for piping the meringue.

Sift the flour, ground almonds and icing sugar together on to a piece of baking parchment and mix them well. This will prevent the almonds forming clumps when folding them into the egg whites. Place the egg whites and caster sugar into a large bowl and whisk to a firm meringue, using an electric beater. With a large metal spoon, gently fold the sifted dry ingredients into the egg whites a third at a time, taking care not to lose any volume. Finally, mix in the vanilla.

Transfer the meringue to a piping bag fitted with a 5mm/$^1/_4$ inch nozzle and pipe 24 discs of meringue on to the baking parchment, following the templates: start at the centre of each circle and pipe in a spiral fashion until you reach the edge. Bake in the centre of the oven for about 20 minutes, until the meringue is golden brown and crisp. It will crisp more as it cools. Leave to cool on the tray. Once they are cold, you should be able to lift the discs from the parchment without them breaking.

Place the butter cream in a piping bag fitted with a 1cm/$^1/_2$ inch plain nozzle and pipe a large bulb of butter cream on to one of the discs. Place another disc of dacquoise on top and squash them together so the butter cream reaches the edges of the discs. Spread the nougatine out on a baking tray lined with baking parchment and roll the edges of the sandwiched discs in it to cover the butter cream. Put them on another clean tray and place them in the fridge to firm for 20 minutes. Remove from the fridge and dust the tops with the 2 tablespoons of icing sugar to cover them completely in a thin, even layer. Serve on small plates with a pastry fork.

Claire's Notes
• You can make the nougatine in advance if you store it in a sealed container, away from moisture (i.e. not in the fridge). If the container is airtight, it will keep for a week before going soft. The butter cream, too, can be made in advance; store it in a plastic container in the fridge for 3–4 days and remove from the fridge 2 hours before using it, so it has time to soften.
• Instead of hazelnuts, you could use 80g/2$^3/_4$oz chocolate hazelnut spread, such as Green & Black's or Nutella, to flavour the butter cream.

CITRUS MERINGUE QUIFFS

4 medium egg whites
240g/8^{1}/$_{2}$oz caster sugar
^{1}/$_{4}$ teaspoon white wine vinegar
1 tablespoon warm water

For the citrus curd
juice of 1 lime
juice of 1 pink grapefruit
125g/4^{1}/$_{2}$oz caster sugar
125g/4^{1}/$_{2}$oz unsalted butter, cut
   into cubes
4 medium eggs

For the citrus sauce, segments
   and candied zest
2 navel oranges
2 pink grapefruit
1 lime
1 lemon
50g/1^{3}/$_{4}$oz caster sugar
1 tablespoon cornflour

SERVES 8

There is a technique and a skill to making the quiffs on this meringue but don't be put off by this; you can always spoon or pipe the meringue instead. Serve with Lemon Sorbet (see page 201) and a glass of Pimm's for the perfect end to a lazy summer afternoon.

The real secret here is in the cooking of the meringue. It should be done at a low temperature so the surface is crisp and the inside is like marshmallow. This allows you to fill the quiffs with a sweet citrus curd that balances the sharpness of the lime and grapefruit.

Preheat the oven to 120°C/250°F/Gas Mark ^{1}/$_{2}$. Place the egg whites, caster sugar and vinegar in a large bowl and whisk with an electric mixer on a medium setting until the meringue holds soft peaks. Add the warm water and whisk on a high setting until the meringue holds medium to firm peaks.

Line a baking sheet with baking parchment. Use a large tablespoon to make the quiffs. Place the spoon in the bowl and scoop up a large amount of meringue but do not lift the spoon completely out of the meringue. When you have a large mound of meringue on the spoon, wobble the spoon from side to side so the surface of the mound becomes smooth. Now lift the spoon from the bowl. Hold the spoon in your left hand (or in your right hand if you're left handed) and point it downwards on to the baking sheet. The meringue should be too firm to drop from the spoon. Take a second tablespoon and push the meringue on to the tray with the back of it. This spoon should also be facing downwards toward the tray. As the last of the meringue leaves the spoon, flick the meringue that is now on the second spoon over the top of the bulb you have just made to make the quiff. Make 8 meringues in this way.

Bake in the centre of the oven for 20–25 minutes, until the outside of the meringue is crisp and the inside is soft, like marshmallow. When they are ready, they will come away from the paper when gently pulled up. Leave to cool on the tray.

Now make the citrus curd. Put the lime and pink grapefruit juice in a small pan with the sugar and butter. Bring to the boil over a medium heat, stirring constantly. Beat the eggs together in a small bowl, then pour the boiled mixture over them, whisking continuously. Return the mixture to a clean pan and whisk over a low heat with a balloon whisk until the curd thickens enough to leave a trail on the surface when the whisk is lifted; this should be just before it reaches boiling point, but do be careful not to let it boil. Remove from the heat and pass through a fine sieve into a bowl. Cover the surface with cling film to prevent a skin forming and leave to cool. Place in the fridge to firm.

Now deal with the fruits for the sauce, segments and candied zest. Cut one orange and one pink grapefruit in half and juice them. Cut the tops and bottoms off the remaining fruits so they sit flat on the work surface and then slice off all the peel and pith with a small, sharp knife, working downwards in small sections. The fruit should not have any white pieces of pith still attached to it. Place the peel in a small bowl for later. Pick up each fruit and cut out each segment from between the membranes, keeping the knife as close to the membrane as you can – do this over a bowl to catch any juice that comes out of the fruit. Now roughly chop the segments into small pieces, again reserving any juice, and set aside.

Take the reserved pieces of peel. You will not need it all – a couple of strips from each fruit will be more than enough. Run a sharp knife between the peel and pith to take off the zest. Cut the zest into very thin strips, place in a small pan of water and simmer for 10 minutes, until soft but not falling apart. Drain the zest through a fine sieve, then refresh under cold running water while still in the sieve. Place the zest in a small pan with a tablespoon of the sugar and 2 tablespoons of water, bring to the boil and simmer gently for about 5 minutes, until the liquid becomes a thin syrup. Leave the zest in the syrup to cool.

Put all the fruit juice in a small pan with the remaining sugar and bring slowly to the boil, stirring occasionally. Mix the cornflour with a tablespoon of water to make a thin paste. Pour a little of the boiling juice on to the cornflour and then return it to the pan with the rest of the juice. Mix well and bring back to the boil, whisking constantly, until the sauce thickens slightly. If it becomes too thick, add a little extra juice (you will need additional fruit for this). Simmer for 1–2 minutes over a low heat, then pour through a fine sieve into a small bowl. Leave to cool completely.

Make a hole in the base of each meringue quiff, using the tip of a 1cm/$^1/_2$ inch piping nozzle or the end of a small spoon. Place the citrus curd in a piping bag fitted with a 1cm/$^1/_2$ inch plain nozzle and pipe the equivalent of a large teaspoonful into each quiff. The quiffs should be soft in the middle, which will enable you to do this.

Place each quiff on an individual serving plate and spoon a ring of the chopped segments around it. Spoon some of the sauce over the segments and decorate with a few pieces of candied zest.

Claire's Notes
• The meringue quiffs can be made a day or two ahead and kept in an airtight container. However, after 3 or 4 days the inside of the quiffs will become harder and less like marshmallow.
• If you are worried that the citrus curd will overheat and separate, cook it in a bowl placed over a pan of simmering water rather than directly in the pan.
• Once you get the hang of segmenting citrus fruits it only takes a few minutes, but allow yourself plenty of time if you have not done it before.
• The zest, sauce and segments can all be prepared a day in advance.

100g/3^1/$_2$oz ground hazelnuts
12g/^{1}/$_2$oz plain flour
200g/7oz caster sugar
6 medium egg whites

For the chocolate mousse
150ml/5fl oz whipping cream
250g/9oz milk chocolate (30–40
    per cent cocoa solids), finely
    chopped
150g/5^1/$_2$oz unsalted butter
4 large egg whites
50g/1^3/$_4$oz caster sugar
30g/1oz cocoa powder
50g/1^3/$_4$oz praline paste or
    chocolate hazelnut spread such
    as Green & Black's or Nutella

For the chocolate leaves
20–25 fresh rose leaves, in good
    condition
300g/10^1/$_2$oz tempered dark
    chocolate (see pages 212–213)

SERVES 6

This literally translates as 'autumn leaves'. It consists of layers of hazelnut meringue sandwiched with a hazelnut chocolate mousse and covered in crisp chocolate leaves. The leaves are so easy to make and look really impressive. We used to do a version of this at Le Cordon Bleu in London while I was teaching there but it involved heating and cooling baking trays, spreading them with chocolate and chilling them just enough to scrape the wafer-thin chocolate into strips, which would then be wrapped quickly around the assembled cake. The classroom always ended up smeared with chocolate – on every fridge door, oven handle and work surface. The memory of it alone was enough to make me change the finish for this book to something less stressful, which involves a considerable amount less cleaning of the kitchen afterwards.

Preheat the oven to 170°C/325°F/Gas Mark 3. Make a template for the hazelnut meringue. Using a 15cm/6 inch cake ring, 5cm/2 inches deep, and a felt-tip pen, draw 3 templates of the ring on a sheet of baking parchment. Flip the paper over and lay it on a baking sheet.

Sift the ground hazelnuts, flour and half the sugar on to a piece of baking parchment. Place the egg whites and the remaining sugar in a large mixing bowl and, using an electric mixer, whisk to a firm meringue. If you are making the meringue by hand, add a third of the sugar to the egg whites and whisk to soft peaks before adding another third of the sugar and whisking to firm peaks. Make sure the meringue is smooth, shiny and at firm peaks before adding the remaining sugar.

Fold in the sifted dry ingredients with a large metal spoon. Take care not to overmix or be too heavy handed. The mix should remain fluffy and not lose volume.

Spoon the meringue into a piping bag fitted with a 5mm/^{1}/$_4$ inch plain nozzle. Starting in the centre of each circle template, pipe in a spiral, moving outwards until you reach the edge of the template. The spiraling lines should be touching, to form a neat disc of hazelnut meringue.

Bake in the centre of the oven for 35–40 minutes, until the meringues are firm to the touch and golden brown. As soon as they come out of the oven, place the cake ring over the discs and press down firmly to cut away any excess; this ensures they are not larger than the ring, as sometimes the meringue expands when baking. As the meringue cools, it will firm up even more, to form crisp discs that can be lifted from the baking parchment. Leave to cool on the baking sheet.

To make the mousse, semi-whip the cream until it forms soft peaks and store it in the fridge. Melt the chocolate in a bowl set over a pan of simmering water, making sure the water doesn't touch the base of the bowl. Melt the butter in a small saucepan. Keep the chocolate and the butter warm.

Whisk the egg whites with the caster sugar until they form stiff peaks. Sift the cocoa powder into a small bowl, add the warm melted butter and whisk to a smooth paste. Pour this paste into the egg white with the warm melted chocolate and fold them both in very gently. Fold in the praline paste, followed by the semi-whipped cream, to make a light, fluffy chocolate mousse.

Place one of the discs of hazelnut meringue on a tray lined with baking parchment and sit the cake ring over it. Use the chocolate mousse to fill a piping bag fitted with a 5mm/^{1}/$_4$ inch nozzle. Pipe a layer of mousse over the disc, then cover with a second disc of meringue and another layer of the chocolate mousse. Place the final disc of meringue over the mousse and press down firmly. You should have about 3–4 tablespoons of mousse left for masking the cake. Place the tray in the fridge for about 1 hour for the mousse to set.

Meanwhile, make the chocolate leaves. Clean and dry the rose leaves; they need to be completely dry on both surfaces. Using a pastry brush, brush the top side of each leaf with tempered chocolate. Take care that the chocolate does not drip or coat the underside of the leaf or it will be hard to peel away when the chocolate sets. Set the brushed leaves flat on a tray lined with baking parchment. Make sure the chocolate is set, then cover the tray with cling film and leave in the fridge for about 30 minutes.

Remove the cake ring with a blowtorch, if you have one, holding it about 15cm/6 inches away from the ring and warming it until it releases the cake, being careful not to leave the torch in any one spot for more than a few seconds. Alternatively, wrap a hot, damp towel around the outside of the ring until the cake releases itself from the mould.

Coat the top and sides of the cake with the remaining chocolate mousse and level it with a palette knife to give a smooth finish. Peel the rose leaves away from the chocolate; they should release with ease. Stick them to the sides and top of the cake. I like to lay the leaves in an upright position so they overlap slightly around the outside of the cake and place a few random ones on the top.

Claire's Notes
• You can make the chocolate leaves in advance. They will keep for at least a week in a sealed plastic container in the fridge. Layer them between sheets of baking parchment to stop them getting knocked and losing their shine.
• If making the leaves seems too much work, buy some chocolate decorations instead. There are some good products available in cake decorating shops and speciality kitchen shops.
• If you cannot find ground hazelnuts, either grind your own or substitute ground almonds, which are more readily available.
• Serve with Vanilla Ice Cream (see page 192) sprinkled with chopped roasted hazelnuts.

CUSTARDS
AND CREAMS

THE SECRETS OF SUCCESS

Custards fall into two groups, stirred and baked, which reflect the method by which they are cooked. Both need careful, gentle cooking to achieve a smooth texture and to prevent curdling in the case of stirred custards, and souffléing and boiling in the case of baked ones.

STIRRED CUSTARDS

A basic stirred custard is a milk sauce thickened slightly with egg yolks and sweetened with sugar. Crème anglaise is a richer version, containing more egg yolks and sometimes made with cream rather than milk. A rich crème anglaise forms the basis of many ice creams (see pages 190–219). Pastry cream, also known as confectioner's custard or crème pâtissière, differs in that it is thickened with flour and/or cornflour as well as eggs, which prevents it curdling. Unlike custard, it can be brought to the boil, and must be simmered for a few minutes while whisking continuously to cook out the starch and prevent it breaking down once it is cold. Pastry cream is very thick and may be lightened with the addition of a little whipped cream. It is used to fill tarts and choux pastries, such as Tutti Frutti Vol-au-Vents (page 90) and Crème Puffs (page 93).

Below is a recipe for a classic crème anglaise. The French liked our custard so much that they named the sweet, smooth vanilla sauce English cream. Strangely, even we, the British, now call it crème anglaise. I was brought up on Bird's custard – invented by Alfred Bird, a nineteenth-century pharmacist, for his wife, who had an allergy to eggs. It was so easy to make, and became so popular, that eventually making a custard from scratch began to seem like more trouble than making the pudding itself. I am pleased that the fresh egg version has found its way back into many households and restaurants.

People can be nervous of making custard, because of the risk of it curdling. Keep the following points in mind and it should be fine:

• Use a heavy-based pan, keep the heat low and stir the custard constantly, so it heats evenly.
• If you are worried that you won't be able to tell when the custard has reached the correct stage, check it with a sugar thermometer; the temperature should not rise above 86°C/185°F.

• If the custard looks as if it is on the verge of separating, a quick whiz with a handheld blender is often sufficient to bring it back together. However, if the custard has become hotter than 86°C/185°F, it cannot be rescued.
• As soon as the custard thickens, strain it through a very fine sieve into a clean bowl and place it over a bowl of ice to prevent further cooking.
• In order to feel completely confident that the sauce won't overheat and separate, you could cook it in a double boiler (or a bowl placed over a pan of gently simmering water). It takes longer and you will need more patience but it works well.

CRÈME ANGLAISE

SERVES 8

1 vanilla pod
500ml/18fl oz whole milk (or, for a richer sauce, 250ml/9fl oz double cream and 250ml/9fl oz milk)
6 medium egg yolks
125g/4$\frac{1}{2}$oz caster sugar

Slit the vanilla pod down its length with a small knife and scrape out the seeds. Place both the seeds and the pod in a saucepan with the milk and bring slowly to the boil over a medium heat.

In a bowl, lightly mix the egg yolks and sugar together with a whisk. Do not leave the sugar sitting on the yolks without mixing them together straight away. If you do, you will notice tiny specks of egg yolk in the mixture; this is known as burning and even if you strain the sauce afterwards, the specks will remain.

Gradually pour the boiled milk on to the egg yolk and sugar mixture, stirring well. Return the mix to a clean pan and cook over a gentle heat, stirring constantly with a wooden spoon, until you can see it begin to thicken slightly; it will change from a watery consistency to a smooth sauce and should be thick enough to coat the spoon. Run your finger down the custard on the back of the spoon – the path should remain separated. It is vital that you do not let the sauce reach boiling point or it will split and curdle.

As soon as the sauce thickens, pour it through a fine sieve into a bowl, then place the bowl over a bowl of crushed ice. Serve hot or cold.

The vanilla pod can be washed, dried and put in a jar of sugar. You will be amazed how it takes on the aroma and flavour of the vanilla. Use the sugar to make pastries and desserts.

BAKED CUSTARDS

These are rich in eggs and cream or milk and have a smooth, creamy texture. Some, such as Crème Caramel (see page 123), call for whole eggs or a mixture of eggs and yolks, while others use just the yolks – Crème Brûlée (page 124) is a classic example. Whole eggs give a firmer, smoother consistency and egg yolks a soft, rich, dense consistency.

Baked custards should be cooked slowly, at a temperature of 150–170°C/300–325°F/Gas Mark 2–3 in a protective bath of water (a roasting tin will do fine) to prevent curdling and to ensure they heat evenly. The water should come at least half way up the side of the dish containing the custard. Various recipes call for warm, cold or even hot water – it depends how quickly the custard needs to be cooked and how long it will be in the oven.

Although baked custards are among the simplest desserts to make, you need to pay a little attention to detail to ensure they have the correct texture. Here are a few tips:

• It helps if you put the pan of water in the oven first and then add the dish or dishes to the water, rather than try to transport a full bath of water and dishes to the oven, as this often causes the water to spill into the custard dishes themselves.
• The water helps insulate the custards and prevents the edges cooking too quickly. Two or three sheets of kitchen paper can be placed in the bottom of the water bath to stop the dishes sliding around and to protect them from the heat at the base of the pan.
• When a custard is cooked, the surface should no longer be wobbly and a knife inserted in the centre should come out clean.

• Remember to remove the dishes from the water bath immediately they are done, to prevent further cooking. The custard should be well chilled before serving, as it sets further during the chilling process.
• I often use a wide, shallow dish for crème brûlée, as it helps with even cooking and takes less time to cook all the way to the centre.

LEMON POSSET

4 lemons
250g/9oz caster sugar
500ml/18fl oz double cream

To decorate
30g/1oz toasted flaked almonds
icing sugar
30g/1oz candied lemon peel strips

SERVES 4

With only three ingredients, this has to be the easiest recipe in the book. Its simplicity, however, yields a surprisingly decadent, smooth and silky cream that will leave your dinner guests trying to guess how you made it.

Squeeze the juice from the lemons and strain it through a fine sieve. Place in a pan with the caster sugar and bring to the boil over a low heat, stirring continuously until the sugar has dissolved. Keep this warm on the side of the stove.

Bring the cream to the boil in a heavy-bottomed pan, then pour it over the warm lemon and sugar mixture. Whisk gently to mix. Pass the mixture through a fine sieve into a jug and pour into individual serving dishes. Place in the fridge for 2 hours, until set.

Decorate with toasted flaked almonds or pistachio nuts, icing sugar and candied lemon peel.

Claire's Notes
• For a perfectly smooth, bubble-free surface, blowtorch the top of the cream mixture for 10 seconds before leaving it to set in the fridge.

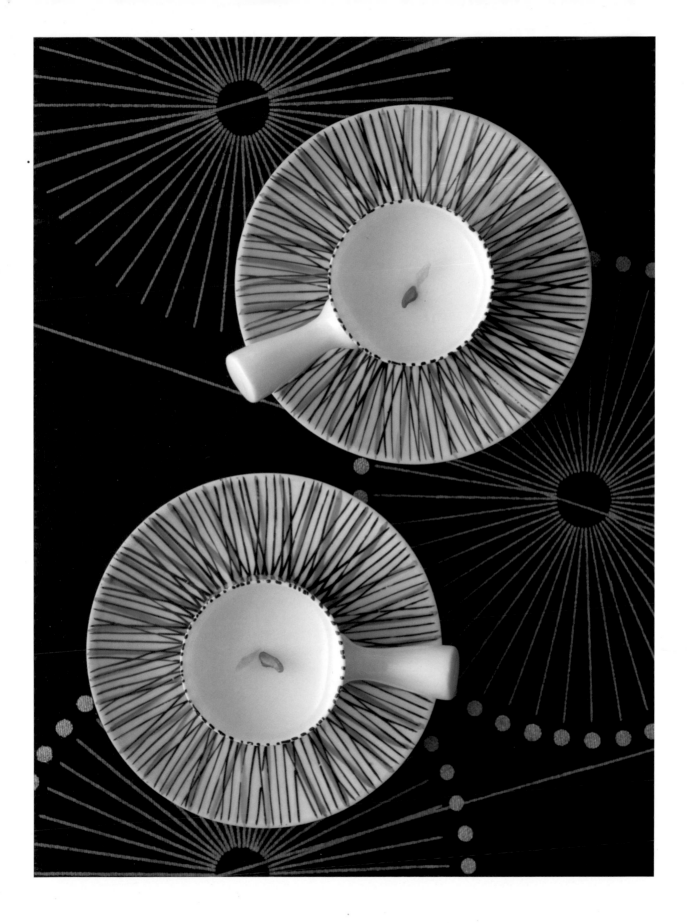

CRÈME CARAMEL

a little vegetable oil for greasing
   the moulds
1 vanilla pod
500ml/18fl oz whole milk
3 medium eggs
2 medium egg yolks
100g/3$^1/_2$oz caster sugar

For the caramel
100g/3$^1/_2$oz caster sugar
1 tablespoon water

SERVES 6

In England crème caramel often features on the practical exam for budding young pastry chefs. It combines the cooking of sugar with the cooking of a custard in a water bath – two skills that require concentration and dexterity.

The firmness of the custard depends on the proportion of egg whites used. Crème caramel should be set enough to turn out of the mould but remain creamy and smooth. For this reason, I include a couple of egg yolks as well as whole eggs.

First grease 6 moulds, such as dariole moulds or ramekins.

To make the caramel, put the sugar in a small, heavy-based saucepan and place over a medium heat. As the sugar starts to melt around the edges, begin to stir slowly but constantly. Once the sugar has melted completely and is a golden caramel colour, carefully remove the pan from the heat and add the water. Great care should be taken at this stage, as the caramel will be dangerously hot. Allow the sugar and water a few seconds to bubble together, then mix them with a spoon. Immediately pour the caramel into the moulds, adding just enough to cover the base. Put the moulds in a deep roasting tin. They should be spaced apart so they are not touching and the heat can circulate evenly around them.

Next make the custard. Preheat the oven to 170°C/325°F/Gas Mark 3. Slit the vanilla pod open lengthways with a knife and scrape out the seeds, then put the pod and seeds in a pan with the milk and bring to the boil. In a large bowl, beat the eggs and egg yolks with the sugar but not so much that they foam. Pour the boiled milk over the beaten egg mix, stirring well. Pass through a very fine sieve.

Fill the prepared moulds with the mixture to just below the top. Pour enough hand-hot water into the roasting tin to come two-thirds of the way up the sides of the moulds, then bake in the centre of the oven for about 20 minutes, until a knife inserted in the centre comes out clean. Do not try to turn the custards out while they are warm. Let them cool thoroughly, then run a knife around the edge of each mould and invert§ them on to a plate for serving.

Claire's Notes
• You can use 4–5 drops of good-quality vanilla extract if you don't have a vanilla pod.
• If you have any caramel left after preparing the moulds, add another tablespoon of water and bring it back to the boil over a low heat to make a caramel sauce. You can serve this on the side.
• Serve with a crisp, buttery biscuit to add texture. Langues de Chat (see page 216) are perfect.

CRÈME BRÛLÉE

500ml/18fl oz double cream
2 vanilla pods
9 medium egg yolks
50g/1³/₄oz caster sugar, plus
    about 100g/3¹/₂oz caster sugar
    for glazing

SERVES 8

The origin of the classic crème brûlée is hotly debated. The Cambridge burnt cream, or Trinity cream, was created in the 1600s at Trinity College in Cambridge. Trinity even has a hot iron, embedded with the college crest, which is used to burn the sugar top. It wasn't until much later that the French translated the words 'burnt cream' to crème brûlée and the dish became popular, causing many to believe, incorrectly, that it is French in origin.

I have so many recipes for crème brûlée but my favourite is the traditional version that uses just egg yolks, cream and sugar, with a touch of vanilla, and is smooth, rich and creamy. There is nothing better than cracking the thin crust of golden caramelised sugar with the back of your spoon and scooping out the soft custard below.

Preheat the oven to 150°C/300°F/Gas Mark 2. Put the cream in a saucepan. Slit the vanilla pods open lengthways and, using the back of a small knife, scrape the seeds from inside the pod into the cream. Add the pods to the cream and bring to the boil. Meanwhile, mix the egg yolks and sugar together lightly, just enough to combine them. Pour the boiled cream over the eggs and sugar, mix well and pass through a very fine sieve.

Fill 8 small ramekins to the top with the custard and place them in a roasting tin. Fill the tin with enough cold water to come two-thirds of the way up the sides of the ramekins, then place in the oven and bake for about 30 minutes, until the custard is set. To test, gently shake the ramekins; the custard should not wobble. If you are not sure, you can insert a knife to see if the custard is cooked in the centre of the dish.

Lift the ramekins from the roasting tin and place on a small tray. Leave to cool, then chill. When they are completely chilled, they are ready for glazing. Using a teaspoon, spread enough sugar over the top of each custard to make a smooth, thin, even layer. With a blowtorch, burn the sugar until it melts and creates a thin sheet of golden caramel. Let the caramel cool and harden before serving; this will only take a minute or two.

Claire's Notes
• You can use shallower *sur le plat* dishes instead of ramekins, if you wish, but remember to reduce the cooking time accordingly.
• Do not let the custard boil, as this will give it an unpleasant curdled texture.
• If you have too much sugar on top of the custards, it will not colour evenly or create a thin crust of caramel. If necessary, reduce the amount until it glazes perfectly; you should not be able to see the custard but there should be no build-up of sugar.
• You can flavour the custard, if you wish. Try infusing a little orange or lemon zest in the cream. Rose and violet oils work well too, but remember to use them sparingly and add to the custard once all the ingredients have been combined, before you fill the dishes.

SPICED PUMPKIN CUSTARD WITH ORANGE-INFUSED GRANOLA

300ml/10fl oz milk

375g/13oz peeled, deseeded pumpkin flesh, chopped

125ml/4fl oz double cream

3 medium eggs

60g/2$\frac{1}{4}$oz caster sugar

35g/1$\frac{1}{4}$oz soft dark brown sugar

$\frac{1}{4}$ teaspoon freshly grated nutmeg

$\frac{1}{4}$ teaspoon ground ginger

$\frac{1}{4}$ teaspoon ground cinnamon

50g/1$\frac{3}{4}$oz unsalted butter, melted

For the granola

200g/7oz demerara sugar

125ml/4fl oz honey

75ml/2$\frac{1}{2}$fl oz golden syrup

110g/3$\frac{3}{4}$oz unsalted butter

1 capful of natural vanilla extract

180g/6oz desiccated coconut

150g/5$\frac{1}{2}$oz pecan nuts, roughly chopped

75g/2$\frac{3}{4}$oz shelled peeled pistachio nuts

100g/3$\frac{1}{2}$oz flaked almonds

250g/9oz large rolled oats

85ml/2$\frac{1}{2}$fl oz sunflower oil

grated zest of 4 oranges

SERVES 6

Try this as an alternative to pumpkin pie at Thanksgiving. You can use other members of the squash family, too, such as butternut or red kuri. I really enjoy the smoothness of the custard with the crunchy granola. This recipe makes more granola than you need but it keeps well in an airtight container. It is excellent on its own as a breakfast dish with plain yoghurt.

First make the granola. Preheat the oven to 180°C/350°F/Gas Mark 4. Put the sugar in a large pan with the honey, golden syrup, butter and vanilla extract and bring slowly to the boil, stirring to dissolve the sugar. Remove from the heat and add the coconut, pecan nuts, pistachios, flaked almonds and oats. Mix well, and then quickly stir in the sunflower oil and orange zest. Turn out on to a baking sheet covered with a nonstick baking mat and spread out evenly. Bake for 25–30 minutes, until golden brown, turning frequently to ensure even colouring. Remove from the oven and, as the granola cools, break it up into pieces.

For the pumpkin custard, preheat the oven to 170°C/325°F/Gas Mark 3. Bring the milk to the boil and add the pumpkin. Reduce the heat and simmer until the pumpkin is tender, adding more milk if necessary to keep it covered. Drain the pumpkin, reserving 125ml/4fl oz of the milk. Purée the pumpkin in a blender, then pass through a fine sieve.

Whisk together the cream, eggs and reserved milk. Add the pumpkin purée, both the sugars and all the spices and mix well. Add the melted butter and pass the mixture through a fine sieve again.

Pour into 6 individual ovenproof dishes, such as ramekins, and put them in a roasting tin. Pour enough hot water into the tin to come half way up the sides of the dishes, then place in the oven and bake for 20–25 minutes, until the custards are set. The surface should feel firm when pressed and no liquid should come to the top. Do not allow them to boil.

Remove the dishes from the roasting tin and leave to cool, then chill. Serve the custards with the granola sprinkled on top – or serve it on the side in a separate dish. For an extra-special treat, add a scoop of cinnamon or vanilla ice cream.

FRUIT FOOL

125ml/4fl oz fruit purée or pulp
(you can use a blender or a food
processor for this; a blender will
give a smoother texture)
caster sugar to taste (for the fruit)
250ml/9fl oz double cream
icing sugar to taste (for the cream)
fresh fruit, to decorate

For the coloured sugar (optional)
1 tablespoon vegetable oil
250g/9oz granulated sugar
50ml/2fl oz water
a little powdered food colouring
(available in cake decorating
shops)

SERVES 6

Claire's Notes
• For the best results, use fruit
that is in season and as ripe as
possible.
• Honey can be used to sweeten
the cream instead of icing sugar,
or you could add a little white wine
or fruit-based liqueur for a dinner-
party dessert.

I love the visual aspect of these delightful English creams. They look very striking and are so easy to make. The classic fool is a combination of crushed, mashed or puréed fruit, sugar and whipped cream. As fruits have varying degrees of sweetness, there is no exact measurement for the sugar. Just add enough to sweeten to your liking.

Fruits such as rhubarb and gooseberries should be cooked to a pulp in a little water first, then sweetened and left to cool. Ripe berries and soft fruits need no cooking. If you like a little texture in the fool, don't sieve the fruit purée. I like to sieve anything with a lot of seeds, such as raspberries and blackcurrants, but mango, kiwi, papaya, etc. all work well just mashed to a pulp.

Sieve the purée to remove seeds, if you like, then add enough caster sugar to sweeten and mix well.

Whip the cream to soft peaks, being careful not to overwhip it. Sweeten with icing sugar if desired and use to fill a piping bag fitted with a 1cm/ $^1/_2$ inch nozzle. Place about $1^1/_2$ tablespoons of the fruit purée in each of 6 serving glasses. Place the piping bag in each glass so the nozzle is nearly touching the purée. Now squeeze the bag; as you do so, it will push the purée to the edge of the glass and create a spiral effect of cream and fruit purée. As the glass fills with cream, lift the bag towards the top of the glass, stopping when it is nearly full. Chill the fools in the fridge for an hour. Decorate with fresh fruit or coloured sugar, if liked, and serve with any remaining fruit purée.

For the coloured sugar, lightly oil a nonstick baking mat with the vegetable oil. Put the sugar and water in a small, heavy-based pan, stir well, then heat, stirring, until the sugar has dissolved. Put a sugar thermometer in the pan and bring to the boil over a high heat. Boil until the mixture reaches the hard-crack stage (150–155°C/300–310°F). While it is boiling, clean the sides of the pan 4 or 5 times with a clean pastry brush dipped in cold water, running the brush around the edges of the pan to keep it free from sugar crystals that might fall back into the sugar and cause the caramel to crystallise. When it reaches the required temperature, remove the pan from the heat and place on a pot-holder to cool slightly.

Using a small paintbrush, very lightly dab little specks of powdered food colouring on to the mat. Pour the slightly cooled sugar syrup on to the mat over the colour to create a thin layer of sugar, which should look like glass. Do not allow the sugar to cool so much that it thickens before you pour it. It should flow in a thin layer over the colour. Leave to cool and then break it into pieces to decorate the fools.

WHITE CHOCOLATE, BUTTERSCOTCH AND MACADAMIA NUT WHIPS

250g/9oz macadamia nuts
$1/4$ teaspoon fine salt

For the butterscotch sauce
200g/7oz caster sugar
100ml/3$1/2$fl oz water
200ml/7fl oz double cream
4 teaspoons rum

For the white chocolate mousse
500ml/18fl oz double cream
250g/9oz white chocolate, finely
    chopped
75ml/2$1/2$oz water
25ml/1fl oz liquid glucose

SERVES 8

Claire's Notes
• Be very careful when making the butterscotch sauce, as the caramel is dangerously hot. Never leave the pan unattended while the sugar is boiling. Make sure you use a bigger saucepan than you need, so the caramel will not bubble over the top when the cream is added.
• For a sophisticated finish, layer the ingredients with chocolate sponge soaked in Bailey's Irish Cream Liqueur (you could use the chocolate sponge in the Black Forest Trifle on page 143) and finish it with Chocolate Décor (see page 194).
• If you are not a fan of white chocolate, then milk chocolate works well with both the butterscotch and the nuts. Be sure to use a good-quality chocolate.

When I worked in the banqueting section at the Hilton London Metropole Hotel, we loved to make up desserts from the sponge trimmings and banqueting sauces that were left over after plating the 1,000-plus portions of whatever the previous day's dessert had been. This was one of our most successful creations. I use macadamia nuts in this recipe, one of the most expensive nuts in the world. At The French Laundry they are flown in directly from Hawaii and they are a whopping 'grade zero'. I had never seen such large macadamia nuts in my life before! You can replace them with pecans, walnuts or whole hazelnuts, if you prefer.

Preheat the oven to 180°C/350°F/Gas Mark 4. Place the nuts on a baking tray lined with baking parchment and sprinkle with the salt. Bake for 10–15 minutes, until golden brown. Leave to cool completely, then chop roughly.

To make the butterscotch sauce, put the sugar and water in a medium, heavy-based pan and mix well to dissolve the sugar. Bring to the boil, then boil over a high heat, without stirring, until the mixture turns a golden caramel colour (see page 137). While it is boiling, clean the sides of the pan 4 or 5 times with a clean pastry brush dipped in cold water, running the brush around the edges of the pan to keep it free from sugar crystals that might fall back into the sugar and cause the caramel to crystallise.

While the sugar is cooking, bring the cream to the boil in a separate pan. Once the syrup turns a golden caramel colour, remove it from the heat and leave it a few seconds to colour more. It will do this naturally as it cools. As soon as it reaches a dark caramel, gradually add the hot cream. Do this very slowly, adding a little at a time, as the sugar will still be very hot and will spit and bubble up. Once all the cream has been added, return the pan to the heat and whisk gently until it boils and all the sugar has dissolved. Stir in the rum, then pour the sauce into a clean bowl or jug and leave to cool completely.

For the mousse, whip the cream to very soft peaks and then place in the fridge. Put the chocolate in a small bowl. Bring the water and glucose to the boil and pour them over the chocolate. Whisk together to form a soft, batter-like mix. Do not allow it to cool. Using a soft bowl scraper or a rubber spatula, gently but thoroughly fold a third of the cream into the chocolate mix. If you add too much cream at the beginning, it will cause the chocolate mix to seize and go lumpy, then split. Gently fold in the remaining cream.

Spoon a tablespoonful of the nuts into each glass or individual serving dish, followed by a spoonful of cold butterscotch sauce. Place the mousse in a piping bag fitted with a 1cm/$1/2$ inch nozzle and pipe it over the sauce until the glass is half full. If you press the tip of the nozzle into the sauce as you pipe, it will press the sauce up the side of the glass, which makes it very attractive. Spoon in a few more nuts, followed by more sauce, then fill the glass to just below the rim with more mousse. Leave in the fridge for 1–2 hours, until firm and set. Decorate with a generous sprinkling of nuts just before serving.

SYLLABUS

5 medium egg yolks
125g/4^1/$_2$oz caster sugar
500ml/18fl oz double cream
150ml/5fl oz dry sherry or a floral
    white wine (I like Brown Brothers
    Orange Muscat & Flora)
^{1}/$_2$ teaspoon ground cinnamon
^{1}/$_4$ teaspoon ground nutmeg
juice of 1 lemon
50g/1^3/$_4$oz toasted flaked almonds
a little icing sugar for dusting

SERVES 6

Syllabub almost certainly started out in England as a sweet drink flavoured with nutmeg and cinnamon, made with cider or ale rather than white wine or sherry. A delightful story is told of a young Somerset milkmaid who put fresh milk straight from the cow's udder into a pail of ale, sweetened it with honey and added spices for flavour. After an hour or so, a curd formed over the ale, with cream on top. Her creation became popular, and the syllabub began to be served in glasses: the solids that formed on top would be eaten with a spoon, then the ale at the bottom would be drunk from the glass.

Later, a more dignified version evolved in wealthy households, where sherry or wine was used instead of ale and the milk was whipped to a froth with a birch whisk. It must have been some time later when a household cook realised that the syllabub stayed firmer when the proportion of wine to milk was reduced and the two did not separate. My modern recipe includes egg yolks and lemon juice.

Whisk the egg yolks and caster sugar together until pale and thick. Add the double cream and continue to whisk until the mixture forms soft peaks. Whisk in the sherry or wine, plus the spices and lemon juice. The consistency should be that of thick double cream that is barely pourable; very soft peaks are acceptable but it should not be like whipped cream.

Pour or pipe the mixture into 6 glasses and chill for 2–3 hours, until firm. Decorate with the toasted flaked almonds and dust with icing sugar. Serve with Langues de Chat (see page 216).

Claire's Notes
• Serve in pretty glass dishes or long-stemmed glasses.
• The syllabub is very good with poached peaches or crushed strawberries in the bottom of the glass. Crushed amaretti soaked in some of the sherry or a little black coffee also work well.

YOGHURT AND BUTTERMILK PANNA COTTA

2 gelatine leaves
500ml/18fl oz plain yoghurt
125g/4¹/2oz caster sugar
150ml/5fl oz crème fraîche
50ml/2fl oz buttermilk

SERVES 4–6

This recipe was created by Sebastian Rouxel, the pastry chef at Per Se in New York and my predecessor at The French Laundry. It is deliciously light but needs to be served in its dish rather than turned out on to a plate, as it barely holds its shape. The beauty of this recipe is that it is not gelatinous and rubbery, as so many of the panna cottas I have tried seem to be. A good panna cotta should bow slightly when it is turned out of the dish. I am very weary of ones that stand proud on the plate.

Soak the gelatine in cold water for about 5 minutes, until soft. Remove from the water, squeeze out the excess liquid and set aside.

Put 100ml/3¹/2fl oz of the yoghurt in a small pan with the sugar and warm through, just enough to melt the sugar.

Warm the gelatine in a small pan with 1 tablespoon of water until it has completely melted. Do not let it boil. Pour the warm yoghurt on to the gelatine and mix well, then add the rest of the yoghurt. Pass the mixture through a fine sieve into a medium bowl. Set this bowl over a larger bowl that has ice in the bottom. Whisk the mix gently as it cools and begins to set slightly. Do not let it set completely, and whisk continuously to prevent lumps. Remove the bowl from the bowl of ice when it is cold, but not so firm that you cannot fold in the crème fraîche.

Semi-whip the crème fraîche until it reaches soft peaks. Whisk it into the yoghurt mixture with the buttermilk to form a soft, pourable mix. Pour quickly into serving dishes and chill for 2–3 hours, until set.

Claire's Notes
• As this is a plain-looking dessert, why not make it in pretty patterned coffee cups and serve with hot Chocolate Sauce (see pages 148–149) and wild berries in separate dishes? The sauce and berries can be spooned on to the panna cotta by your guests.

DESSERTS,
MOUSSES
AND JELLIES

THE SECRETS OF SUCCESS

BOILING SUGAR

Sugar is a staple of any pastry department, and even a small, 15-table restaurant like The French Laundry gets through more than 150 kilos a week. Whether the sugar is dissolved into a syrup or boiled to make a caramel, it forms the basis of many of the recipes in this book – as a caramel sauce, in mousses, butter creams and fillings, or in sweets such as fudge and marshmallows.

WARNING! Cooking sugar can be dangerous. Observe the following rules in order to cook sugar as safely as possible:

• Never leave a pan of cooking sugar unattended. It turns into caramel very quickly and then goes black as quickly again. It is extremely hot and dangerous at this stage.
• Take the pan off the heat when the sugar syrup reaches a light caramel; the heat from the pan will cause the sugar to continue to cook and colour.
• Keep a bowl of ice nearby at all times. The pan can be placed on the ice to prevent further cooking, if necessary. It's also worth keeping an ice pack to hand, to ease any burns.
• If you manage to get caramel or very hot boiling sugar on your skin, first plunge the affected area into a bath of cold water and then remove the sugar. Keep the affected area immersed in water to reduce the heat and redness.
• Never pour cold water or cream into hot caramel, as it will cause it to spit violently. Always warm the liquid first.
• When stirring, use utensils that do not conduct the heat, such as wooden or heat-safe plastic ones. Metal spoons will get very hot and can burn you during the cooking process.

MAKING SUGAR SYRUP

The easiest type of sugar boiling is simple syrup (also known as stock syrup), where equal amounts of sugar and water are brought to the boil and left to cool before use. If you boil the syrup for longer, the water evaporates, and it becomes hotter and more concentrated until it finally changes colour and becomes caramel.

It is vital to use a sugar thermometer to ensure the syrup reaches the correct temperature for each recipe. A few degrees can make all the difference, especially at the early levels, such as soft ball through to hard ball.

SUGAR STAGES

Depending on the temperature it reaches, sugar syrup has various uses, as follows:

Thread or small gloss (100°C/212°F)
Used for syrups.
Soft ball (118°C/245°F)
Used for fondant, Italian meringue and some sweet making.
Firm ball (120°C/248°F)
Used for marshmallows and soft caramels.
Hard ball 124°C/255°F
Used for fudge.
Crack (144°C/291°F)
Used for dipping candied fruits and marzipans.
Hard crack (152°C/305°F)
Used for making some fruit-based sauces where the acidity is high.
Caramel (210°C/410°F)
Used for caramel sauce.

To make sugar syrup, put the sugar and water in a heavy-based pan, mix well to help the sugar dissolve, then place over a high heat. You can stir it as it comes to the boil, if you want, to ensure that the sugar is completely dissolved. However, once the syrup reaches boiling point, it should not be stirred or agitated as this causes crystals to form.

When the syrup comes to the boil, put a sugar thermometer in the pan to get a precise reading. Have a jug of warm water ready to put the thermometer in as soon as the syrup reaches the desired temperature; this helps keep the worktop clean and also helps dissolve the sugar sticking to the thermometer immediately, thus making it easier to clean.

If you do not have a sugar thermometer, you can test the sugar by picking up a small amount on a teaspoon and dropping it into a bowl of ice-cold water, where it will immediately form the shape and firmness of the ball or crack described above. This is the way professionals are taught to test sugar but it does require a great deal of experience to judge it correctly – I would always recommend a thermometer for home use. There is no need to use a thermometer for caramel, however, as this is always judged by its colour.

Use a clean pastry brush dipped in cold water to brush and wash down the sides of the pan before and during boiling. This keeps the sides of the pan free from sugar crystals, which can cause the syrup to crystallise or become cloudy.

MAKING CARAMEL

There are two methods for making caramel: direct and indirect. Direct caramel is made without any water and is the quicker of the two methods. It can be tricky if the sugar heats up unevenly, and it is important to use a really good, heavy-based pan. Add the sugar to the pan a little at a time (unless you are making just a small amount of caramel, in which case the sugar can be added all at once) and stir it continuously over a medium to high heat as it melts and colours. Stir gently to avoid splashing yourself with hot sugar. Each addition of sugar should have completely melted before you add more. It turns a caramel colour very rapidly, so don't be alarmed. Turn down the heat if it gets dark too quickly; the next addition of sugar will cool it down.

Indirect caramel is made with a mixture of sugar and water, usually with at least twice as much sugar as water. Follow the instructions for making sugar syrup above, boiling the syrup until it takes on the colour specified in the recipe. A light caramel will not have a rich intense flavour and tends to look a little wishy-washy, especially if being used for Crème Caramel (see page 123). However, a dark caramel that is close to black will taste bitter and unpleasant. Aim for something between the two.

Both direct and indirect caramel can be cooled quickly by carefully placing the pan in a bowl of ice.

USING GELATINE

Gelatine is a setting agent that is used to help firm jellies to a wobble and set soft mousses so they retain their lightness. It can also be used to firm up whipped cream so it does not lose its shape (see Black Forest Trifle on page 143) and even help unwhipped cream or yoghurt hold its shape, as in Panna Cotta (see page 132).

Gelatine should always be used in moderation, otherwise it can make mousses rubbery and jellies too firm. The perfect mousse should hold its shape and melt in the mouth when eaten. I use chocolate or butter to firm a few of the mousse recipes in this book, so less gelatine is required.

I favour leaf gelatine because it dissolves easily and is more refined but you can substitute powdered gelatine if necessary. One teaspoon of powder is equivalent to two gelatine leaves. Leaf gelatine is standardised and has the same gelling capacity regardless of its thickness or dimensions.

Powdered gelatine must be sprinkled over a small amount of cool water or liquid for a minute or two to soften. The liquid is then gently heated until the gelatine dissolves. Take care not to let it boil or the gelatine will burn.

Gelatine leaves should be soaked in cold water first until they become soft and limp – usually about five minutes. They should then be squeezed to remove excess water and heated with a little of the water or liquid called for in the recipe until they dissolve. Once again, it's important not to let it boil.

The following tips will help you use gelatine successfully:

• Incorporate the dissolved gelatine while it is still warm or into warmed mousse bases, as the recipe recommends.
• Gelatine can be reheated only if it has not boiled. A high heat reduces its thickening qualities.
• Acid can prevent gelatine from setting, so if you are using acidic fruits, more gelatine will be required. This is taken into account in the recipes – Blood Orange, Cara Cara and Mandarin Jellies (page 170), for example, require 20 leaves of gelatine.
• Always pass dissolved gelatine through a fine sieve before adding it to a mixture, as there may be some

particles that have not dissolved properly. Do this directly into the jelly or mousse base, so as not to lose any.
• When making mousses that contain only gelatine and no chocolate or butter, you will need to stir the base frequently over a bowl of ice after the gelatine has been added, to speed up the gelling process. Let the base cool and thicken to a soft consistency before adding the cream – this ensures that the mousse has maximum volume and lightness.

WHIPPING CREAM

Double cream, whipping cream and crème fraîche can all be whipped. Double cream will be thicker and hold its shape better, as it has a higher fat content and whips to a very firm consistency. Whipping cream will be lighter and more aerated. It still holds its shape but it will drop if left for more than a few hours.

Whipping by hand, with a balloon whisk or rotary whisk, takes more time than an electric mixer but incorporates more air and produces a greater volume. However, a machine is quicker and easier and gives very satisfactory results.

• Always make sure the cream is very cold before whipping, to give greater volume and to prevent it turning buttery and grainy. Ideally it should be well chilled for at least 12 hours before whipping. Use a large, round-bottomed bowl and a balloon whisk or an electric mixer.
• Cream for mousses should generally be only semi-whipped, to the stage where it just holds its shape.
• Cream for piping should be firmly whipped, so it holds a firm shape.
• Take care not to overwhip the cream, or it will become grainy and separate.
• After cream has been whipped, it should be placed back in the fridge immediately to keep it cold if you are not using it straight away.

ASSEMBLING DESSERTS

It is important to remember that pâtisserie is a sequence of building blocks, and a dessert without firm foundations will not hold up. Each building block must be correctly made and assembled as per the recipe. Take time to form the layers of a complex dessert and pay attention to detail. If one aspect is wrong it could ruin the whole dessert.

In pastry kitchens, we hardly ever prepare all the items for a dessert on the same day. We make the various bases, such as butter creams, sponges, ganache, chocolate glazes, soaking syrups and pastes, etc., on one day and simply assemble them the next. It take the stress out of production and also ensures that pastes have time to rest and sponges are cool and easy to cut and handle. Syrups can be easily warmed up with no quality loss.

Before embarking on a complex dessert, I really recommend that you read the recipe thoroughly before you start and decide what you can do to make the production as easy as possible and as enjoyable as possible. After all cooking is supposed to be fun.

BAKED VANILLA CHEESECAKE

1kg/2$\frac{1}{4}$lb Philadelphia cream
cheese
250g/9oz caster sugar
6 medium eggs, lightly beaten
1 vanilla pod
1 capful of vanilla extract
2 tablespoons icing sugar

For the base
260g/9$\frac{1}{4}$oz digestive biscuits
70g unsalted butter

For the topping
175ml/6fl oz crème fraîche
25g/1oz caster sugar
$\frac{1}{4}$ vanilla pod

SERVES 10–12

I consider this to be 'the cheesecake of all cheesecakes'. It is certainly the easiest to make and it produces perfect results time after time. I was given the recipe by a friend's mother, when I was working at the Wolseley on Piccadilly, in London, and needed a cheesecake that would be creamy, light and traditional.

I always use Philadelphia cream cheese and a combination of fresh vanilla and vanilla extract. The result is a smooth, creamy, extremely vanilla-y cheesecake. Don't be tempted to skip the topping. It really does make a difference and it takes only a few minutes to prepare.

Preheat the oven to 180°C/350°F/Gas Mark 4. Line the base of a 25cm/ 10 inch springform cake tin with baking parchment.

First make the base. Place the biscuits in a large plastic bag and use a rolling pin to crush them into fine crumbs. Melt the butter in a pan, then remove from the heat and stir in the crumbs until well combined. Spoon the mixture into the prepared cake tin, pressing it down firmly to make sure the base of the tin is evenly covered. Bake for 15–18 minutes until the mixture is lightly coloured and forms a firm base. Remove from the oven and leave to cool.

Reduce the oven temperature to 150°C/300°F/Gas Mark 2. Beat the cream cheese and sugar together until smooth, using either an electric mixer or a wooden spoon. Add the beaten eggs a little at a time, beating well between each addition. If using an electric mixer, make sure you scrape down the sides of the bowl as you add the eggs to keep the mix smooth.

Cut the vanilla pod in half lengthways and, using the back of a small knife, scrape out the seeds into the cream cheese mixture. Add the vanilla extract and stir well to combine. Spoon the mixture over the biscuit base and level the top with a spatula. Bake in the centre of the oven for about 1 hour, until the cheesecake is set – a knife inserted in the centre should come out clean. Check after 30 minutes that the cheesecake is not rising in the tin. If it is, lower the temperature of the oven to 140°C/275°F/Gas Mark 1 and continue baking.

Let the cheesecake sit for 10 minutes after baking. Meanwhile, make the topping. Combine the crème fraîche with the sugar and the seeds from the vanilla pod. Spread this mixture over the top of the cheesecake and level it with a palette knife. Return the cheesecake to the oven and cook for 10 minutes.

Leave the cheesecake to cool at room temperature, then transfer it to the fridge for about 2 hours to firm up. To remove the cheesecake from the tin, run a small knife around the edge, keeping it very close to the tin, before opening the springform. Cut with a knife that has been warmed in a jug of hot water. The cheesecake will keep in a sealed container in the fridge for 3 days.

Claire's Notes
• This also works really well as individual cheesecakes. Use small, individual cake tins with removable bases and wrap some foil around the base of each one to prevent leakage.
• Sprinkle fresh blueberries on to the crème fraîche topping before you bake it. They burst in the oven and some of the juice colours the topping, which looks and tastes great.

BLACK FOREST TRIFLE

For the chocolate sponge
200g/7oz plain flour
1 teaspoon bicarbonate of soda
25g/1oz dark cocoa powder
200g/7oz caster sugar
2 teaspoons white wine vinegar
250ml/9fl oz water
250ml/9fl oz cold black coffee
40ml/1^1/$_2$fl oz vegetable oil
1 teaspoon vanilla extract

For the cherries
2 x 425g/15oz cans of black
    cherries
juice of 1 orange
2 tablespoons kirsch
^{1}/$_2$ cinnamon stick
70g/2^1/$_2$oz caster sugar
1 tablespoon cornflour

For the kirsch syrup
100g/3^1/$_2$oz caster sugar
100ml/3^1/$_2$fl oz water
25ml/1fl oz kirsch

For the cream
2 gelatine leaves
600ml/20fl oz whipping cream
25g/1oz icing sugar

To decorate
a few chocolate curls (see pages
    213–214)
a few fresh cherries
a little icing sugar

SERVES 8

Claire's Notes
• Once you have made the
basic products for the trifle,
you can assemble it very quickly.
The sponge can be frozen for up
to 3 weeks and the thickened
cherries and kirsch syrup will
keep in the fridge for 3 days.

This is a fun twist on a classic dessert. Typically a Black Forest gâteau consists of several layers of chocolate cake soaked in Kirschwasser, a cherry-based spirit, plus whipped cream, cherries and chocolate shavings. This brilliant recipe allows you to make a stunning-looking dessert quite simply.

Preheat the oven to 170°C/325°F/Gas Mark 3. Lightly grease a 15cm/6 inch square cake tin and line the base with baking parchment.

Sift the flour, bicarbonate of soda and cocoa powder into a large mixing bowl. Add the caster sugar and mix well to combine, then make a well in the centre. Combine the white wine vinegar, water, coffee, oil and vanilla in a small bowl and pour into the well in the dry ingredients. Mix well with a wooden or plastic spoon to give a smooth batter. You can do this in an electric mixer fitted with the paddle attachment but take care not to overmix the batter.

Pour the batter into the prepared cake tin and bake in the centre of the oven for 20–30 minutes, until the surface springs back to the touch and a skewer inserted in the centre comes out clean. Leave to cool in the tin.

Drain the juice from the cherries and pour two-thirds of it into a small saucepan. Add the orange juice, kirsch and cinnamon stick and bring slowly to the boil. Mix the sugar and cornflour together in a bowl. Gradually add enough of the remaining cherry juice to make a smooth, loose paste. Pour the boiled cherry juice on to the paste and whisk until smooth. Return the mixture to the pan and bring back to the boil over a low heat, whisking continuously. Lower the heat and simmer for 2–3 minutes, until thickened. Pour the thickened sauce over the cherries in a bowl and leave to cool completely. Once the cherries have cooled a little, cover the bowl with cling film to stop a skin forming.

To make the kirsch syrup, put the sugar and water in a small pan, stir well to dissolve the sugar, then bring to the boil. Remove from the heat immediately, add the kirsch and leave to cool.

For the cream, soak the gelatine leaves in a bowl of cold water for about 5 minutes, until completely softened. Remove them from the water, squeeze out excess liquid and keep to one side. Bring 50ml/2fl oz of the cream to the boil in a small saucepan. Remove from the heat, add the softened gelatine and stir until the gelatine has dissolved. Leave until the cream is just warm, then add it to the remaining cream with the icing sugar and whisk to firm peaks.

To assemble the trifles, cut the chocolate sponge into 2.5cm/1 inch cubes. Place a couple of pieces of sponge in each of 8 serving glasses or dishes and, using a pastry brush, soak them well with the kirsch syrup. Place a large spoonful of the thickened cherries on top of the sponge. Using a piping bag fitted with a 1cm/^{1}/$_2$ inch plain nozzle, pipe the whipped cream into the glasses: keep the piping tip next to the side of the glass and pipe several vertical lines up to the edge of the glass. As you pipe, press the tip into the cherries so some of the thickened juice moves up the sides of the glass.

Place more thickened cherries into the glass, especially between the lines of piped cream. Place another cube or two of sponge into the centre of the glass. Finish by piping cream over the top of the cherries and sponge and smoothing it flat with a palette knife. Decorate with chocolate curls, a few fresh cherries and a little of the thickened cherry juice. Dust with icing sugar.

BAKED CHOCOLATE MOUSSE

100g/3¹/₂oz dark chocolate
(70 per cent cocoa solids), finely
chopped
50g/1³/₄oz dark chocolate
(72 per cent cocoa solids), finely
chopped
100g/3¹/₂oz unsalted butter
1 medium egg
30g/1oz caster sugar

To serve
150ml/5fl oz crème fraîche
50ml/2fl oz double cream
¹/₂ teaspoon vanilla extract
15g/¹/₂oz icing sugar, plus a little
extra for dusting
Butterscotch Sauce (see page 130)

SERVES 8

This rich, intense mousse is not for fainthearted chocolate lovers. Although it is simple to make, the cooking time and serving temperature are critical to its success. If you can master them, it makes a really impressive dinner-party dessert. You do need to serve it with crème fraîche or an ice cream that will cut through the richness of the mousse. I have served the mousse with cherries and also with orange, but my favourite way is with a scoop of crème fraîche and a little butterscotch sauce.

You will need eight 5cm/2 inch ring moulds, 2.5cm/1 inch high. I know these sound small but believe me, it is so rich you need only a small amount. If you do not have individual rings, it also works in a 20cm/8 inch flan ring, when it will take 8–10 minutes to cook. You will need to get it just to the right temperature to cut it though, which is not always an easy task.

Preheat the oven to 170°C/325°F/Gas Mark 3. Prepare the ring moulds by giving them a base of aluminium foil. Cut 8 squares or circles of foil 2.5cm/1inch bigger than your ring moulds. Sit each mould in the centre of a piece of foil and neatly bring the excess to the edges of the mould, scrunching it to form a ring that comes 5mm/¹/₄ inch up the sides of the mould. This will ensure the mixture does not leak during baking. Put the moulds on a baking tray.

Put both chocolates and the butter in a bowl set over a pan of simmering water, making sure the water doesn't touch the base of the bowl. Leave to melt, stirring occasionally. Keep warm.

Whisk the egg and caster sugar together until pale and thick and increased in volume (as it's only a small amount, you'll probably need to do this by hand). Pour the warm melted chocolate and butter into the whisked mixture and fold together gently, using a rubber spatula or a large metal spoon. Make sure the two are well combined, taking care not to overmix otherwise you might lose volume. Spoon the mixture into the prepared moulds and bake in the top of the oven for 8 minutes exactly. No more. Check the oven after 4 minutes and, if they are beginning to form a large, slightly risen ring of bubbles around the edge of the mould, lower the oven temperature very slightly and leave the oven door slightly ajar for the remaining 4 minutes of the cooking time. When they are done, the mousses will still look wobbly and soft; the surface should be smooth and may be covered in what looks like very small bubbles.

Cool the mousses completely, leaving them on the baking tray and in their rings. When they have cooled, place the baking tray in the fridge to allow them to set. They should be very firm and hard before you try to unmould them.

(continued on page 146)

(continued from page 144)

About 4 hours before you want to serve them, unmould the mousses. You can do this with a blowtorch, if you have one, holding it about 15cm/ 6 inches away from the mould to warm it and turning the mould as you do so. Be careful not to leave the blowtorch in one spot for any length of time or the mousse will melt and lose its shape. If you don't have a blowtorch, wrap a hot, damp cloth around each ring until it can be easily removed.

Place each mousse on a serving plate. It is very important you use the plates you intend to serve them on, as once they reach the correct serving temperature they will be too soft to move. Leave the mousses to sit on the plates at room temperature for up to 4 hours, until they become soft. They should still hold their shape but be very soft, almost scoopable, when you serve them.

Just before you are ready to serve, combine the crème fraîche, double cream, vanilla and icing sugar in a bowl and whisk until they form firm peaks. Using 2 dessertspoons that have been warmed in a jug of hot water, scoop up some of the cream in one spoon, then shape it into an oval by scraping it from one spoon to the other. Place one scoop on top of each mousse. Drizzle a little butterscotch sauce over the top and dust with a little icing sugar.

FEUILLETINE CARAMEL

315ml/10$\frac{1}{2}$fl oz double cream

300g/10$\frac{1}{2}$oz milk chocolate (33–40 per cent cocoa solids), finely chopped

1 quantity of Butterscotch Sauce (see page 130)

1 quantity of Chocolate Sauce (see pages 148–149)

Chocolate Décor (see page 194)

For the feuilletine

50g/1$\frac{3}{4}$oz nibbed almonds

2 teaspoons brandy

1–2 tablespoons icing sugar

65g/2$\frac{1}{4}$oz dark chocolate (70 per cent cocoa solids)

125g/4$\frac{1}{2}$oz sugared cornflakes, such as Sugar Frosties

250g/9oz chocolate hazelnut spread, such as Green & Black's or Nutella

SERVES 6

Claire's Notes

• The feuilletine will keep for a week if stored in a sealed container in the fridge.

• Make the butterscotch sauce and the chocolate sauce the day before to speed up the assembly.

• Serve with a handful of candied peanuts (see page 78) – it's like eating the best Snicker bar in the world!

• Make sure the ganache is poured into the glasses while it is still hot, so it makes an even layer.

My love of chocolate and caramel inspired me to create this dessert. I am addicted to chocolate-coated caramels and, not having a Thornton's chocolate shop close to my home town of Napa – or indeed anywhere in America – to get my fix, I set about making my own dessert version of a milk chocolate caramel. The recipe evolved from one thing to another before I was happy with the version that finally made its way on to The French Laundry menu. I knew that I wanted the centre to be liquid caramel, and it took several attempts before I finally created a little chocolate cup to hold the caramel. The method for making the cup is a little too longwinded for this book, so I have adapted the recipe for making in glasses or individual dishes. I suggest you use small martini glasses or extra small ramekins. It is a sweet dessert and very rich.

Preheat the oven to 180°C/350°F/Gas Mark 4. Start by preparing the almonds for the feuilletine. Place them in a small bowl, add the brandy and mix well. Add the icing sugar and combine thoroughly. If the nuts look slightly wet, add a little more icing sugar until they are dry. Spread the nuts out on a baking tray lined with baking parchment, place in the centre of the oven and bake for 15 minutes, until golden brown. Leave to cool on the tray.

Semi-whip 125ml/4fl oz of the double cream and store, covered, in the fridge until later.

Back to the feuilletine: melt the dark chocolate in a bowl placed over a pan of simmering water, making sure the water doesn't touch the base of the bowl. Keep warm. Put the cornflakes in a plastic bag and crush with a rolling pin as finely as you can. Add them to the dark chocolate and mix well. Stir in the chocolate hazelnut spread and the cooled roasted almonds.

Use a teaspoon to spoon small amounts, about the size of a hazelnut, on to a tray lined with baking parchment. Place in the fridge for about 20 minutes to set.

Meanwhile, put the chopped milk chocolate in a bowl. Place the remaining double cream in a small saucepan and bring to the boil over a medium heat. As soon as it comes to the boil, pour it over the milk chocolate and whisk gently to form a smooth, shiny ganache. Pour half the ganache into 6 small glasses or dishes to form a neat, even layer. Place them in the fridge to firm. Fold a third of the semi-whipped cream into the remaining ganache, using a large metal spoon or a rubber spatula. The first addition of cream sometimes melts a little, but this is fine, so do not panic. Make sure it is well combined, then fold in the remaining cream, taking care to be very gentle and not overmix.

Take the glasses from the fridge and drop several chilled feuilletine pieces into each one. Spoon over a generous amount of butterscotch sauce. Put the chocolate mousse in a piping bag fitted with a 1cm/$\frac{1}{2}$ inch plain nozzle and pipe a neat, even layer of mousse over the sauce. Add a few more feuilletine pieces to each glass and cover with a generous spoonful of chocolate sauce. Pipe another layer of mousse into each glass. Place the glasses in the fridge for about 2 hours to allow the mousse to set.

To decorate, spoon some of the butterscotch sauce over the mousse and finish with chocolate décor.

CHOCOLATE AND RASPBERRY DOME

For the poached raspberries
350g/12oz raspberries
100g/3^1/$_2$oz caster sugar
100ml/3^1/$_2$fl oz water
1 teaspoon framboise liqueur
   (optional)

For the raspberry sauce
200g/7oz raspberries
80g/2^3/$_4$oz icing sugar
a little lemon juice

For the mousse
275g/9^3/$_4$oz Chuao or similar dark
   chocolate
650ml/22fl oz whipping cream
115g/4oz caster sugar
3 large egg whites
4 gelatine leaves

For the chocolate sauce
250ml/9fl oz double cream
200g/7oz Chuao chocolate, finely
   chopped

For the garnish
300g/10^1/$_2$oz tempered dark
   chocolate (see pages 212–213)
   – optional
1 punnet of raspberries
a little icing sugar

SERVES 12

I recommend you use Scottish raspberries for this, if possible. Scotland produces some of the best raspberries in the world, and over the years Scottish farmers have invested time and money in developing new varieties that suit the climate there. This recipe is the ideal showcase for good raspberries, as they are softly poached and the flavour intensifies as they steep in the syrup, which is also used to make the mousse.

I love all chocolate but my absolute favourite is the sublime Chuao, which is produced by a small brother and sister company called Amedei, based in Tuscany. Chuao was first brought to my attention by the lovely Laura King, who not only supplied me with my beloved Amedei but just happens to be the largest importer of caviar into England. Chuao oozes with aromas and essences of raspberries, cherries and plums, making it perfectly in tune with this dessert. It is so rich and powerful that the taste lingers in your mouth like a good wine for several minutes afterwards. If you have trouble finding Chuao, choose a good chocolate with 70 per cent cocoa solids. Check the blurb on the back of the packet, as most describe the product. Anything that has similar characteristics to the Chuao will work well.

First prepare the poached raspberries. Wash the raspberries in a colander and then dry them gently on a clean tea towel. Place them in a large mixing bowl. Combine the sugar and water in a small saucepan and stir well. Bring to the boil, remove from the heat and add the framboise. Pour this syrup over the raspberries and leave to cool. The heat of the syrup will draw the juice from the raspberries, turning it a pretty shade of pink.

To make the raspberry sauce, place the raspberries in a blender with the icing sugar and blitz until smooth. Pass the sauce through a fine sieve to remove the seeds. Add a little lemon juice a drop or two at a time to adjust the sweetness and balance of the sauce.

Next make the mousse. Grate 25g/1oz of the chocolate straight from the block on to a piece of baking parchment, using a cheese grater or a microplane. Finely chop the remaining chocolate and melt it in a bowl set over a pan of simmering water, making sure the water doesn't touch the base of the bowl. Keep warm. Semi-whip the cream, keeping it at soft peaks, and store it in the fridge until later.

If you have an electric mixer, you can combine all the sugar with the egg whites and whisk to a stiff meringue on a medium to fast speed. If you are doing it by hand, place the egg whites in a large mixing bowl, add a third of the sugar and whisk until the meringue forms soft peaks. Add another third of the sugar and continuing whisking until the meringue reaches firm peaks. Add the remaining sugar and whisk just enough to combine.

Soak the gelatine in a large bowl of very cold water for about 5 minutes, until it is completely soft. Remove from the water and squeeze out the excess. Take 25ml/1fl oz of the poaching liquid from the raspberries and heat it to boiling point in a small saucepan. Remove from the heat, add the soaked gelatine and stir until dissolved. Making sure the mixture is still warm, fold it gently into the meringue with a large metal spoon or a rubber spatula. Then fold in the melted chocolate, taking care not to lose any volume. Mix half the semi-whipped cream into the chocolate meringue and then fold in the rest. Lastly add the grated chocolate and mix gently.

To assemble the dessert, spoon some of the poached raspberries into 12 individual serving dishes and cover with a spoonful of the raspberry sauce. Spoon a little of the chocolate mousse into the dishes, then push a small spoonful of poached raspberries down into the centre of the mousse. Spoon in more chocolate mousse and, using a palette knife or spatula, shape into a smooth dome. Chill for 2 hours, until firm.

Make the chocolate sauce while the domes are chilling. Bring the cream to the boil, then remove from the heat. Pour it over the chopped chocolate and mix gently to make a smooth sauce.

If you are making the chocolate decoration, spread a little tempered chocolate on to a clean sheet of acetate and smooth it out as thinly as possible with an angled palette knife. It should set in a few minutes. Once the chocolate is set, flip the acetate over on to a tray lined with baking parchment, so the chocolate is facing the parchment. Store in a cool place or wrapped in cling film in the fridge. When you want to decorate the mousses, the chocolate should peel away easily from the acetate in a single sheet. Break it into abstract pieces.

Just before serving, spoon a large tablespoon of chocolate sauce over each dome. Decorate with the fresh raspberries and the chocolate pieces, then dust with a little icing sugar.

Claire's Notes

• I like to use glass coupe dishes or pretty china dishes that are deep enough to make a dome.
• Framboise is a clear raspberry spirit that adds a kick to the poaching liquid for this dessert. The remaining poaching liquid is too good to throw away. Serve it chilled in shot glasses with a small scoop of raspberry sorbet, as an accompaniment to the dessert.
• The domes will keep, covered, for 2 days in the fridge. Finish with the chocolate sauce and decorate them on the day.

TIA MARIA AND COFFEE DELICE

For the almond sponge
250g/9oz white marzipan
25g/1oz icing sugar
3 medium eggs
60g/2^1/$_4$oz unsalted butter
25g/1oz plain flour
25g/1oz cornflour

For the syrup and filling
100g/3^1/$_2$oz caster sugar
100ml/3^1/$_2$fl oz water
100ml/3^1/$_2$fl oz Tia Maria
200g/7oz amaretti biscuits

For the feuilletine
75g/2^3/$_4$oz milk chocolate (at least
    30 per cent cocoa solids)
125g/4^1/$_2$oz sugared cornflakes,
    such as Sugar Frosties
250g/9oz chocolate hazelnut
    spread, such as Green & Black's
    or Nutella

For the coffee mousse
375ml/12^1/$_2$fl oz double cream
400g/14oz milk chocolate (at least
    30 per cent cocoa solids)
1^1/$_2$ gelatine leaves
50ml/2fl oz liquid glucose
50ml/2fl oz water
12g/^{1}/$_2$oz ground coffee

To finish
100g/3^1/$_2$oz ground hazelnuts or
    almonds
8 amaretti biscuits

SERVES 8

I have been making this dessert for over 20 years. The recipe belongs to the great Swiss patissier Ernest Bachmann, one of my mentors and idols, and I have adapted it over time, making various combinations of different chocolates, sponges and coffees. The almond flavour of the amaretti biscuits works well with the caramel qualities in the milk chocolate, while the Tia Maria adds a little kick.

You can make individual ones if you have rings or assemble it in a cake tin and cut it into slices. Either way, it is a very impressive dessert.

Preheat the oven to 170°C/325°F/Gas Mark 3. Line the base of a 15cm/ 6 inch square cake tin with baking parchment.

To make the almond sponge, break the marzipan into small pieces and placing it in a freestanding electric mixer fitted with the paddle attachment. Sift the icing sugar and add to the bowl, then mix together on a low speed until combined.

Separate 2 of the eggs. Beat the yolks with the remaining whole egg in a small bowl, just to combine. Add to the marzipan a little at a time, still mixing on a low speed. Make sure you scrape down the sides of the bowl between each addition and the marzipan remains smooth. If you add the egg too quickly, it will become lumpy.

Melt the butter in a small pan and keep hot. Sift the flour and cornflour on to a piece of baking parchment.

Whisk the egg whites in a clean bowl until they form firm peaks. Fold the egg whites into the creamed marzipan with a large metal spoon or rubber spatula. Fold in the sifted flours, taking care not to lose any volume. Pour the warm melted butter down the side of the bowl so it flows on to the surface of the mix without sinking in. Fold it in using the same metal spoon or rubber spatula. Spoon the mix into the prepared cake tin and bake in the centre of the oven for 20–25 minutes, until the cake is golden brown and springs back to the touch when pressed gently. Leave to cool in the tin.

Spread the ground hazelnuts or almonds for finishing the délices on a tray lined with baking parchment. Bake in the centre of the oven for about 10 minutes, until golden brown. Cool on the tray.

Next make the syrup. Put the sugar and water in a small pan and place over a medium heat, stirring until the sugar has dissolved. Bring to the boil, then remove from the heat and add the Tia Maria. Leave to cool.

To make the feuilletine, melt the chocolate in a bowl placed over a pan of simmering water, making sure the water does not touch the base of the bowl. Place the sugared cornflakes in a plastic bag and crush them as finely as possible with a rolling pin, then transfer to a small bowl. Stir in the melted chocolate. Add the chocolate hazelnut spread and combine well. Take 2 sheets of baking parchment each about 300 x 210mm (12 x 8 inches).

(continued on page 152)

(continued from page 150)

Spoon the feuilletine in the centre of one of them, place the other piece on top and then roll out the feuilletine mixture between the sheets of paper until it is about 5mm thick. Place the feuilletine, still between the 2 pieces of parchment, on a tray and place in the freezer to chill until firm.

Turn the almond sponge out of the tin and use a 4cm/1^1/$_2$ inch plain pastry cutter to cut out 8 discs. Place eight 4cm/1^1/$_2$ inch ring moulds, about 5cm/2 inches deep, on a tray lined with baking parchment and put a disc of sponge in the base of each one. Using a pastry brush, soak each disc with the Tia Maria syrup.

Remove the sheet of feuilletine from the freezer. It should be cold and firm to the touch. Peel off the paper on one side and flip it over on to another piece of baking parchment. Remove the parchment from the second side. Work quickly, as the feuilletine will go soft and be difficult to handle if it gets warm. Cut out 8 discs with the pastry cutter and place on top of the sponge in the ring moulds.

Place the remaining Tia Maria syrup in a small bowl. Break the amaretti for the filling in half and dunk them one at a time in the syrup to soak them. They should be soft but not falling apart. Now place 4 or 5 pieces in each ring mould around the side of the ring.

Finally make the coffee mousse. Whip the cream to soft peaks and set it aside in the fridge. Melt the chocolate in a bowl placed over a pan of simmering water, making sure the water does not touch the base of the bowl. Soak the gelatine in a large bowl of cold water for about 5 minutes, until soft. Remove the gelatine from the water, squeeze out excess liquid and set aside. Put the glucose, water and coffee in a small pan over a medium heat. As soon as it comes to boiling point, remove from the heat and add the soaked gelatine. Whisk until dissolved. Strain the hot mixture through a fine sieve over the melted chocolate and whisk gently to combine to a smooth paste.

Using a large metal spoon or a rubber spatula, fold a third of the semi-whipped cream into the chocolate mixture. Make sure it is mixed in thoroughly before adding any more. Add the cream in 2 more batches, taking extreme care to be as gentle as possible and not overmix. Place the mixture in a piping bag fitted with a 1cm/^{1}/$_2$ inch plain nozzle and pipe into the prepared moulds. Level the top of each mould with a palette knife or spatula, then place the tray in the fridge. Leave for about 2 hours, until the mousse is firm and set.

To finish, place the ground nuts in a tea strainer or fine sieve and dust the top of each mousse in an even layer. Unmould the mousses. You can do this with a blowtorch, if you have one, holding it about 15cm/6 inches away from each mould to warm it, turning the mould as you do so. Be careful not to leave the blowtorch in one spot for any length of time or the mousse will melt and lose its shape. If you don't have a blowtorch, wrap a hot, damp towel around the outside of each ring to warm it. Finish with an amaretti biscuit on each mousse.

Claire's Notes

• Once the chocolate has melted, remove it from the pan of hot water to prevent it becoming burnt. Milk chocolate is more susceptible to burning than dark chocolate. Keep the bowl warm by sitting it on top of the oven whilst the oven is on.

• If you do not have individual moulds, assemble the cake in the same fashion in the tin in which you baked the sponge. Once it is set, trim the edges neatly with a hot knife and cut it into squares or oblongs.

GREEN TEA AND JASMINE DELICE

For the pistachio cake
80g/2³/₄oz shelled peeled
  pistachio nuts
80g/2³/₄oz softened unsalted
  butter
75g/2²/₃oz caster sugar
1 large and 1 small egg
10g/¹/₄oz plain flour
10g/¹/₄oz cornflour

For the jasmine tea mousse
3 tablespoons water
2 tablespoons jasmine tea
300ml/10fl oz double cream
2 gelatine leaves
150g/5¹/₂oz white chocolate, finely
  chopped
2 tablespoons liquid glucose

For the green tea mousse
3 tablespoons water
2 tablespoons green tea
300ml/10fl oz double cream
2 gelatine leaves
150g/5¹/₂oz white chocolate, finely
  chopped
2 tablespoons liquid glucose

SERVES 12

The growing popularity of herbal and fruit teas inspired me to try to incorporate them in my desserts. This one has a balance of floral and chocolate, delicate and rich. At The French Laundry we serve it with a very small amount of passionfruit jelly, which is just enough to cut the creaminess. A passionfruit sorbet or sauce would also work well.

Preheat the oven to 170°C/325°F/Gas Mark 3. You will need a 20 x 15cm/ 8 x 6 inch square cake tin with a removable base. Line the base with baking parchment. Chop the pistachio nuts as finely as you can, the smaller the better. You can do this in a food processor, if you have one, but take care not to over grind them or they will become oily.

Cream the butter and sugar together until light and fluffy. If doing this in a freestanding electric mixer, use the paddle attachment. Lightly beat the large egg and add it to the creamed mixture a little at a time, mixing well between each addition. Sift the flour and cornflour together and mix them with the pistachio nuts. Fold these into the cake batter a tablespoon at a time, taking care not to over fold and tighten the mix. Beat the small egg and add to the mix, folding it in gently with a large metal spoon. Transfer the mixture to the lined cake tin and level the top with a spatula or palette knife; the mixture should be about 5mm/¹/₄ inch thick. Bake in the centre of the oven for 15–20 minutes, until the cake springs back when gently pressed or a skewer inserted in the centre comes out clean. Leave to cool in the tin.

Both the mousses are made in the same way but it is important that you make them one at a time. Start with the jasmine mousse. Boil the water, pour it over the tea and leave to steep for 10 minutes. Strain the tea to remove the leaves. Whip the cream to soft peaks and place in the fridge.

Soak the gelatine leaves in a bowl of cold water for about 5 minutes, until very soft. Remove from the water and squeeze out excess liquid. Put the chopped chocolate in a large bowl. Place the tea and liquid glucose in a small pan and bring gently just to the boil. Remove from the heat, add the soaked gelatine and stir well to dissolve. Pass the mixture through a fine sieve directly on to the chopped chocolate. Leave for 30 seconds, then whisk gently to combine all the ingredients. The chocolate should be completely melted.

Using a rubber spatula, gently fold in a third of the semi-whipped cream. Make sure the cream is fully incorporated but do not overmix. The cream will melt a little in the hot chocolate. Fold in another third of the cream; this time the mix will feel a little firmer. Take extreme care when folding in the final third of the cream; be as gentle as possible and do not overmix. The mixture should have the consistency of a soft mousse.

(continued on page 155)

(continued from page 153)

Spoon all but 3 tablespoons of the mousse on to the pistachio cake and level it with a spatula or a palette knife. The mousse should be the same depth as the sponge. Place the tin on a tray and refrigerate for 45 minutes, until the mousse is set. Put the remaining jasmine mousse in a small bowl, cover and leave in a cool place, but not the fridge.

Make the green tea mousse in exactly the same way as the jasmine mousse and make a second layer on the cake, using all the mousse this time. Place the tin back in the fridge for about 1 hour, until set and firm to the touch.

Remove the délice by running a small knife around the edge of the tin and lifting the délice, still on the removable base, from the tin.

Spread the remaining jasmine mousse thinly over the top and level with a palette knife. Do not worry if it goes a little over the sides, as these will be trimmed off later. Comb the mousse with a comb scraper and place back on a tray in the refrigerator to set.

To serve, neaten the délice by trimming off the edges with a serrated bread knife that has been warmed in hot water and then dried. Cut into individual portions.

Claire's Notes
• If you can find them, use the green Sicilian pistachios; they are an incredibly vibrant green colour.
• When you're making the mousse, it can split easily and there is nothing you can do to bring it back, so make sure these key steps are followed:
– The cream should be at soft peaks, no more.
– The chocolate mix should be warm.
– Fold the first third of the cream into the chocolate mix gently but thoroughly.
– Be as gentle as possible when folding in the cream and do not overmix.
– Make sure your sponge is completely cold before starting to make the mousse; it needs to be cold before you put the mousse on it and you don't want the second mousse to set in the bowl before you can put the first one on the cake.

BITTER CHOCOLATE, PRALINE BRÛLÉE, ESPRESSO TORTE

For the chocolate sponge
125g/4$^{1}/_{2}$oz dark chocolate
   (72 per cent cocoa solids), finely
   chopped
125g/4$^{1}/_{2}$oz unsalted butter
4 medium eggs
185g/6$^{1}/_{2}$oz caster sugar
60g/2$^{1}/_{4}$oz plain flour

For the praline brûlée
300ml/10fl oz double cream
4 medium egg yolks
25g/1oz caster sugar
2 tablespoons chocolate hazelnut
   spread, such as Green & Black's
   or Nutella

For the bitter chocolate mousse
160g/5$^{3}/_{4}$oz dark chocolate
   (72 per cent cocoa solids), finely
   chopped
30g/1oz unsalted butter
450ml/16fl oz double cream
8 medium egg yolks
150g/5$^{1}/_{2}$oz caster sugar
75ml/2$^{1}/_{2}$fl oz water
25g/1oz ground espresso coffee
145g/5oz dark cocoa powder

To finish
100g/3$^{1}/_{2}$oz dark chocolate
   (72 per cent cocoa solids)

SERVES 10–12

This dessert is only for serious chocolate lovers who like their chocolate dark and bitter. The mousse is rich and heavy, part truffle, part ganache. The coffee enhances the strength of the chocolate and gives a seriously X-rated feel to this dessert, while the praline brûlée adds a creamy, luxurious mouth feel. Even the sponge is laden with chocolate and butter. It sums up everything I so love about my occupation. It is extravagant, luxurious, serious but playful, decadent, rich and totally irresistible.

Preheat the oven to 180°C/350°F/Gas Mark 4. Grease a 20cm/8 inch springform cake tin and line the base with a disc of baking parchment.

To make the chocolate sponge, place the chopped chocolate and the butter in a bowl and place it over a pan of boiling water, making sure the water does not touch the base of the bowl. Stir the chocolate and butter until they have melted. Remove the bowl from the pan of hot water but keep it warm by the side of the stove.

Using an electric mixer, whisk the eggs and sugar until light and fluffy. The mixture should triple in volume and be thick enough to leave a trail on the surface when drizzled from the whisk. Using a large metal spoon or a rubber spatula, gently fold the warm chocolate and butter into the whisked eggs and sugar, keeping as much volume as possible. Sift the flour on to a piece of baking parchment and gently fold that in too.

Transfer the mixture to the prepared cake tin. Level the surface with a spatula and bake in the centre of the oven for 20 minutes, until the cake springs back when lightly pressed or a skewer comes out clean when inserted in the centre. Leave to cool in the tin.

Sit a 20cm/8 inch cake ring, 5cm/2 inches high, on a tray lined with baking parchment. Remove the sponge from the cake tin and place in the bottom of the ring.

Next make the praline brûlée. Have a blender or food processor set up ready to go. Bring the cream to the boil in a small pan. Meanwhile, mix the egg yolks and sugar together in a small bowl. As soon as the cream boils, pour it on to the egg yolks and sugar, mixing well. Transfer the mixture to a clean pan, place over a low heat and whisk gently until it begins to thicken slightly. Just before it reaches boiling point, remove the pan from the heat and pour the mixture into the blender or food processor. Add the chocolate and hazelnut spread and blend on a low to medium speed for 30–45 seconds. This helps to aerate the mix. Pour it into a small bowl and cover the surface with cling film. Once it has cooled, place it in the fridge to chill.

Now for the bitter chocolate mousse. Melt the chocolate and butter in a small bowl over a pan of simmering water, stirring until they have completely melted. Remove the bowl from the pan of water and keep warm on the top of the stove. Semi-whip the cream until it is just holding firm peaks. Keep in the fridge until later

Using a handheld electric mixer, whisk the egg yolks and sugar until pale and thick. Bring the water to the boil and pour it over the coffee. Add to the whisked egg yolks and sugar and mix well. Sift the cocoa powder into a small bowl and whisk in the warm melted butter and chocolate to make a smooth paste. Pour the chocolate mix into the whisked egg mix and combine using a large metal spoon or a rubber spatula. Gently fold in the semi-whipped cream in 3 batches, making sure you fold it in gently and all the ingredients are well combined before you add the next batch.

Spoon half the mousse on top of the sponge in the cake ring until it is half full. Level the surface with a spatula and place the torte in the fridge for about 15 minutes to set the mousse. Keep the remaining mousse in a warm place where it will not set. Remove the torte and spread the cooled brûlée over the top, then return to the fridge for another 15 minutes to firm it up. Spoon on the remaining chocolate mousse and level the top with a spatula. Place the completed torte back in the fridge and leave to firm up for about 1 hour.

Remove the ring by running a blowtorch quickly over the outside to warm it gently. Do not hold the torch in any one place for more than a few seconds or the mousse will melt. Push the ring upwards and over the top of the torte. If you don't have a blowtorch, you can use a hot, damp kitchen towel instead, holding it around the outside of the ring to warm it so that it slides off cleanly.

To finish, finely grate the dark chocolate on a microplane grater and use to dust the top of the torte. When serving, cut the torte into neat, even slices, using a serrated bread knife that has been dipped in a jug of hot water and then dried. Serve to someone you care about, with an enormous scoop of Vanilla Ice Cream (see page 192).

Claire's Notes
• Make the sponge and brûlée a day in advance and assemble the torte the day you want to serve it. The brûlée will keep for a day in the fridge and the sponge can be frozen for up to 2 weeks.
• Place the dark chocolate for grating in the freezer so it gets really hard; this makes it easier to grate and gives a very fine finish.

OPÉRA

For the butter cream
180g/6oz caster sugar
65ml/2$\frac{1}{4}$fl oz water
2$\frac{1}{2}$ teaspoons liquid glucose
3 medium egg whites
250g/9oz unsalted butter, at room
    temperature
1 tablespoon liquid coffee (e.g
    Camp coffee essence)

For the coffee syrup
500g/1lb 2oz caster sugar
500ml/18fl oz water
2 heaped tablespoons ground
    coffee

For the joconde
6 medium eggs, separated
250g/9oz caster sugar
125g/4$\frac{1}{2}$oz ground almonds
125g/4$\frac{1}{2}$oz plain flour

For the chocolate ganache
300g/10$\frac{1}{2}$oz dark chocolate
    (60–70 per cent cocoa solids),
    finely chopped
150ml/5fl oz double cream

For the glaze
150g/5$\frac{1}{2}$oz dark chocolate (70
    per cent cocoa solids), chopped
90ml/3fl oz double cream
12g/$\frac{1}{2}$oz caster sugar
2 teaspoons liquid glucose

To finish
50g/1$\frac{3}{4}$oz dark chocolate (70 per
    cent cocoa solids), melted
gold leaf (optional)

SERVES 12

This is one of my favourite cakes to make. I really enjoy the challenge of getting the layers perfectly even and imbibing (soaking) the sponge. I am not a coffee lover but I do like coffee cake and this combination of coffee and rich chocolate is seriously adult. If cakes were listed according to their indulgence factor, this would be top of the list in the adult section.

Many believe Opéra was created by Louis Clichy, baker and owner of the Clichy pâtisserie in Paris in the 1930s. However, another pâtisserie made a very similar cake known by the same name, which was created in honour of the Paris Opera House.

You will need an angled palette knife for a professional finish. You can make the layers of joconde (almond sponge), butter cream and ganache without one but it is not as easy and takes twice as long. The finished cake should stand not much more than 2.5cm/1 inch in height.

Start by making the butter cream. Place the sugar, water and glucose in a heavy-based pan and mix to dissolve. Place the pan over a medium heat and stir until it comes to the boil. Put a sugar thermometer in the pan and boil, without stirring, until the syrup reaches soft-ball stage (118°C/245°F). To prevent crystallisation, brush down the sides of the pan 4 or 5 times with a clean pastry brush dipped in a little cold water.

While the sugar syrup is cooking, start to whisk the egg whites in a freestanding electric mixer, or in a large bowl with a handheld electric beater. When the egg whites are well risen and firm, reduce the speed of the machine to medium. Once the sugar syrup has reached the correct temperature, remove the thermometer and pour the syrup slowly and carefully on to the whisking egg whites. Avoid pouring it directly on to the whisk as it turns in the bowl, or it will throw the syrup around the sides of the bowl. Whisk until the mixture is nearly cold, then add the butter a tablespoon at a time, whisking well between each addition. Continue to whisk until the butter cream is smooth and shiny. Add the coffee essence and mix in well. Cover the butter cream with cling film but do not refrigerate it.

To make the coffee syrup, put the sugar, water and ground coffee in a pan and mix well, then bring slowly to the boil, stirring to dissolve the sugar. As soon as it reaches a rolling boil, remove from the heat. Transfer to a plastic container or bowl and cool completely.

Next make the joconde. Preheat the oven to 200°C/400°F/Gas Mark 6. Line two 45 x 30cm/18 x 12 inch baking trays with baking parchment. Whisk the egg yolks with half the caster sugar until pale, thick, fluffy and doubled in volume. In a freestanding electric mixer, whisk the egg whites with the remaining caster sugar until they form a stiff meringue. Whilst the egg whites are whisking, sift the ground almonds and flour together on to a piece of baking parchment. Remove the egg whites from the machine. Using a large metal spoon, fold a third of the whites into the whisked egg yolk mix. Now fold in a little of the sifted dry ingredients. Repeat until all the egg whites and dry ingredients have been folded in. Take care not to be heavy handed and overmix the batter. Divide the mix equally between the 2 lined baking trays, then level the top with an angled palette knife. Bake for 10–12 minutes, until the joconde is light brown and springs back when lightly pressed. Leave to cool in the baking trays.

While the sponge is cooking, make the ganache. Place the finely chopped chocolate in a bowl. Bring the cream to the boil and pour it over the chocolate. Whisk very gently to make a smooth, shiny ganache. Cover with cling film, but do not refrigerate.

Cut each sponge cake in half. Brush one piece with the melted dark chocolate on one side. Let the chocolate set and then turn the joconde over on to a lined baking tray so the chocolate is on the bottom. This will form the base of the cake. Using a pastry brush, soak this layer very well with the coffee syrup. You should not see any white sponge; it should be the colour of coffee and when pressed the sponge should feel soft.

Using the angled palette knife, spread an even layer of butter cream over the soaked sponge. Place another piece of sponge on top of that and soak well with the coffee syrup. Spread this layer with an even layer of the chocolate ganache. Place another piece of sponge on the ganache and soak again. This time cover it with an even layer of butter cream. Place the last piece of sponge on the butter cream and, using the back of the baking tray, press down gently on the cake to make a flat, even surface. Soak the top with a little less syrup than the rest of the cake and spread with a slightly thinner layer of butter cream. Level with the palette knife.

Place the cake, still on the tray, in the fridge for 30 minutes to firm up. Once the cake has firmed, make the glaze. Put the chopped chocolate in a bowl. Bring the cream to the boil with the sugar and glucose, then pour it over the chopped chocolate and mix very gently to form a smooth, shiny glaze. Pour the glaze over the top of the cake and level with the angled palette knife, leaving the glaze quite thick so you can level it again to a smooth finish with a clean metal ruler. Run the ruler over the glaze to make it a thin, even layer. I try to smooth it in just one or two goes, as the more you work the glaze, the more it will lose its shine and become dull. Do not worry if the glaze falls over the edges of the cakes, as you will be trimming them off later. Keep any excess glaze in a small bowl.

Put the cake back in the fridge for about 20 minutes to firm up the glaze. Using a serrated bread knife that has been warmed in a jug of hot water and then dried, trim off the edges of the cake to show the neat layers. The word Opéra is classically piped on to the cake – I use some of the excess glaze or ganache for this. You can pipe it on top of the whole cake or cut individual slices and pipe on each one, as shown in the picture. If you are not happy to pipe the word Opéra, simply finish with gold leaf, which still looks stunning. Pick up the gold leaf on the tip of a knife and place the tip into the cake; the gold leaf will stick to the cake.

The cake will keep in a sealed container in the fridge for 5–6 days.

Claire's Notes

• For ease of production, make the sponge, butter cream and syrup the day before you are going to assemble the cake. Don't keep the butter cream in the fridge, however, as it will get too hard.

• Opéra keeps extremely well in the freezer, as long as you freeze it before doing the glaze. Finish the cake when needed and be sure to defrost it well before attempting the glazing.

• If you overcook the sponge and it is a little crisp, which does happen sometimes, remove the sponge from the baking tray as soon as it comes out of the oven and leave to cool on a wire rack. It will still absorb a lot of coffee syrup, so make sure you soak it well and check it is soft by pressing it gently.

CHARLOTTE ROYAL

For the Swiss roll

For the Swiss roll

3 medium eggs

75g/2³/₄oz caster sugar, plus extra
for sprinkling

75g/2³/₄oz plain flour

4 tablespoons seedless raspberry
preserve

For the strawberry mousse

300g/10¹/₂oz strawberries for
puréeing, plus 6 strawberries,
hulled and cut into small pieces

3 gelatine leaves

250g/9oz caster sugar

250ml/9fl oz water

1 teaspoon lemon juice

250ml/9fl oz double cream

To decorate

3 tablespoons apricot preserve

6 strawberries, cut into halves or
quarters

MAKES 10

This dessert is less complex than it looks but it does involve quite a bit of skill. Classically it is filled with a kirsch bavarois – a custard-based mousse flavoured with cherry liqueur. My recipe is for a fruit-based strawberry mousse that is very light and creamy. It looks so pretty and is the very essence of summer.

You will need 10 individual dome moulds, about 7.5cm/3 inches in diameter, to make these. I suggest investing in the stainless steel ones. They are better than the flexi moulds because they can be warmed easily and the mousse will pop out effortlessly. If you have inexpensive teacups, they will make good moulds too.

Preheat the oven to 180°C/350°F/Gas Mark 4. Grease a Swiss roll tin and line it with baking parchment.

Using an electric mixer, beat the eggs and sugar together until they are pale and fluffy and have tripled in volume; the mixture should be thick enough to leave a trail on the surface when drizzled from the whisk. Sift the flour on to a piece of baking parchment. Using a large metal spoon, gently fold it into the mixture a spoonful at a time, taking care to disperse the flour over the entire area of the egg foam; this helps to prevent lumps. Keep as much volume as you can and try not to overmix. Transfer the mixture to the prepared Swiss roll tin and level the surface with an angled palette knife. It is important that the sponge is as level as possible on the tray so it cooks evenly, so take your time to smooth out the mix without knocking out the volume.

Bake for 10–12 minutes, until the sponge is golden brown and springs back to the touch when gently pressed. Do not overcook, or it will become brittle and hard. Remove the sponge from the tray as soon as it comes out of the oven and place on a wire rack to cool. It should still be on the parchment.

Once the sponge is completely cold, turn it over on to a piece of baking parchment that has been lightly sprinkled with caster sugar; this will prevent the sponge sticking to the paper. Peel off the backing paper and spread the sponge evenly with a thin layer of raspberry preserve. The shorter end of the oblong should be facing you. Cut away about 5mm/¹/₄ inch of the sponge to make a neat, even, clean line. Roll the sponge up as tightly as you can until it forms a coil about 2.5cm/1 inch wide. Using a large knife, cut across the sponge to release the roll from the rest of the sponge. Repeat this process until there is no more sponge; you should have 4 or 5 coils. Wrap them individually in baking parchment and place in the freezer for about an hour.

Remove the coils of sponge from the freezer and allow them to defrost only a little; they will be easier to cut if they are still slightly frozen. Slice discs of Swiss roll about 5mm/¹/₄ inch thick. Place one disc in the centre of

(continued on page 164)

(continued from page 162)

each dome mould, then continue to cover the mould completely with the cut discs, working around the central one. Keep the discs as close together as you can, so there are not too many gaps. Once the moulds are fully lined, place them on a tray in the fridge while you make the mousse.

Purée the 300g/10^1/$_2$oz strawberries in a food processor or blender and then pass through a fine sieve to remove the seeds. Weigh the purée; you will need 250g/9oz. Keep any remaining purée covered in a small bowl in the fridge.

Soak the gelatine leaves in cold water for about 5 minutes, until soft and pliable, then remove from the water and squeeze out the excess liquid. Keep them in a small bowl to one side.

Place the sugar and water in a heavy-based pan and bring slowly to the boil, stirring to dissolve the sugar. Remove from the heat and add the soaked gelatine, stirring well to combine. Pass this syrup through a fine sieve into a large mixing bowl, add the strawberry purée and lemon juice and mix well.

Semi-whip the cream until it just holds soft peaks. Leave in the fridge while you cool the mousse base. Place the bowl containing the mousse base over a larger bowl full of ice and whisk it gently as it cools. It is important to keep the mix moving so it does not set on the side of the bowl and form lumps.

Once the mixture is completely cold and has begun to thicken slightly, remove it from the ice. Using a large metal spoon or a rubber spatula, fold in a third of the semi-whipped cream. Once it has been incorporated, mix in the remaining two-thirds. Spoon the mixture into the prepared moulds to fill them half way. Place the chopped strawberries on top of the mousse, then fill up the moulds with the remaining mousse. Level with a palette knife and place them on a small tray in the fridge for 2–3 hours to set.

Once the mousse is set, you can turn the charlottes out of their moulds by dipping them into a small basin of hot water for a few seconds, then flipping them over on to a tray lined with baking parchment. The moulds should lift off easily, leaving the charlottes on the tray.

Bring the apricot preserve to the boil in a small pan with a tablespoon of water, then pass through a fine sieve. Place back in a clean pan and bring to the boil again. Brush the domes with the preserve to make them shiny and to prevent the sponge drying out. Transfer the domes to individual serving plates and serve with the cut strawberries and any leftover strawberry purée.

Claire's Notes

• The Swiss roll coils can be made in advance and will keep in the freezer for up to 4 weeks.
• For an extra kick, add 2 teaspoons of kirsch or Cointreau to the mousse base before folding in the cream.
• These keep really well in the freezer. Freeze them unglazed and defrost thoroughly before glazing them.

PASSIONFRUIT AND MANGO TERRINE WITH EXOTIC FRUITS

1 punnet of strawberries

1 punnet of blackberries

1 punnet of blueberries

1 punnet of raspberries

15–20 red or green small seedless grapes

2 peaches

2 plums

1 mango

1 papaya

For the mousse

10 gelatine leaves

6 passionfruit

125g/4^1/$_2$oz caster sugar

125ml/4fl oz water

4–6 mangoes

375ml/12^1/$_2$fl oz double cream

SERVES 10—12

This is a good choice if you have a lot of people to feed, as one terrine produces 10–12 slices. It is a great summer dessert, it looks stunning and is also very light to eat. I first came across it when I was at London's Intercontinental Hotel, and it made its way with me to the House of Commons, where I worked some years later. I once overheard a couple of ladies in the powder room near the famous terrace, where they had been lunching, raving about the fruit custard slice they had just eaten. I was trying to think what that might have been and suddenly realised it was the passionfruit terrine. I was a little disappointed that they referred to my work of art as a custard slice but it was followed with lots of praise so I let it go – without introducing myself as the producer of their dessert.

Always use fresh fruits, not frozen ones. You can use virtually whatever tropical fruits you like but make sure they are properly ripe and avoid pineapple, figs, citrus fruits and kiwi fruits – these will break down the gelatine and the terrine will fall apart when cut. I make mine as colourful as possible, with the fruits listed opposite.

You will need a terrine mould, about 30 x 7.5cm/12 x 3 inches. I use a heavy Le Creuset mould but they are available in all sorts of materials, from plastic to metal, and come with flat, round and tunnel-shaped bases. All work well, so pick whichever shape you like best.

First prepare all the fruit for the terrine. Wash and dry the berries and grapes, cutting the strawberries into halves or quarters if large. Peel and pit the peaches, plums and mango, then peel and deseed the papaya. Cut them into long slices about 5mm/^{1}/$_4$ inch thick and set aside.

Next make the mousse. Soak the gelatine in a large bowl of cold water for about 5 minutes, until it is very soft, making sure you separate out the leaves as you put them in the bowl so they do not clump together. Cut the passionfruit in half and scoop out the insides. Place in a fine sieve and press well to release as much juice as possible.

Put the sugar and water in a small pan and bring to the boil, stirring to dissolve the sugar. Remove from the heat and measure out 125ml/4fl oz, reserving the rest of the syrup for later. Squeeze out excess liquid from the soaked gelatine. Add the gelatine to the hot 125ml/4fl oz of syrup, stirring to dissolve, then pass it through a fine sieve. Keep warm, but don't put it back on the heat.

Peel the mangoes for the terrine, then place a knife on the top of the fruit and press down gently so you can feel where the stone is. Cut either side of it with a sharp knife to remove the flesh. Place the mango flesh in a blender and blitz until smooth. Push it through a fine sieve and weigh out 125g/4^1/$_2$oz. Add the 125g/4^1/$_2$oz mango purée to the passionfruit juice and mix well. Stir the mango preparation into the warm gelatine syrup.

(continued on page 167)

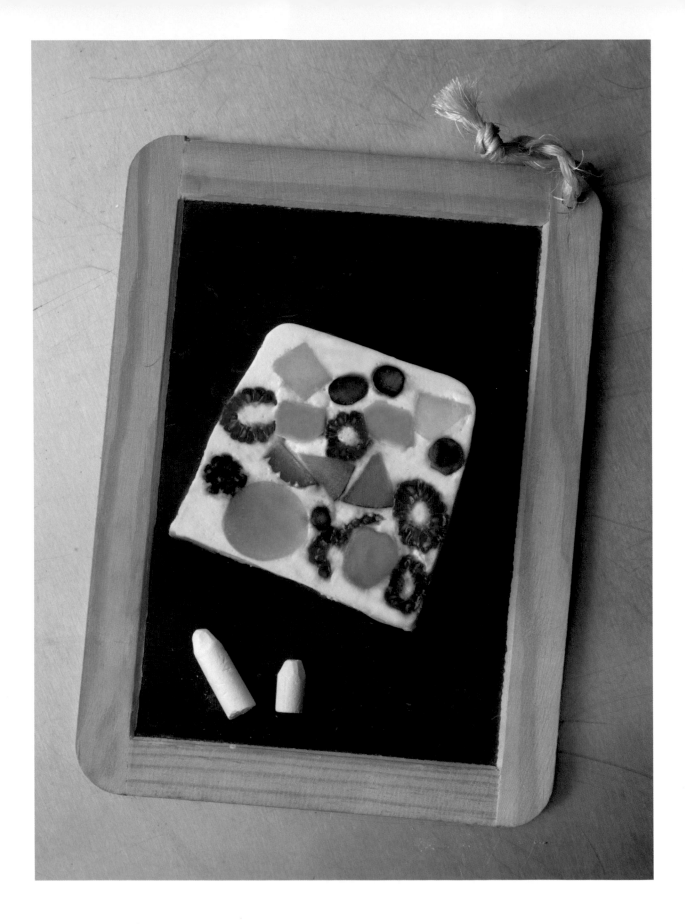

(continued from page 165)

Whip the cream to soft peaks and fold it through the mango and passionfruit base. If you are using a plastic mould, line the bottom and sides with cling film. Metal and other moulds do not need to be lined. Spoon a 5mm/^{1}/$_4$ inch layer of the mousse into the bottom of the mould, then add enough fruit to cover it. You really need to pack the fruits in well. Try to keep them from touching the sides of the mould but go as close to it as you can to fit in as many as possible. Keep layering the terrine mould with fruits and mousse until you reach 5mm/^{1}/$_4$ inch from the top. Finish with a layer of mousse and smooth it level with a palette knife or spatula. Place the terrine in the fridge for 4 hours to set. Combine the remaining mango purée with the leftover syrup to make a sauce. I often put in the passionfruit seeds as well, as they still have a lot of flavour.

To unmould the terrine, first run a small knife around the top edge of the mould, then sit the terrine in a bowl of very hot water for a few seconds. Release the terrine at one end by sliding a spatula into the mould and pushing the terrine away from the side. You should be able to see that the terrine is loose. Place a tray or suitable flat serving dish over the top of the terrine and flip it over, holding on tightly to both the terrine mould and the tray. The terrine should plop out on to the tray.

Cut the terrine into even slices with a sharp serrated bread knife. Serve with any extra berries you could not fit in the terrine when assembling, plus the mango sauce.

Claire's Notes
• You can use about 250g/9oz raspberries or strawberries as your base for the mousse instead of mango, if you prefer. After puréeing and sieving them, weigh out 125g/4^1/$_2$oz, as for the mango above.
• If you need to make the terrine in advance, it will keep for 2 days in the fridge in its dish. Once the terrine has set, cover the top with cling film to keep it fresh.
• The terrine does not freeze well, as the fruits take on too much water. When the terrine defrosts, it will weep fruit juice.
• Before you add the whipped cream to the mousse base, make sure the base has not set. If it has begun to firm up, place the bowl over a pan of hot water, making sure the water does not touch the base of the bowl, and warm it slightly. Take care not to let it get so hot that it melts the cream and becomes liquid.

HIBISCUS JELLIES WITH RED BERRIES

500g/1lb 2oz mixed red berries,
  such as strawberries,
  redcurrants, raspberries, etc.,
  plus a few extra to serve
12 gelatine leaves
600ml/20fl oz water
250g/9oz caster sugar
1–2 tablespoons dried hibiscus
  flowers
125g/4^1/$_2$oz raspberries
300ml/10 fl oz dry white wine

SERVES 8–10

I buy dried hibiscus flowers from the local Chinese supermarket but they can also be found in some healthfood shops. If red berries are not in season, you can layer the jelly with other fruits, such as pomegranate seeds, black seedless grapes and blueberries.

This dessert looks good made in individual jelly moulds, if you can find them. However, you can also use tall shot glasses or pretty Champagne or dessert coupes.

Wash and dry the berries. Cut any strawberries into quarters.

Soak the gelatine in a large bowl of cold water for about 5 minutes, until it is completely soft, separating the leaves out as you place them in the water so they do not clump together. Remove from the water, squeeze out excess liquid and set aside.

Put the water, sugar and hibiscus flowers in a pan and bring to the boil, stirring to dissolve the sugar. Remove from the heat and leave to stand for 10 minutes, then strain through a fine sieve to remove the flowers. Add the 125g/4^1/$_2$oz raspberries to the liquid, return the pan to the heat and bring back to the boil. Remove from the heat, add the gelatine and stir until dissolved. Add the white wine. Whiz the mixture in a blender until smooth (you will probably have to do this in batches), then pass through a fine sieve to remove the raspberry seeds.

Put 8–10 jelly moulds or glasses on a tray and pour a little jelly into each one. Sprinkle in an assortment of berries. They should make a layer in the jelly. Place the tray in the fridge to set the jelly. Once the jelly is set, continue to layer with jelly and fruit until the dishes are full.

If using jelly moulds, sit each one in a bath of hot water for a few seconds to help release the jelly; when you turn it over, it should fall easily out of the mould on to a plate. Serve the jellies with more berries and a little fresh fruit sauce, if liked.

Claire's Notes
• If you want the jelly to set quickly, cool it over a bowl of ice before filling the glasses.
• If you are serving the jellies in glasses, you can reduce the amount of gelatine from 12 to 10 leaves. It is fine to make the jelly a little softer, as you will not be turning it out.
• For a really floral jelly, replace 25ml/1fl oz of the white wine with elderflower syrup.

BLOOD ORANGE, CARA CARA AND MANDARIN JELLIES WITH PINK GRAPEFRUIT HACHE

200ml/7fl oz blood orange juice
(4–5 oranges)
200ml/7fl oz cara cara orange
juice (4–5 oranges)
200ml/7fl oz mandarin juice (5–6
mandarins)
200ml/7fl oz pink grapefruit juice
(2–3 grapefruit)
juice of 1 lemon
20 gelatine leaves
500g/1lb 2oz caster sugar
500ml/18fl oz water
3 pink grapefruit

SERVES 10

Sometimes called red navel oranges, cara cara oranges are a lovely golden colour with a pink hue. They were originally grown in Venezuela but I see them more and more in market stalls here in California. If you cannot find them, use navel oranges instead.

I love jelly as a simple, clean and refreshing way to finish any meal. It takes only a few minutes to prepare and can look fabulous in a pretty glass or serving dish. You can make them in individual glasses or do a large one for a help-yourself buffet-style effect. I loved the bowl in the photo and went for a modern finish, with Space Age splashes. However, the jelly also looks great, and perhaps a little more refined, layered in crystal glass dishes.

Strain all the fruit juice through a very fine sieve, keeping the various juices separate.

Soak the gelatine in a large bowl of cold water for about 5 minutes, until it is very soft, making sure you separate out the leaves as you put them in the bowl so they do not clump together.

Put the sugar and water in a pan and bring to the boil, stirring to dissolve the sugar. As soon as it reaches a rolling boil, remove it from the heat. Measure out 800ml/28fl oz of this syrup in a measuring jug; reserve the excess syrup. Squeeze out excess water from the soaked gelatine and add it to the hot measured syrup. Pass the syrup through a fine sieve.

Measure 200ml/7fl oz of the hot gelatine syrup and mix it with the 200ml/7fl oz of blood orange juice. Repeat this for each of the remaining fruit juices, keeping them separate. Use the lemon juice to adjust the sweetness of each fruit.

Pour one of the jellies into a large serving dish or 10 individual glasses. Save a little of each for the top design. Place the dish or glasses on a tray and place in the fridge to set. Repeat for each fruit, making sure each layer is set before you start the next.

For the final layer, splash on the various jellies to make a funky design – do this one at a time, letting each jelly set before adding a splash of the next one.

For the haché, slice the top and bottom off the 3 pink grapefruit and peel them, removing all the white pith. Cut the segments out from between the membranes. Chop them finely and place in a small dish. Warm the remaining sugar syrup and pour it over the haché. Serve with the jellies.

Claire's Notes
• This is a fabulous alternative to Christmas pudding and it is the perfect time of year to make the jelly, as there are so many satsumas, tangerines and clementines available. Substitute seasonal citrus fruits for the ones in the recipe and make a non-Christmas-pudding-eater happy.

PUDDINGS

MARMALADE BREAD AND BUTTER PUDDING

1 small panettone (about 450g/1lb)

150g/5^1/$_2$oz unsalted butter, melted

1 vanilla pod (optional)

300ml/10fl oz double cream

300ml/10fl oz milk

4 medium eggs

4 medium egg yolks

175g/6oz caster sugar

4 tablespoons marmalade

SERVES 6—8

Claire's Notes

• Be careful not to let the custard boil during baking. If it begins to soufflé in the dish, reduce the oven temperature to 150°C/300°F/Gas Mark 2.

• You can prepare the custard the day before and keep it in the fridge. The panettone can be put in the dishes the day before too, and the melted butter poured over. Remember to add 10–15 minutes to the baking time, as the ingredients will be cold.

'Blessed be he that invented pudding,' declared the French writer, Misson, when he visited England in the 1690s, and rightly so because the humble English pudding is a heavenly experience. Originally they were based on meat but by the seventeenth century, eggs, sugar, butter, milk, suet and bone marrow were being used to make an assortment of steamed, boiled and baked puddings. Frugal cooks who did not want to waste stale bread sliced it and soaked it in milk, then sweetened it with honey or sugar and baked it to make a pudding. This has evolved to include eggs, dried fruit and spices, and nowadays the stale bread might be replaced by buttery brioche, fruit-laden panettone and even Madeira cake for a luxurious dish.

My version uses panettone, which eliminates the need for a lot of different ingredients. Buy a good-quality panettone. I always make sure mine is flavoured with lemon and vanilla and includes a good assortment of dried fruits.

Preheat the oven to 170°C/325°F/Gas Mark 3. Cut the panettone into slices about 1cm/^{1}/$_2$ inch thick. If you plan to make the pudding in individual dishes, cut the slices into pieces. You can make them different heights and widths so they sit abstractly in the dishes: 3–4 pieces is normally enough for a ramekin. If using a single large dish (you will need one about 15 x 20cm/ 6 x 8 inches), cut each panettone slice into quarters and lay them neatly overlapping in the dish. I do not cut off the crust, as it adds texture and colour to the dish once it is baked. Pour the melted butter over the panettone.

If using the vanilla pod, slit it open lengthways and scrape out the seeds with the back of a knife. Bring the cream and milk to the boil with the vanilla pod and seeds. Meanwhile, combine the eggs, egg yolks and sugar in a mixing bowl and whisk gently. Pour the boiled milk and cream over the egg mix and whisk to a smooth custard, then pass through a fine sieve. Pour the custard over the panettone.

Put the dish or dishes in a roasting tin and pour enough hot water into the tin to come two-thirds of the way up the sides of the dishes. Place in the centre of the oven and bake for 30–40 minutes, until the top is golden brown. If you insert a knife into the pudding, there should not be any liquid below the panettone top.

Remove from the roasting tin. Put the marmalade in a small pan with a tablespoon of water and bring to the boil. Brush it over the surface of the pudding with a pastry brush. Serve hot, with Crème Anglaise (see page 118) or a large dollop of Vanilla Ice Cream (see page 192).

STEAMED TREACLE SPONGE

110g/3¾oz softened unsalted butter, plus extra for greasing
110g/3¾oz caster sugar
150g/5½oz self-raising flour
a pinch of salt
grated zest of ½ lemon
2 large eggs
1 small tin of golden syrup

SERVES 6–8

I cannot remember where I read this but someone once described the steamed pudding as, 'a bosomy symbol of domesticity, a warming item of succor, contentment and winter evenings by the fire'. How true. For me, it is all those things and certainly has to be the way to a man's heart. I think of the beloved Mrs Beeton as the queen of puddings. My mind conjures up an idealised picture of her standing at a bleached wooden table in her Victorian kitchen, creaming, mixing and steaming the most divine English puddings.

This recipe is wonderful. It is blissfully simple to make, and every inch is light and fluffy. Your only dilemma will be what to do in the 2½ hours it is steaming.

Grease a 1 litre/35fl oz pudding basin well with softened butter.

Place the butter, sugar, flour, salt and lemon zest in a large mixing bowl, break in the eggs and combine everything with a handheld electric mixer set on a medium-high speed until you have a good soft, creamy mixture. If you are doing this by hand instead, use a large wooden or plastic spoon and make sure the butter is as soft as it can be without being melted. Cream the ingredients together well for 3–4 minutes.

Put 3–4 large tablespoons of golden syrup into the bottom of the prepared pudding basin. Spoon the pudding mixture over the syrup and level it with the back of the spoon. Cover the basin with a piece of baking parchment or well-greased foil, making a 2.5cm/1 inch pleat in the middle. Tie securely around the rim with string. Place the pudding in a steamer and steam for 2½ hours, checking half way through cooking that the water in the steamer is not getting too low. Top up as necessary.

Remove the pudding basin from the steamer, take off the paper or foil and place a shallow serving dish over the top of the pudding. Holding both tightly together, invert the pudding on to the dish and remove the basin. Bring the remaining golden syrup to the boil and serve with the steaming pudding, along with oodles of Crème Anglaise (see page 118).

Variations

Mincemeat Place 3 large tablespoons of mincemeat in the pudding basin instead of the golden syrup.

Apple and cinnamon Place 3 tablespoons of sweetened stewed Bramley apples mixed with 25g/1oz sultanas in the pudding basin instead of the syrup and add a teaspoon of ground cinnamon to the pudding batter.

Chocolate chip Add 100g/3½oz chopped dark chocolate to the pudding batter. Serve with chocolate custard (follow the recipe for Crème Anglaise on page 118, stirring in 200g/7oz chopped chocolate at the end).

Summer berry Place 3 tablespoons of assorted summer berries in the pudding basin instead of the golden syrup. Serve with a large scoop of clotted cream.

Plum Place 5–6 stoned and quartered plums in the pudding basin instead of syrup.

Claire's Notes
• Use a serving dish with a slight well and pour some of the extra hot syrup around the pudding before serving.
• If you do not have a steamer, use a large saucepan with a tight-fitting lid. Place an old cloth in the bottom of the pan, sit an old plate on the cloth and place the pudding on the plate. Fill with 7.5cm/3 inches of boiling water and remember to keep it topped up during cooking.

STICKY TOFFEE PUDDING

175g/6oz Medjool dates, pitted
  and chopped
300ml/10fl oz water
1 teaspoon bicarbonate of soda
50g/1³/₄oz softened unsalted
  butter, plus a little extra for
  greasing
175g/6oz caster sugar
2 medium eggs, lightly beaten
175g/6oz self-raising flour

For the toffee sauce
350ml/12fl oz double cream
50g/1³/₄oz soft dark brown sugar
1 tablespoon black treacle
25g/1oz dark chocolate (70–72 per
  cent cocoa solids), grated

SERVES 6

Calories, calories, calories and worth every single one! This pudding oozes with lusciousness, served with generous spoonfuls of toffee sauce made with treacle, cream and dark brown sugar. The recipe is said to have come from a farmer's wife in Lancashire but there are also stories of the landlady of The Gait Inn in Millington, Lancashire, having had the recipe before that – perhaps she was a friend of the farmer's wife and passed it on to her. Without a doubt, though, it was Francis Coulson, at Sharrow Bay Hotel in the Lake District, who developed and refined this dessert in the 1970s, making it one of Britain's best-loved puddings.

Use Medjool dates, if you can find them – most supermarkets stock them these days. They have a wrinkly appearance and don't have a tough skin. However, all kinds of dates will work. I add a little chocolate to my toffee sauce to take the edge off the sweetness but you can omit it if you want the purest version.

Preheat the oven to 180°C/350°F/Gas Mark 4. Lightly grease a 750ml/25fl oz ceramic pudding basin or 6 individual timbales or basins with a little butter.

Put the dates and water in a pan, bring to the boil and simmer for 4–5 minutes, until the dates are soft. Remove from the heat and add the bicarbonate of soda. Don't panic if it turns a strange, murky green colour. Leave to cool slightly.

Cream together the butter and sugar until light and fluffy. Add the eggs a little at a time, beating well between each addition. Add the warm date mixture, including all the liquid, and mix well. Sift the flour into a large bowl and gradually pour the warm batter on to the flour, whisking constantly. You can do this in 3 or 4 stages if you don't have a friend there to help you pour while you whisk. Make sure all the ingredients are well combined.

Spoon the mixture into the basin or dishes and bake for 25–30 minutes for a large pudding, 12–15 minutes for individual ones, until well risen and just firm to the touch. Meanwhile, make the sauce by bringing the cream, sugar and treacle to the boil in a pan and simmering for 1–2 minutes, until thickened. Add the grated chocolate and stir well.

Turn the puddings out on to individual serving dishes and spoon over the sauce. Serve with Crème Anglaise (see page 118) or Vanilla Ice Cream (see page 192).

Claire's Notes
• This pudding really is best eaten immediately after it comes out of the oven but you can stone and chop the dates and weigh your ingredients out the day before if you want to save time.
• Any leftovers make great crumbs, which will store well in an airtight container in the fridge. Spoon them over Greek yoghurt, add some toasted pecan nuts and serve with any leftover toffee sauce, gently warmed up.

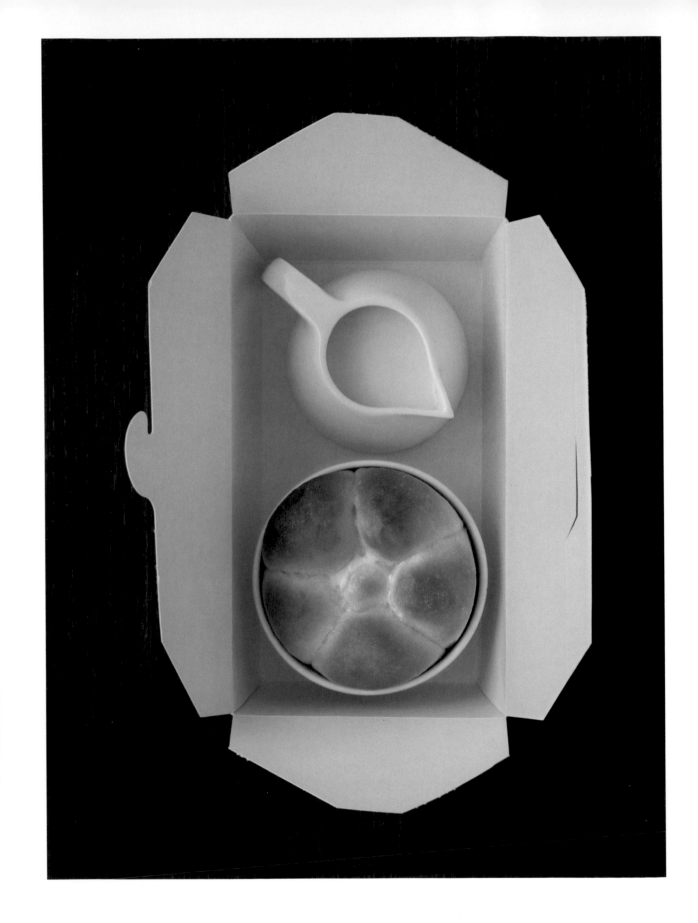

DUMPH NOODLE

375g/13oz strong white flour
25g/1oz fresh yeast
200ml/7fl oz milk
70g/2^1/$_2$oz unsalted butter
70g/2^1/$_2$oz caster sugar
1 teaspoon salt
grated zest of 1 lemon
2 medium eggs

For the topping
55g/2oz unsalted butter
55ml/2fl oz double cream

SERVES 8

I learned how to make this unusual pudding whilst studying under Professor John Huber. I think that one of the many reasons I so enjoyed John's classes was because he would always throw in a couple of extra recipes from his homeland, and boy, were they good. I remember sitting unauthorised on the work station at the end of class, scoffing warm, buttery dumph noodle and admiring the Swiss-German ability to make sweet dough taste so good. When I took up my first head pastry chef position, at London's Portman Hotel, it was one of the first hot dishes I put on the trolley, and it is still one of my favourite yeast-based desserts. Some years later, I taught at Le Cordon Bleu, where I would put it in the bakery class as an extra. There are students who will remember me turning a blind eye while they sat on the worktops and scoffed their day's work.

Grease the base and sides of a 20 x 30cm/8 x 12 inch baking tray, 2.5–4cm/1–1^1/$_2$ inches deep.

Sift the flour into a large bowl and make a well in the centre. Crumble the fresh yeast into the well. Warm the milk to 37°C/98°F or until it is just lukewarm, then pour it over the yeast. Stir the yeast and milk together so the yeast dissolves. Take a little of the flour from the outside of the well and sprinkle it in a light, even layer over the yeast mixture. Cover the bowl tightly with cling film and leave for 15 minutes in a warm, but not hot, place until the flour on top of the yeast mixture shows signs of cracks.

Melt the butter and mix with the sugar, salt, grated lemon zest and eggs, combining all the ingredients well. Add to the flour and yeast and mix with your hand to form a smooth, soft dough. Turn it out on to a lightly floured work surface and knead lightly, just until it is no longer sticky. (You could do all this in an electric mixer fitted with a dough hook.) Return the dough to the bowl, cover with cling film and leave in a warm place for 20–30 minutes, until the dough has doubled in size.

Knock back the dough by kneading it gently on a lightly floured work surface. It should be smooth and shiny and not sticky. Working in a warm, draught-free environment, shape the dough into a long sausage, 4cm/1^1/$_2$ inches wide. Cut it into pieces about 2.5cm/1 inch thick and roll these into balls. To make neat balls, cup your hand around a piece of dough on the worktop and move your hand in a circular motion, keeping the dough on the worktop and pressing gently whilst spinning the dough. This should smooth the surface of the ball and make it rounder at the same time. Place the dough balls in the greased baking tin to form neat lines. They should be just touching.

Place a piece of lightly oiled cling film over the baking tray. Take care that the cling film is resting on top of the dough balls and not stretched over the edges of the tin itself, so the dough can rise freely. Leave in a warm place for a further 15 minutes, until doubled in size. Preheat the oven to 200°C/400°F/Gas Mark 6.

(continued on page 180)

(continued from page 179)

Melt the butter for the topping. Remove the cling film and very gently brush the melted butter over the surface of the buns, reserving any leftover butter. Place in the oven and bake for 15 minutes, then reduce the heat to 180°C/350°F/Gas Mark 4 and continue baking for about 15 minutes, until the buns are golden brown. If you are unsure, pull one of the buns from the tray and break it open; it should not be doughy in the middle.

Brush the remaining butter and the double cream over the top and return to the oven for 3–4 minutes. Serve piping hot with lots of Crème Anglaise (see page 118) or, for a richer dessert, hot Chocolate Sauce (see pages 148–149).

500ml/18fl oz milk
75g/2³⁄₄oz unsalted butter
60g/2¹⁄₄oz plain flour
¹⁄₄ teaspoon salt
8 medium eggs, separated
125g/4¹⁄₂oz caster sugar
150g/5¹⁄₂oz dark chocolate (65–70 per cent cocoa solids), finely chopped
12g/¹⁄₂oz cornflour
icing sugar for dusting

For the sponge fingers
2 large eggs
125g/4¹⁄₂oz caster sugar
125g/4¹⁄₂oz plain flour
50ml/2fl oz Cointreau

For the soufflé dishes
100g/3¹⁄₂oz softened unsalted butter
100g/4¹⁄₂oz caster sugar

SERVES 8

I worked under Ernest Bachmann, the head pastry chef at the Intercontinental Hotel on Hyde Park Corner in London, for three years and it was there I learned to make hot soufflés. The head chef was a very meticulous Swiss-German called Peter Kromburg, for whom I had the highest regard. Not the least because during my time there, I blew up the pastry oven, which resulted in the ceiling tiles coming down and the whole of the kitchen being covered in a fine layer of soot, not to mention the ball of fire travelling through the pastry section and past his office door. Although at the time he seemed rather irate and did yell a few unpleasant words, he nevertheless kept his cool and the pastry section was able to function again within a few hours even if it was without me. I had to go to hospital because the blast had knocked me out! He let me keep my job, and my respect for him was so great I even called my much-loved Maine Coon cat Kromburg.

The main restaurant, which held a Michelin star in the early 1980s, was named Le Soufflé and the menu included many soufflés, both savoury and sweet. The hotel could accommodate banquets for up to 900 people. It was not an unusual occurrence to be making hot soufflés for 500 or more, and I have not been fazed by making a soufflé since. This recipe works as well for eight as it does for 800.

Start by making the sponge fingers. Preheat the oven to 180°C/350°F/ Gas Mark 4. Using an electric mixer, whisk the eggs and sugar together until pale, thick and tripled in volume. The mixture should be thick enough to leave a trail on the surface when drizzled from the whisk. Sift the flour on to a piece of baking parchment and fold it into the whisked mixture a third at a time, using a large metal spoon. Be careful not to overmix. The mixture should retain its volume.

Using a piping bag fitted with a 1cm/¹⁄₂ inch plain nozzle, pipe the mixture in 5cm/2 inch lengths on to a baking sheet lined with baking parchment.

Bake in the centre of the oven for 8–10 minutes, until firm and light brown. Leave on the tray to cool; the sponge fingers should peel away from the parchment when cold. Turn up the oven to 200°C/400°F/Gas Mark 6 for the soufflés.

Prepare 8 large ramekins, about 250ml/9fl oz in capacity. With a small pastry brush, coat the inside of each one with the softened butter. Once you have a good coating, go back and brush the butter in an upward motion. This creates an even layer that is travelling in the same direction as the soufflé as it rises. Make sure the butter goes all the way to the rim and covers the entire dish. Fill up one of the ramekins with the caster sugar. Roll the ramekin around so the sugar goes up to the rim. Hold it over a bowl and flip it over, so the excess sugar is tipped into the bowl. There should be a fine, even coating of sugar inside the ramekin. Repeat to coat all the dishes.

(continued on page 183)

Claire's Notes

• You can make the basic mix the day before, up to the point where you put it in a bowl and cover it with cling film, and keep it in the fridge overnight. Warm it in a bowl set over a pan of hot water when you want to use it.

• Make sure there is no mixture on the edge of the ramekins when they go into the oven. When you are filling the dishes, take extra time and be careful to avoid spillages that will cause them to stick and rise unevenly.

• Use a timer when cooking the soufflés. Never leave the oven, but refrain from opening the oven door during cooking.

• I always bake at least one extra soufflé so I can test whether it is cooked. I break it open and check how it looks inside.

(continued from page 181)

To make the soufflés, bring the milk to the boil and keep it hot. Melt the butter in a medium pan and heat until it begins to bubble. Quickly stir in the flour and salt to make a roux and keep stirring for a minute to cook out the flour. Over a moderate heat, and now using a whisk, add the milk a little at a time, whisking well between each addition to keep the mix smooth and lump free. Once all the milk has been incorporated, bring the soufflé base to the boil, whisking constantly. Remove from the heat and leave to cool slightly.

Mix the egg yolks with 25g/1oz of the sugar. Add to the cooling soufflé base and whisk until smooth. Return to the heat and bring back to the boil, whisking constantly. Remove from the heat, add 75g/2³/₄oz of the chopped chocolate and mix in well. Transfer the mixture to a large mixing bowl and cover the surface with cling film.

Put the egg whites in a large bowl. Mix the cornflour with the remaining 100g/3¹/₂oz of caster sugar and add to the egg whites. Whisk with an electric mixer until they form firm peaks. (If you are whisking the egg whites by hand, add the sugar mixture a third at a time, making sure the egg whites are holding a soft peak before the second addition and a medium peak before the third one.)

Gently whisk the chocolate soufflé base to soften it and then fold in a third of the beaten egg whites, using a large metal spoon and turning the bowl as you go. Make sure they are well folded in without losing any volume. Fold in the remaining egg white a third at a time following the same procedure.

Break the sponge fingers and place 1–2 in the base of each prepared ramekin. Brush them lightly with the Cointreau. Take the remaining chopped chocolate and divide it between the dishes, sprinkling it over the soaked sponge fingers. Using a piping bag fitted with a 2.5cm/1 inch nozzle, pipe the soufflé mixture into the prepared dishes so it comes to just below the rim. Place on a baking sheet and bake in the centre of the oven for 8–10 minutes, until well risen and firm to the touch. A true soufflé should be a little soft in the middle but not sunken, and the top should not give when very gently pressed. When you open the soufflé with a spoon it should be ever so slightly runny in the very centre. Serve the soufflés immediately, dusted with a little icing sugar.

WARM CHOCOLATE FONDANT

200g/7oz softened unsalted butter, plus a little melted butter for greasing the moulds

a little caster sugar

a little spray oil

200g/7oz Chuao chocolate, finely chopped

200g/7oz icing sugar, sifted, plus extra for dusting

4 medium eggs

4 medium egg yolks

55g/2oz plain flour

35g/1^1/$_4$oz cocoa powder

SERVES 8

Claire's Notes

• Select a dark, extra bitter cocoa powder for the best colour and flavour.

• Sift the dry ingredients together and mix them well before folding them into the creamed mix. Cocoa powder is heavier than flour and by mixing them well you will limit the chance of the cocoa powder clumping and forming lumps in the finished mix.

• If by any chance you have any left over, these fondants are great cold the next day. Store them in a tin and they become delicious little chocolate cakes, the centres less liquid and fudgier.

There are many recipes for these lovely little cakes that ooze puddles of warm, molten chocolate lava. Some involve making two different mixes, freezing the mixture, using complicated moulds, and technical procedures that even the most skilled pastry chef would have trouble executing well. I tend to think, why make it complicated when it can be so easy? This recipe is simple to make and limited to just a handful of choice ingredients.

Do try to get hold of the Venezuelan Amedei Chuao chocolate (see page 148). It has notes of red fruits, berries and plums, and it really does make all the difference here. If you are unable to find this heaven-sent chocolate, however, Valrhona Manjari is a close second.

Preheat the oven to 190°C/375°F/Gas Mark 5. Prepare 8 dariole moulds or ramekin dishes by brushing them well with melted butter, then dusting them with caster sugar – the best way to do this is to fill one of them to the top with sugar, then tip out all the sugar into the next mould, continuing in this way until you have sugared all the moulds. They should be completely covered with a thin coating of sugar. Lightly spray them with oil to give you extra confidence that the puddings will turn out without sticking.

Put the chocolate in a bowl set over a pan of hot water, making sure the water doesn't touch the base of the bowl. Let it melt, then keep warm.

Using an electric mixer, cream the butter and icing sugar together until pale and fluffy. Mix the eggs and egg yolks together and add them a little at a time to the creamed butter and sugar, beating well between each addition. Lower the speed of the mixer and add the warm melted chocolate. Sift the flour and cocoa powder and fold them in with a large metal spoon, being careful not to overwork the mixture. Spoon it into the prepared moulds; they should be just over half full. Place in the oven and bake for 8–11 minutes. The cooking time is vital to the molten-lava centre, so set a timer and do not leave the oven unattended. After 8 minutes, remove one of the puddings and check that it is set around the edges and the middle still looks a little loose – it should be slightly concave. You can insert a skewer to test it; the centre should still be liquid. If you think it needs a little longer, return it to the oven for 3 minutes.

Remove the puddings from the oven and let them sit for 30 seconds, then carefully turn each one over on to a serving plate. They should just drop out, so be careful. Dust with icing sugar and serve immediately, with hot Crème Anglaise (see page 118) or ice cream.

APPLE AND CINNAMON CHARLOTTE

1 white loaf, thinly sliced (use
    bread that is 1–2 days' old)
250g/9oz unsalted butter, melted
6–8 large cooking apples, peeled,
    cored and roughly chopped
pared zest of 1 lemon
25g/1oz caster sugar, or to taste
1 teaspoon ground cinnamon

SERVES 8

I know nothing for certain of the history of this dessert except that it was known as a good way to use up stale bread. Some say Queen Charlotte, the wife of George III, was an apple lover and that is how it got its name. Making a charlotte involves cutting the bread into neat, even strips and lining a mould by arranging them vertically overlapping. The bread is dipped in butter first, so it browns in the oven and gives a crisp outer coating to the softly stewed, cinnamon-scented apples within. Insufficient cooking, poor lining of the mould or wet apples can cause the charlotte to collapse when turned out. This recipe uses individual dariole moulds so there is less chance of the charlotte collapsing, and they are so good as a winter dessert, perfect after a Sunday roast dinner.

Preheat the oven to 180°C/350°F/Gas Mark 4. Cut the crusts off the bread. Cut out 8 discs of bread to fit the base of the dariole moulds, dip them in the melted butter and then place in the moulds. Cut the remaining slices of bread into 4 equal strips each. Don't stack the slices up to do this, as you don't want to squash them while you are cutting them. Trim the strips so they are the exact height of your dariole moulds. Dip them into the butter one at a time, then use to line the darioles, slightly overlapping them. Tuck the last strip behind the first one so it is neatly finished.

Place the apples in a large pan with about 3 tablespoons of water to prevent them burning. Add the lemon zest, bring to the boil, then cover the pan and reduce the heat to a simmer. Simmer until tender, stirring from time to time to prevent sticking. Once the apples are soft, remove the lid and continue to cook until they are free of excess liquid. It's important to stir continuously at this stage so the apples do not burn. Stir in the sugar and cinnamon and remove the lemon zest.

Spoon the hot mixture into the bread-lined dariole moulds almost to the top. Using a cutter the same size as the top of the dariole moulds, cut out 8 rounds of bread. Dip them in the melted butter and place on top of the apples.

Take a small piece of baking parchment and lay it on the work surface. Turn over each filled dariole one at a time and press down firmly to squash the bread flat. If you have overfilled the moulds, apple will come out of the top and it will not sit flat. Remove some of the apple if this happens.

Place the moulds on a baking sheet and bake in the centre of the oven for 20–25 minutes, until the bread is golden brown. They do puff up a little during cooking but don't worry if they go down when they cool slightly. To test if they are done, turn one of the moulds over and shake it gently. The charlotte should come out easily and should be evenly coloured. Serve warm with Crème Anglaise (see page 118) or ice cream.

Claire's Notes
• You can assemble the puddings a day in advance and leave them in the fridge until you want to bake them. Add 10 minutes to the baking time.
• The charlottes are good cold the next day but you can reheat them in a moderate oven if you want them warm.

BRAMLEY APPLE AND CINNAMON RISOTTO

50g/1³/₄oz unsalted butter
100g/3¹/₂oz risotto rice, rinsed
600ml/20fl oz Bramley apple juice
2 Bramley apples, peeled and
   grated
a pinch of freshly grated nutmeg
a pinch of ground mixed spice
caster sugar, to sweeten

For the cinnamon custard
500ml/18fl oz double cream
7 medium egg yolks
50g/1³/₄oz caster sugar
1 teaspoon ground cinnamon

To decorate
4 Bramley apples, peeled, cored
   and roughly chopped
150ml/5fl oz organic cider
a little sugar

SERVES 4–6

Claire's Notes
• When making the custard, have
the blender already set up and
ready to go – you need to transfer
the custard quickly to the blender
so it does not continue to cook
and separate. If the custard does
separate, then as long as you whiz
it up in the blender straight away,
it will come back together into a
creamy sauce.
• For a restaurant finish like the
one in the photo, decorate the
risotto with a few apple balls
poached in cider and pour over a
little caramel sauce (follow the
caramel recipe in Crème Caramel
on page 123, adding a tablespoon
of water to it as described in the
Notes).
• Serve with a glass of chilled
Pedro Ximénez sherry. It's also
very good with Shortbread (see
page 12).

Great Britain is lucky to have some of the world's best apple varieties, and Bramleys have to be my favourite. I love their tartness and the way they cook down so quickly almost to a purée. This makes them a great choice for this particular recipe. When I first arrived in America, I was introduced to Donald Schmitt, the original owner of The French Laundry when it was only a two-table restaurant. Donald now owns an apple farm with over 150 varieties of organic apples and, would you believe it, he even managed to provide me with a couple of boxes of my beloved Bramleys? He is without a doubt my favourite supplier.

Melt the butter in a nonstick frying pan, add the rice and stir over a medium heat until it is coated in the butter. Add a third of the apple juice and all the grated apple and stir well. Lower the heat and cook slowly until the apples break down and the juice has been absorbed. Keep adding more juice as it is absorbed and remember to give the rice a stir from time to time. When all the juice has been absorbed, check to see if the rice is cooked. If not, add a little extra juice and continue to cook until the rice is soft.

Remove from the heat and add the spices and enough sugar to sweeten to your taste. I like it to be a little sharp, so I tend to keep the sugar to a minimum. Spoon into glasses or individual dishes and level the top with the back of a spoon. Leave to cool, then chill until set.

To make the cinnamon custard, bring the cream to the boil in a saucepan. Beat the egg yolks with the sugar in a bowl. Once the cream has come to the boil, pour it over the yolks and sugar, stirring all the time. Mix well and return to a clean pan. Over a low heat, stir the custard with a wooden spoon until it thickens slightly and just begins to boil around the edge of the pan; do not let it boil rapidly. Immediately remove from the heat, pass through a fine sieve and transfer to a blender. Add the cinnamon and blitz for a few seconds, until the custard becomes lighter and slightly more viscous. Spoon or pipe it on top of the risotto immediately, then place back in the fridge.

Put the chopped apples in a pan, add the cider and cook gently until soft. The apples should break down completely to form a soft compote. Continue cooking until any excess liquid has evaporated, then sweeten to taste and leave to cool completely. Spoon on top of the set cinnamon custard before serving.

VANILLA ICE CREAM WITH CHANTILLY CREAM AND HOT CHOCOLATE SAUCE

2 vanilla pods
500ml/18fl oz whole milk
500ml/18fl oz double cream
12 medium egg yolks
250g/9oz caster sugar

For the Chantilly cream
300ml/10fl oz whipping cream
25g/1oz icing sugar, sifted
a few drops of vanilla extract

To serve
100g/3^1/$_2$oz flaked almonds
Chocolate Sauce (see pages
  148–149)

SERVES 4–6

Claire's Notes
• Have the fine sieve and the bowl of ice ready before you start the cooking process, so you can cool the custard quickly and there is less risk of it separating.
• The ice cream will keep in a sealed plastic tub in the freezer for a week.
• To make banana splits, cut bananas in half and place them in long banana split dishes. Scoop 3 balls of vanilla ice cream in between each cut banana. Pipe the Chantilly cream over the ice cream, sprinkle with the flaked almonds and drizzle with the chocolate sauce.

Vanilla ice cream has to be one of my favourite desserts. It is so simple and so good. There are three main types of vanilla pod available and they vary greatly in aroma and taste. The Bourbon pods are long, slender and very rich, with an abundance of tiny seeds and a sweet, hay-like scent. Mexican pods are similar to the Bourbon ones in appearance, though they have a spicy, woody fragrance, while Tahitian pods are noticeably shorter and thicker, with a fruity aroma. I suggest that you experiment to determine which flavour you like most. Be sure to choose moist, plump vanilla pods; hard, dry ones are very inferior.

To make the smoothest ice cream, you need an ice-cream machine. Look at all the ones available and think about how often you are going to use it before making your choice. With the cheaper models, you have to freeze the bowl before churning the ice cream, so you will need freezer space for it. The larger, more expensive models freeze in the machine without a separate chamber and turn the ice cream at a higher speed, which makes it smoother and creamier. They do, however, take up considerable counter space and are heavy and bulky.

Slit the vanilla pods open lengthwise with a small, sharp knife, then scrape out the seeds with the back of the knife. Put the pods and seeds in a pan with the milk and cream and bring to the boil.

Meanwhile, put the egg yolks and sugar in a large bowl and mix well. Gradually pour the boiled milk and cream over the egg and sugar mixture in a steady stream, stirring constantly. Return the mixture to a clean pan and cook over a low heat, stirring with a wooden spoon, until the mixture is thick enough to coat the back of the spoon; it should register 86°C/185°F on a sugar thermometer. Do not allow it to boil or it will separate. Pass this custard immediately through a fine sieve into a bowl, then place the bowl over a larger bowl of ice to prevent the custard cooking further. Leave to cool completely, then churn in an ice-cream machine.

Meanwhile, preheat the oven to 180°C/350°F/Gas Mark 4. Spread the flaked almonds out on a baking tray lined with baking parchment, place in the oven and bake for about 10 minutes, until the almonds are golden. Leave to cool completely.

For the Chantilly cream, whisk the cream with the sifted icing sugar and vanilla until it holds firm peaks.

To serve, scoop the vanilla ice cream into bowls or sundae dishes and pipe on the Chantilly cream using a piping bag fitted with a 1cm/^{1}/$_2$ inch star nozzle. Sprinkle with a generous handful of toasted flaked almonds and top with hot chocolate sauce.

QUICK STRAWBERRY ICE CREAM

600g/1lb 5oz strawberries
320g/11$^{1}/_{2}$oz caster sugar
500ml/18fl oz double cream

SERVES 4–6

One day when I was teaching at Le Cordon Bleu, my friend and fellow pastry lecturer, Matthew Hardy, was in the basement, busily prepping for our ice-cream demonstration the next day. I was shocked to see him making strawberry ice cream without any eggs, and was convinced it wouldn't be as luxurious as my recipe. I was, however, pleasantly surprised, as it was every bit as rich and creamy as mine. Whenever I make a fruit ice cream now, whatever the flavour, I use this recipe. The quality of the fruit is paramount. It should be as ripe as possible, as any greenness will come through in the taste after the ice cream has been churned.

Wash and hull the strawberries. Purée them in a blender and then pass through a fine sieve to remove the seeds.

Mix half the sugar with the cream and bring to the boil. Pour this mixture over the fruit purée and mix well, then stir in the rest of the sugar. Leave to cool completely. Churn in an ice-cream machine according to the manufacturer's instructions. Soften slightly before serving, so the ice cream will scoop easily.

Claire's Notes
• This ice cream makes a delicious Wimbledon knickerbocker glory. Layer it in tall glasses with strawberry sauce, whipped cream and sliced strawberries or warm strawberry compote. Finish with chocolate shavings and/or toasted flaked almonds for a completely over-the-top summer dessert, perfect for a lazy summer Sunday afternoon.

DELUXE COFFEE ICE CREAM

500ml/18fl oz whole milk
500ml/18fl oz double cream
3 tablespoons freshly ground
  espresso coffee
12 medium egg yolks
250g/9oz caster sugar
Chocolate Sauce (see pages
  148–149) or Crème Anglaise
  (see page 118), to serve

For the chocolate décor
300g/10^1/$_2$oz tempered dark
  chocolate (see pages 212–213)
300g/10^1/$_2$oz tempered white
  chocolate (see pages 212–213)

SERVES 4–6

The quality of the coffee is critical to the overall flavour of this ice cream. Use only whole coffee beans and grind them yourself or have the shop grind them for you. I use espresso beans, as they have a bitter, sharp taste that complements the richness and creaminess of the ice-cream base.

If you make the chocolate decoration, you will need a sheet of acetate, about 300 x 210mm (12 x 8 inches).

Bring the milk and cream to the boil with the ground coffee. As soon as it boils, turn off the heat and leave to infuse for 10 minutes. Return to the heat and bring back to the boil, then turn off the heat again and infuse for another 10 minutes. Pass through a fine sieve into a measuring jug. Bring the coffee mix back up to 1 litre with extra milk if necessary. Return to a clean pan and bring to the boil.

Put the egg yolks and sugar in a large bowl and mix well. Pour the coffee-flavoured milk over the mixture in a steady stream, stir and return to the pan. Cook over a low heat, stirring constantly with a wooden spoon, until the mixture is thick enough to coat the back of the spoon, or reaches 86°C/185°F on a sugar thermometer. Do not allow it to boil or it will separate. As soon as it thickens, pour it through a fine sieve into a bowl. Place the bowl over a larger bowl of ice to prevent the custard cooking further.

When the custard is completely cool, churn it in an ice-cream machine.

For the chocolate décor, randomly drizzle the dark chocolate from a fork or the back of a spoon on to a sheet of acetate to make the pattern of your choice. Leave it to set. Spoon several tablespoons of the tempered white chocolate over the dark chocolate and spread with a palette knife until it is smooth and thin. Let the sheet of chocolate set, then place it on a tray. Wrap the tray in cling film and place in the fridge.

Serve the ice cream decorated with the two-toned chocolate décor, broken into jagged pieces, and accompanied by Chocolate Sauce or Crème Anglaise.

Claire's Notes
• Sheets of acetate can be bought in boxes from most stationery stores.

SALTED PISTACHIO ICE CREAM

1 egg white
250g/9oz shelled peeled pistachio
   nuts
1 teaspoon sea salt
600ml/20fl oz double cream
400ml/14fl oz whole milk
12 medium egg yolks
250g/9oz caster sugar

SERVES 6–8

Pistachios vary from shades of yellow to green, with green ones being the finest. If you can find them, use the pre-shelled, very bright green nuts. They have a wonderful flavour and give the ice cream a dramatic, vibrant colour. Otherwise, choose high-quality salted pistachio nuts in the shell. If you are using the salted variety, omit the salt from the recipe.

This ice cream makes a fantastic accompaniment to the Hot Chocolate Soufflés on page 181. For an all-out experience, serve with a jug of hot Chocolate Sauce (see pages 148–149).

Preheat the oven to 180°C/350°F/Gas Mark 4. Whip the egg white by hand until it makes a light foam. Take a tablespoon of the foam and mix it with the pistachio nuts; it should be just enough to coat them lightly. Add the salt and mix well. Spread the nuts over a baking tray lined with baking parchment and bake for about 5 minutes, until they dry out; they should not change colour. Leave to cool, then chop finely.

Bring the cream and milk to the boil. Meanwhile, mix the egg yolks and sugar together in a large bowl. Pour the cream and milk on to the egg and sugar mixture in a steady stream and stir well. Return the mixture to a clean pan and cook over a low heat, stirring constantly with a wooden spoon, until the mixture thickens enough to coat the back of the spoon; it should register 86°C/185°F on a sugar thermometer. Do not let it boil or the custard will separate. Pass immediately through a fine sieve into a bowl and stir in the chopped salted pistachio nuts. Place the bowl over a larger bowl of ice to prevent the custard cooking further. Leave to cool completely, then churn in an ice-cream machine.

POPCORN SHERBET

35g/1^1/$_4$oz unpopped popcorn
a little salt
120g/4^1/$_4$oz unsalted butter
1 litre/35fl oz whole milk
125ml/4fl oz liquid glucose

SERVES 4—6

A sherbet is a cross between a sorbet and an ice cream. It often contains milk or cream but not usually any eggs. One evening, shortly after I arrived at The French Laundry, Thomas Keller handed me a small piece of card with two words written on it: 'popcorn sorbet'. Not being overly acquainted with popcorn, I went in search of it. The supermarkets in the States have whole aisles allocated to popcorn, and I was so overwhelmed that I returned empty handed. I left the selection of popcorn to a member of my team and focused on creating a composed sorbet dish for the chef, featuring this sherbet recipe. We paired it with a sticky toffee pudding and date sauce and freshly popped popcorn threaded on to sugar sticks. Why not try the Butterscotch Sauce on page 130 to make a similar pairing?

Pop the popcorn according to the instructions on the packet, seasoning with a little salt. Add the butter and stir until it has completely melted and the popcorn is evenly coated in it.

Bring the milk to the boil in a large pan, add the popcorn and bring back to the boil. Cover the pan with cling film and leave for 10 minutes to infuse. Bring back to the boil, remove from the heat and allow to infuse for another 10 minutes. Some of the fat will have risen to the surface as the mixture cools. Remove about 10 per cent of this fat with a ladle and discard it. Add the glucose to the popcorn mixture and stir well. Leave to cool completely, stirring regularly to prevent the fat settling on the top, then churn in an ice-cream machine.

Claire's Notes
• If you have a microwave, you can use microwave popcorn. It saves on mess and extra pans.
• Serve with caramelised salted pecan nuts. Roast 200g/7oz pecan nuts in the oven at 180°C/350°F/Gas Mark 4 with a little sea salt and then leave to cool. Make the caramel in the Crème Caramel recipe on page 123. Just as the sugar turns a golden colour, add the roasted salted pecans and mix gently. Pour them on to a nonstick baking mat, separate them out with a fork and let them cool completely. Chop the nuts roughly, sprinkle them over the sherbet and serve with hot Butterscotch Sauce (see page 130).

BLACKCURRANT SPOOM

400g/14oz frozen blackcurrants
125g/4$^{1}/_{2}$oz caster sugar
150ml/5fl oz water
juice of $^{1}/_{2}$ lime

For the Italian meringue
75g/2$^{3}/_{4}$oz caster sugar
1$^{1}/_{2}$ tablespoons water
2 small egg whites

SERVES 8

Claire's Notes
• If you have any extra
blackcurrant purée, blend it with a
little icing sugar to sweeten it and
spoon it into the glasses before
adding the spoom.
• You could use a ready-made fruit
purée from a supermarket but you
will need to reduce the sugar, as
most commercial purées have
10 per cent added sugar.
• If your sorbet is churned before
the Italian meringue is ready, keep
it in the freezer in a bowl ready for
mixing.

Spoom is the American term for spume, *which is the French word for foam.
It is a very light, fluffy type of sorbet, made with Italian meringue. If you
use sharper fruits it is simply delightful, as they contrast with the sweetness
of the meringue. Blackcurrants, redcurrants, raspberries, gooseberries and
rhubarb all make wonderful spooms.*

*The cooking of the sugar is best done with a sugar thermometer, as it
needs to be very precise. If you do not use your sugar thermometer often,
I recommend you check it first for air bubbles or damage.*

Defrost the blackcurrants and place them in a pan with all the liquid that
comes from them while they are defrosting. Add 100ml/3$^{1}/_{2}$fl oz water and
cook over a very low heat for about 15 minutes, until tender; if the liquid
evaporates during cooking, replace it with water so you do not have less
liquid than you started with. Purée the blackcurrants in a blender until
smooth, then pass though a fine sieve. You should have at least 250g/9oz of
blackcurrant purée.

Put 250g/9oz of the purée in a pan with the sugar and water, mix well
and bring to the boil. Stir in the lime juice, remove from the heat and leave
to cool completely. Churn in an ice-cream machine.

When the sorbet base is nearly ready in the ice-cream machine, start
making the Italian meringue. Put the sugar and water in a small, heavy-
based pan and bring to the boil, stirring to dissolve the sugar. Put a sugar
thermometer in the pan and boil the syrup, without stirring, until it reaches
118°C/245°F. Keep a pastry brush and a jug of cold water near the stove
while the sugar is boiling and wash down the sides of the pan with the wet
pastry brush every 3–5 minutes to prevent the sugar crystallising.

As soon as the sugar syrup starts boiling, begin to whisk the egg whites.
This is best done with a handheld electric beater. When the egg whites are
at soft peaks and the sugar reaches the correct temperature, reduce the
speed of the mixer and carefully pour the sugar syrup on to the egg whites.
Avoid pouring it directly on to the whisk or it will throw the syrup around
the sides of the bowl. Turn the speed back up as soon as you have added
all the syrup and whisk until the meringue is smooth and firm. Remove the
sorbet from the ice-cream machine and carefully fold it into the Italian
meringue, making sure the meringue is no longer warm. I like to leave
it not completely folded into the sorbet, so it looks likes ripples.

Place in a container in the freezer for an hour. Once the spoom has
firmed, it can be piped into glasses or scooped into dishes.

CHOCOLATE AND PISTACHIO SEMIFREDDO

750ml/25fl oz double cream

6 medium egg yolks

50g/1³/₄oz caster sugar

100ml/3¹/₂fl oz honey, preferably Leatherwood honey

100g/3¹/₂oz shelled peeled pistachio nuts, chopped, plus a few extra to serve

Chocolate Décor, to serve (see page 194)

For the ganache

300g/10¹/₂oz dark chocolate (70 per cent cocoa solids), finely chopped

200ml/7fl oz double cream

For the glaze

400g/14oz flan jelly, such as Quick Jel

90ml/3fl oz double cream

40g/1¹/₂oz caster sugar

40ml/1¹/₂fl oz water

225g/8oz dark chocolate (70 per cent cocoa solids), finely chopped

SERVES 10–12

Claire's Notes

• Instead of making individual semifreddos, you could make one large one in a terrine mould. Freeze and glaze as in the recipe, then cut into slices to serve.

• This dessert will keep for up to 2 weeks frozen in the moulds or turned out and stored in a plastic box in the freezer. If you are preparing it for a dinner party, you can make the semifreddos ahead of time and glaze them up to 8 hours before serving. As they sit on the plate coming to temperature, just prior to serving, the shine on the glaze will return.

I was given this recipe by a member of my team of 19 pastry chefs shortly after I started working at Sir Terence Conran's newly opened Bluebird restaurant, on London's King's Road. I was having a spell of all things Italian, and after a week of testing all my recipes and quite a few others I had found in various books, I still could not find one that matched the texture I was looking for. Semifreddo translates as half frozen, or half chilled, and I knew I wanted the texture to be more smooth than iced and more chilled than frozen, and it had to hold its shape and be creamy at the same time. Finally, one of the team, probably exasperated by my failed efforts, left a small, well-used, rather tatty recipe book on my work station with the page propped open at Semifreddo. It was his Italian grandmother's recipe and he was willing to share it with me. Of course, it was just perfect – so perfect that I followed it exactly. Here I've added a glaze and a little decoration.

Bring the cream to the boil. Meanwhile, lightly whisk the egg yolks, sugar and honey together. Gradually pour the boiling cream over the egg mixture, stirring constantly. Return the mixture to a clean pan and cook over a low heat, stirring all the time with a wooden spoon, until it thickens enough to coat the back of the spoon. Pour this custard immediately through a fine sieve into a bowl and place over a larger bowl full of ice to cool slightly.

Now make the ganache. Put the chopped chocolate in a bowl. Bring the cream to the boil, pour it over the chocolate and whisk gently until smooth. Combine the hot ganache with the custard base, which should be slightly warm but not hot, and mix well. Set the bowl over a larger bowl of ice again and whisk gently until the mixture cools and thickens slightly. Stir in the pistachios. Transfer the mixture to 10–12 dariole moulds or other small dishes and place them in the freezer for 24 hours.

To turn out the semifreddos, dip the moulds quickly in hot water, then insert a small knife 2.5cm/1 inch from the base of each one and pull to release from the mould. The semifreddo should stay on the tip of the knife. Remove from the knife and place the semifreddo on a frozen tray lined with baking parchment. Place in the freezer until they are very firm.

Meanwhile, make the glaze. Make up the flan jelly according to the instructions on the packet. Place in a saucepan with the cream, sugar and water, stir well and warm over a low heat until the mix melts to a liquid. Bring to the boil and pour it over the chopped chocolate in a bowl. Stir very gently to combine all the ingredients without creating any air bubbles.

Place the semifreddos on a wire rack, then place the rack over an empty plastic tray or a lined baking tray. Spoon the warm glaze on top. Remove the semifreddos from the wire rack by sliding a palette knife under them, then place them back in the freezer on the frozen lined tray.

To serve, remove the semifreddos from the freezer and place on individual serving plates. Decorate with pieces of chocolate décor and a few shelled, peeled pistachio nuts. Let the semifreddos sit on the plate for 10 minutes before serving so they reach the right consistency.

LEMON SORBET WITH RASPBERRY COMPOTE

finely grated zest of 2 lemons
500ml/18fl oz freshly squeezed
   lemon juice (about 16 lemons)
200g/7oz caster sugar
1 teaspoon liquid glucose

For the raspberry compote
250g/9oz raspberries
100g/3$\frac{1}{2}$oz icing sugar
lemon juice to taste

SERVES 6

Lemon sorbet is not only a wonderful palate cleanser between courses but also a light, refreshing way to end a hearty or rich meal. Select unwaxed organic lemons, preferably with their leaves still attached, as they have an intense flavour and always give a high yield of juice.

You can make sorbet so much more interesting by serving it with a seasonal fruit compote or a light, wafer-type biscuit. Raspberry compote works well with this recipe. Spruce up the presentation by freezing some fancy glasses so they frost over slightly when they are removed from the freezer. Scoop the sorbet directly into the glasses, spoon over the warm compote and serve immediately. Try a little chilled grappa poured over the top for an extra kick.

Bring 200ml/7fl oz of water to the boil in a small pan, then reduce the heat to a simmer and add the lemon zest. Boil for 5 minutes, then tip the mixture through a fine sieve. Refresh the zest by placing the sieve under cold running water for 30 seconds. Transfer to a small container and set aside.

Place the lemon juice and sugar in a pan with 500ml/18fl oz water and stir to combine. Bring to the boil, add the liquid glucose and then pass through a fine sieve. Leave to cool completely, then chill. Add the lemon zest and churn the mixture in an ice-cream machine.

Meanwhile, make the raspberry compote. Place half the raspberries in a blender with the icing sugar and blitz for a few seconds until smooth. Pass through a fine sieve to remove the seeds, then add lemon juice to taste; this helps to brighten the sauce and take away some of the sweetness. Add the remaining raspberries and mix gently. Warm slowly over a low heat, being careful that the fruit doesn't break up.

To serve, scoop the lemon sorbet into bowls and spoon the warm raspberry compote on top.

Claire's Notes
• For summer, freeze the sorbet mixture in ice cube trays to make lemon ice cubes, or use it to fill lolly moulds.

MANGO, LIME AND GINGER SORBETS

For the lime zest and ginger garnish
100g/3$^1/_2$oz caster sugar
100ml/3$^1/_2$fl oz water
a knuckle-sized piece of ginger

For the mango sorbet
4–5 ripe mangoes
juice of 1 lime
250ml/9fl oz water
150g/5$^1/_2$oz caster sugar
25ml/1fl oz white wine

For the lime and ginger sorbet
5g/$^1/_5$oz piece of fresh ginger
250ml/9fl oz water
200g/7oz caster sugar
250ml/9fl oz lime juice (from about 12–15 limes)

SERVES 6–8

I love this combination of sweet, floral mango, the tartness of lime and the zing of fresh ginger. It makes a wonderful finish to a Chinese, Indian or Asian meal. Make sure you use properly ripe mangoes; the quality of the fruit determines the quality and flavour of the sorbet. You can use frozen mango purée if you can find it, but remember to reduce the sugar in the recipe by 10 per cent, as most brands contain 10 per cent added sugar.

The colours of these two sorbets are very striking together, so serve them next to one another in a funky glass or dish. Remember to freeze or chill the serving dishes first.

To make the lime zest garnish, you will need to use the zest from 2 of the limes for the sorbet. Cut the top and bottom from the limes so they sit flat on the chopping board. Using a vegetable peeler or a sharp knife, run the blade down the limes from top to bottom to remove the zest in small strips. Lay the strips of zest on the chopping board and remove any white pith from them, then cut them into fine matchsticks. Place them in a pan of boiling water and simmer for 10–15 minutes. Tip into a fine sieve and refresh by placing the sieve under cold running water for 30 seconds. Put 50g/1^3/4oz of the sugar in a small pan with 50ml/2fl oz of the water and bring to the boil, then add the lime strips and simmer for 10 minutes. Remove from the heat and let the lime cool in the syrup.

Peel the ginger and chop it into neat strips. Bring the remaining sugar and water to the boil in a small pan, add the ginger and cook over a low heat for 5–10 minutes, until soft. Leave to cool in the syrup.

Now make the sorbets. If the mangoes are ripe, you should not have to cook them first. Simply peel off the skins and cut the flesh from around the stones. Blitz to a purée with the lime juice in a blender, then pass the purée through a fine sieve. You will need 500g/1lb 2oz purée. Put the water and sugar in a pan and stir well, then bring to the boil. Remove from the heat and add the white wine. Add this mixture to the 500g/1lb 2oz mango purée and mix well. Churn in an ice-cream machine until frozen.

For the lime and ginger sorbet, peel the piece of ginger and cut it into very small pieces. Put the water, sugar, lime juice and ginger in a pan and bring to the boil. Remove from the heat and leave to infuse for 20 minutes, then pass through a fine sieve and leave to cool completely. Churn in an ice-cream machine until frozen.

Scoop the sorbets and serve in the same dish, decorated with the ginger and lime zest.

PINK CHAMPAGNE GRANITÉ

400g/14oz caster sugar
400ml/14fl oz water
juice of $\frac{1}{2}$ lemon
1 bottle of pink Champagne

SERVES 6—8

This is a great way to make a frozen palate cleanser or a luxurious, refreshing dessert without an ice-cream machine. You will need a deep baking tray in which to freeze the granité, or you could use one of the disposable foil ones intended for roasting meat. They allow you the luxury of using a brand-new tray at a very reasonable price. At home, I keep the foil ones especially for granité and use them more than once. Most brands are very strong and seem able to withstand several sessions of freezing.

Wild strawberries make for a perfect accompaniment. The delicate, sweet, floral taste complements the dryness of the pink Champagne. Redcurrants are also good, as used in the photograph opposite. Arrange the fruit around the edge of each glass, or simply place a large spoonful in the centre of the granité when it is in the glass.

Put a baking tray about 7.5cm/3 inches deep into the freezer; putting the granité in a pre-frozen tray speeds up the freezing process.

Put the sugar and water in a pan and bring to the boil, stirring to dissolve the sugar. Remove from the heat as soon as it boils and add the lemon juice. Let the syrup cool completely. Once it has cooled (and not before), open the Champagne and mix it with the syrup straight away. Pour the mixture into the frozen tray and place in the freezer. It will begin to freeze around the edges of the dish. When you see this start to happen, remove from the freezer and mix the granité well with a whisk. Whisk frequently as it freezes to break up the crystals and make fine flakes of Champagne ice – you will need to do this about every 20 minutes, depending on the efficiency of your freezer.

Once the tray is full of fine flakes that are completely frozen, the granité is ready. Serve in frozen pretty glass dishes or chilled Champagne flutes.

Claire's Notes
• Stored in a sealed plastic container, the granité will keep for a week and only need minimal mixing with a fork to fluff up the flakes.
• Serve between the main course and dessert to cleanse the palate, or after cheese and before dessert.
• I have made this with peach Champagne with great success.

ORANGE AND GRAND MARNIER SOUFFLÉ GLACÉ

8–10 large navel oranges (you will
    need 400ml/14fl oz juice)
800ml/28fl oz double cream
3 medium eggs, separated
150g/5oz icing sugar
1 tablespoon Grand Marnier

To decorate
2 large oranges
200ml/7fl oz double cream
1 tablespoon cocoa powder

SERVES 10

If the thought of making a hot soufflé scares you, then why not try a frozen one? It looks every inch as impressive and is a lovely way to complete a summer lunch. This recipe is very light and refreshing. Although you can make it with almost any flavour you choose, I like citrus flavours best, particularly lemon, lime and orange.

This dessert was a regular feature on our banqueting menu when I was at London's Intercontinental Hotel and, since I was a junior member of the team, it was one of the tasks on the preparation list that always fell to me. I wouldn't like to take a bet on how many I made over the long summer months during my three-year apprenticeship but I can tell you I do make rather a good soufflé glacé.

You will need a 15cm/6 inch diameter soufflé dish, about 7.5cm/3 inches deep, and a strip of white card that is 5cm/2 inches wide and long enough to wrap around the dish.

Using a microplane grater or other fine grater, zest 3 of the oranges. Bring a small pan of water to the boil, add the zest and simmer for 5 minutes. Pour through a small, fine sieve and run cold water over the zest for 30 seconds while it is still in the sieve to refresh and remove any of the bitterness.

Juice all the oranges, measure out 400ml/14fl oz and pass the juice through a fine sieve into a pan. Bring to the boil and simmer over a low heat until reduced by half. Leave to cool.

Whip the cream to soft peaks and store in the fridge.

Put the egg yolks in a bowl with half the icing sugar and whisk with an electric mixer until the mixture is pale and at least doubled in volume. It should be thick enough to leave a trail on the surface when drizzled from the whisk.

In a clean bowl, whisk the egg whites until they form stiff peaks. Add the remaining icing sugar in 3 stages, whisking well between each addition, until you have a firm meringue.

Add the reduced orange juice and the zest to the egg yolk mixture, then mix in the Grand Marnier. Gently fold in the egg whites; do not overmix. Lastly, carefully fold in the whipped cream.

Take the piece of white card and place it on the inside of the soufflé dish, wrapping it around so it overlaps slightly. It should fit snugly on the ridge, just below the rim. Make this as tight and secure as you can; it should be level and firm, not wobbly or slipping down at an angle. Secure it with sticky tape or a staple to keep it in a circle. Spoon the mixture into the soufflé dish and level the top with a palette knife to give a smooth finish. Place the dish in the freezer for 3–4 hours, until completely frozen.

To serve, remove the dish from the freezer and untape or remove the staple from the piece of card. The soufflé must be firmly frozen for you to do this. Run a small knife between the card and the soufflé to release the card. Again, if the soufflé is firmly frozen, this will be easy and the card will come away neatly. Place the soufflé back in the freezer while you prepare the decoration.

With a small, sharp knife, cut the tops and bottoms off the oranges so they sit flat on the work surface. Slice off all the peel and pith, working downwards in small sections. The fruit should not have any white pith still attached to it. Pick up each fruit and cut out each segment from between the membranes, keeping the knife as close to the membrane as you can to make neat, clean orange segments.

Whip the cream to firm peaks. Remove the soufflé from the freezer and pipe 10–12 bulbs of cream around the edge, using a piping bag fitted with a 1cm/$^1/_2$ inch plain nozzle. Lightly dust the cream and the surface of the soufflé with the cocoa powder. Place one orange segment on each bulb of cream.

Leave for 15–20 minutes at room temperature for the soufflé to soften slightly before serving. It should be soft enough to cut into portions and remove from the dish without the portion losing its shape. I use a knife and a palette knife. Insert both into the dish on either side of the first portion you have cut and lift both up at the same time. The first portion is always the hardest to remove, so keep that for yourself and serve the remaining slices to your guests.

Claire's Notes

• Once you have cut the orange segments, put them on a piece of kitchen paper to absorb some of the moisture; they will look better when you place them on the cream.

MINT CHOCOLATE CHIP ICE CREAM SANDWICHES

For the mint chocolate chip parfait

a small bunch of fresh spearmint
250ml/9fl oz whole milk
6 medium egg yolks
200g/7oz caster sugar
350ml/12fl oz double cream
50g/1³/₄oz dark chocolate (55 per cent cocoa solids), finely grated
a little green food colouring (optional)

For the sablé biscuits

260g/9¹/₄oz softened unsalted butter
75g/2³/₄oz icing sugar
1 small egg, lightly beaten
250g/9oz plain flour
50g/1³/₄oz cocoa powder
75g/2³/₄oz ground almonds

MAKES 18

Claire's Notes

• You can make the biscuits on the same day as the parfait and keep them in an airtight tin. When you want to serve them, simply unmould the parfaits and sandwich with the sablés.
• For extra indulgence, sandwich the biscuits with the parfait, then place them back in the freezer for 1 hour to firm. Dunk them in a bowl of melted dark chocolate. As the biscuits are frozen, the chocolate should set almost immediately; if not, place them back in the freezer for a few minutes before serving.
• When using the blowtorch be careful not to leave it in one spot for any length of time or the parfait will melt and lose its shape.

I had never actually made these until I started writing this book but they were inspired by America's famous Oreo cookies. Bouchon Bakery, Thomas Keller's wonderful pastry shop here in Yountville where I live, heaves with fancy cakes, Danish pastries, tarts and cookies. I am unable to visit without sampling one of the goodies from the laden pâtisserie counter and it was here that I tasted my first TKO, Bouchon's own version of the Oreo. The 'Keller Oreo' – a light, crisp cocoa sablé biscuit that melts in the mouth, sandwiched with a generous dollop of mint and white chocolate ganache – is nothing like the ones you buy in supermarkets. I think my weakness for mint chocolate chip ice cream might have had a part to play in my English version of the TKO.

Place the leaves from the bunch of mint in a pan with the milk and bring to the boil. Remove from the heat and leave to infuse for 10 minutes. Bring back to the boil and then pass through a fine sieve.

Mix the egg yolks with the sugar in a bowl and gradually stir in the hot milk. Return the mixture to a clean pan and cook over a low heat, stirring constantly with a wooden spoon, until the mixture thickens enough to coat the back of the spoon. Pass this custard through a fine sieve into a bowl, place the bowl over a larger bowl of ice and leave to cool. Meanwhile, semi-whip the cream to medium peaks and store in the fridge.

When the custard is cold, whisk it with a handheld electric mixer until it is very light. Fold in the semi-whipped cream. Add the finely grated chocolate and a little green food colouring, if desired (you can do this by dipping a cocktail stick into the colouring, then into the parfait mixture, to avoid adding too much).

Line 2 baking trays with baking parchment and place 18 ring moulds, about 7.5cm/3 inches in diameter and 4cm/1¹/₂ inches deep, on them. Fill them with the parfait mixture, using a piping bag, then smooth over the tops with a palette knife or spatula. Freeze for 24 hours.

To make the biscuits, cream together the butter and icing sugar, then beat in the egg. Sift the flour, cocoa powder and ground almonds together and add to the creamed mixture. Bring together to form a dough but do not overwork it. If using an electric mixer, fold in the dry ingredients by hand.

Put the dough on a large sheet of baking parchment and place another sheet on top. Using a rolling pin, roll out the dough between the sheets to about 5mm/¹/₄ inch thick (rolling the dough between parchment makes it easier to handle). Place the dough, still in the paper, on a baking sheet and chill for 2 hours.

Preheat the oven to 180°C/350°F/Gas Mark 4. Remove the top sheet of paper and prick the dough well with a fork. Cut out 36 circles using a 7.5cm/3 inch fluted cutter and place on baking sheets lined with baking parchment. Bake for about 20 minutes, until crisp. Leave to cool on the trays.

Release the parfait from the rings. You can do this with a blowtorch, holding it about 15cm/6 inches away from the mould to warm it and turning the mould as you do so. If you don't have a blowtorch, wrap a hot, damp cloth around each ring until it can be easily removed. Sandwich each one between 2 sablés and serve.

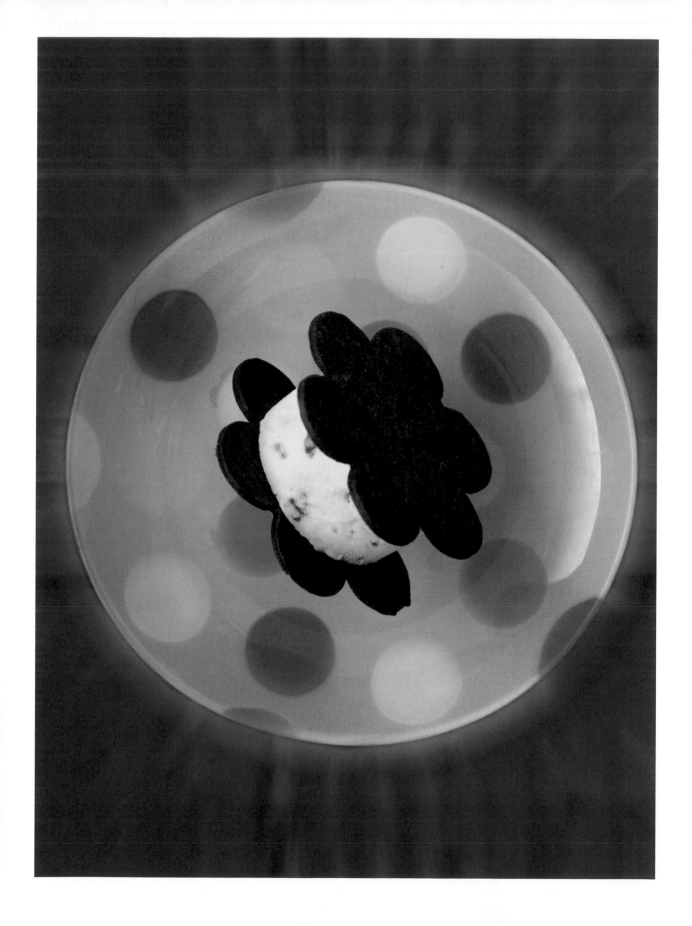

PETITS FOURS

THE SECRETS OF SUCCESS

TEMPERING CHOCOLATE

Tempering is necessary to bring chocolate back to the correct crystalline form once it has been melted. It is essential whenever you are using chocolate to make decorations or for finishing purposes, such as coating cookies and petits fours or dipping chocolate truffles. When the crystals in the chocolate are stable, it will be firm and easy to work with, whereas if it contains too many unstable crystals it will be uneven and streaky. Tempering encourages the formation of the right kind of crystals.

Successfully tempered chocolate has the following desirable properties:

• A high gloss
• A resistance to warmth
• A pleasant aroma
• A smooth mouth-feel
• A longer shelf life
• A good snap – the chocolate is crisp and snaps when broken

Undesirable qualities are:

• A white/grey colour or white streaks
• Vulnerability to warmth
• A dull appearance
• A soft, flexible consistency

Before the chocolate can be tempered, it needs to be melted. Never let it come into direct contact with the heat source: it will burn. The best way to melt it at home is in a bowl placed over a pan of gently simmering water. Here are the correct melting temperatures for chocolate:

Dark chocolate
• Melt until it reaches 40–45°C/104–113°F
• Cool to 27–28°C/80–82°F
• Reheat to a working temperature of 31–32°C/88–89°F

Milk chocolate
• Melt until it reaches 32.5°C/90°F
• Cool to 27–28°C/80–82°F
• Reheat to a working temperature of no more than 30°C/86°F

White chocolate
• Melt until it reaches 30.5°C/87°F
• Cool to 27°C/80°F
• Reheat to a working temperature of 28°C/82°F

You will need a chocolate thermometer in order to get accurate readings of the temperatures. Domestic chocolate tempering machines are available. They are not cheap but they do work very well, and are worth considering if you plan to do large amounts of chocolate work regularly at home.

Although many recipes in this book need only a little tempered chocolate for decoration, 300g/10$\frac{1}{2}$oz is specified in the ingredients list, as it's not practical to temper any smaller an amount. Decorations made from tempered chocolate will keep for 3 months in a sealed container in the fridge. Any leftover tempered chocolate can be poured on to a piece of baking parchment, left to harden and then chopped up ready for cooking in recipes.

What follows is a step-by-step guide to tempering chocolate at home.

1. Working in a cool, draught-free environment (ideally the room temperature should be no more than 21°C/70°F), chop the chocolate as finely as you can with a large, sharp knife. Place a little over two-thirds of the chocolate into a clean bowl, preferably a metal one.

2. Place the bowl over a pan of simmering water, making sure the water does not touch the base of the bowl. There should be no water or steam coming up around the sides of the bowl (if any steam or drops of water came into contact with the chocolate, it would 'seize' and be unworkable). The water should be simmering gently, not boiling.

3. Melt the chocolate to the temperature specified above, using a chocolate thermometer to check it. Stir very gently with a spatula as it melts and do not leave it unattended at any time. When the chocolate is nearly two-thirds melted, remove the bowl from the pan of water and place it on a folded dry kitchen cloth. This prevents the bowl sitting directly on the work surface, which would cool it too quickly, and also keeps the bottom of the bowl dry.

4. Continue to stir gently; the heat of the chocolate and of the bowl will help to melt the remaining pieces of chocolate. Add a tablespoon of the remaining chopped chocolate and stir until it has melted. This process is known as seeding. Keep adding a tablespoon of the finely chopped chocolate and stirring gently. The temperature of the chocolate will be reduced. Be careful not to add so much chocolate that it no longer melts. The aim is to reduce the temperature of the melted chocolate by adding small, room-temperature, crystalline pieces of chocolate.

5. When the pieces of chocolate no longer melt, stop adding them. The precrystallising state has now started, the chocolate is beginning to come down in temperature and the crystals are starting to form a stable structure. The chocolate now needs to cool to a temperature of 27–28°C/80–82°F. If you leave the chocolate in a cool place and stir it from time to time, it will come down in temperature by itself. The amount of time it takes to do this depends on the working environment. The cooler the environment, the quicker the desirable temperature will be reached – as a rough guideline, it should take about 10–15 minutes on a normal British day or in an airconditioned room. Use the thermometer to keep a check on the temperature.

6. Once the chocolate has reached the correct temperature, it is at a stable level and fully tempered, but it is not at the best temperature for working with. So place the bowl back over the pan of simmering water and bring it up to the working temperature given above. As this is only a few degrees higher and you will be tempering a relatively small amount of chocolate, extreme caution should be taken to avoid bringing the chocolate past the ideal temperature. (If this does happen, simply restart the cooling process and bring it back down to 27–28°C/80–82°F.) I suggest you place the bowl back over the simmering water for only a few seconds, as it will heat up very quickly and retain enough heat to bring the chocolate past the ideal temperature. Remove the bowl after 5 seconds and stir gently, then test with the chocolate thermometer. If it is not at the correct temperature, keep placing the bowl back over the pan of simmering water for only a few seconds at a time until the ideal temperature is reached.

7. You can test the chocolate to see if it has all the desirable qualities by dipping the tip of a knife into it and placing the knife in a cool place. It should set in an even manner, be free of white streaks and have a high shine and gloss. If it's not right, simply start the tempering process again.

8. Keep the bowl of tempered chocolate resting on the folded kitchen cloth while you work with it according to the instructions in your recipe. If it begins to cool down, you can warm it again so long as it does not go past the working temperature.

TEMPERING CHOCOLATE IN A MICROWAVE

The microwave is a fast way of tempering a small amount of chocolate (but never less than 250g) but you need to be very careful, as the chocolate is more likely to burn. Follow the steps described above but use the microwave to melt the chocolate and bring it back to working temperature. It is vital that the microwave is on half power. Melt the chocolate gradually, just a few minutes at a time and, when you are trying to achieve the working temperature, just a few seconds at a time. Stir the chocolate frequently during the melting process.

MAKING CHOCOLATE CURLS

It does take a while to get the technique right for chocolate curls but, once you have mastered it, it becomes a quick garnish for so many desserts and cakes. The secret is having the chocolate at the right temperature and using a lower-quality chocolate, such as baker's chocolate, that contains vegetable fat and not cocoa butter. This allows the curls to roll and not splinter as you make them.

You will need a cheese slicer to form the curls. Simply pull the slicer flat over the smooth side of a large block of chocolate so that it peels off in a curl. It's worth buying a couple of blocks of chocolate so you can practise until you have perfected your curls – you will need a block weighing about 250g to make decent ones. Keep the chocolate at room temperature before use. If it seems a little soft, firm it in the fridge for 5–10 minutes; if it splinters and refuses to curl, place the block in a warm place, such as near a radiator or a turned-on stove.

You can store the curls in a sealed plastic container in the fridge. They will keep for at least four weeks.

PIPING

You may wonder why I recommend piping almost everything into moulds or on to baking trays. It is a question of uniformity. Once you have mastered the art of controlling a piping bag, it allows you to pipe even amounts of a mixture, whether it is mousse, meringue, choux paste, cream or sponge batters. This yields regular portions and consistently neat and uniform shapes, such as éclairs, meringue discs and cream rosettes.

USING A PIPING BAG

1. Until you become skilled in using a piping bag, it does help to cut off the end of the bag to insert the piping nozzle. Cut the bag, insert the nozzle, then fold the bag back where the nozzle is and secure with a bulldog clip to keep it in place, so nothing can leak out.
2. Fold back the top of the piping bag over your left hand (assuming you are right handed) and make the opening as wide as possible. For beginners, this can be done by placing the bag in a large measuring jug and folding the top of the bag over the rim of the jug; this leaves both hands free to fill the bag.
3. Fill the bag using a spoon or ladle, but take care not to fill it too high; about half way is sufficient. If the bag is too full, it will be difficult to control.
4. Take the bag from the jug and seal the top by bringing the opening together and twisting it closed. Clench it tightly in your right hand, making sure your hand is sitting firmly around the top of the bag where it meets the filling. This is very important, as the pressure needs to come from the top of the bag. If you squeeze from the middle, the mix above your hand will travel up the bag and come out of the top, which is not being held closed by your hand.
5. Now hold the bag pointing downwards towards the baking sheet or vessel you are filling and squeeze

gently. This needs to be a controlled motion. The more firmly you squeeze, the quicker the mix will come out of the bag. Do not squeeze the bag until it is in the glass or 2.5cm/1 inch from the baking sheet. To stop the mix coming out, simply stop the pressure and lift the tip of the bag upwards.
6. As the bag empties, remember to move your grip on the top of the bag so it is always firmly on top of the mix.

A good way to practise is to use Trex or other vegetable shortening. It is soft enough to pipe straight from the fridge but firm enough to control. Simply pipe out different shapes, such as buns or fingers, on a worktop. You can keep scraping it up and refilling the bag for as long as it takes to master the art.

MAKING A PAPER PIPING BAG

If you are piping small amounts of chocolate, you can make a paper piping bag, as follows:

1. Cut out a rectangle of baking parchment approximately 25 x 20cm/10 x 8 inches. Cut the rectangle in half diagonally to make 2 triangles.
2. Using one triangle, place it flat on the work surface so the right angle of the triangle is pointing towards your right elbow (assuming you are right handed). Curl the top point over to meet the right angle and form a cone shape.
3. Wrap the remaining long side around the outside of the cone, making sure the point of the cone doesn't come open.
4. Fold the points over twice to secure the cone.

Remember not to overfill the piping bag with chocolate, or it will be difficult to handle and will come out of the top of the bag. After filling the bag, roll the top down to secure the chocolate inside whilst piping. Snip the pointed end of the cone to make a small opening – the wider the opening, the thicker the chocolate piping will be.

LANGUES DE CHAT

125g/4^1/$_2$oz softened unsalted
   butter, plus a little melted butter
   for greasing the baking sheet
125g/4^1/$_2$oz icing sugar
1 teaspoon vanilla extract
2 small egg whites
175g/6oz plain flour

MAKES 50

Langues de chat – or 'cat's tongues', as they translate – are buttery biscuits often used to accompany ice creams and sorbets. When fresh out of the oven, they are also wonderful for scooping up leftover lemon curd or homemade strawberry jam, and fantastic for dunking in your mid-morning cup of tea. They should be golden and crisp around the edges, a little paler in the centre.

I like them so much with ices that I hardly ever bother with a spoon, I just use the langue de chat to scoop up the ice cream. Of course, this does mean you will need more than one or two per person, but who's counting!

Preheat the oven to 170°C/325°F/Gas Mark 3. You could cook the langues de chat on nonstick baking mats but I like the crispness a greased baking sheet gives to the underside of the biscuits. Prepare 2 large baking sheets by greasing them well with melted butter, then put them in the fridge to firm the butter.

Put the softened butter in a bowl, sift in the icing sugar and cream together until pale and fluffy. Add the vanilla to the egg whites and mix them into the creamed batter. There is no need to whisk or beat them in, but do make sure they are well incorporated. Sift the flour and fold it into the batter with a large metal spoon. Do not overwork the mixture or it will be tight and heavy. If you are making it in an electric mixer, make sure you fold in the flour by hand.

Transfer the mixture to a piping bag fitted with a 5mm/^{1}/$_4$ inch plain nozzle. Remove the chilled trays from the fridge and dust finely with plain flour. Pipe straight sticks about 10cm/4 inches long, leaving a little space between each biscuit, as they spread during baking.

Bake in the centre of the oven for 8–10 minutes, until the edges are golden and the middle slightly lighter. Cool slightly, then remove from the baking tray and leave on a wire rack to cool completely.

Claire's Notes
• Lemon or orange zest makes a change from the classic vanilla flavouring, especially if you are serving them with a citrus sorbet or the Orange and Grand Marnier Soufflé Glacé on page 206.

HONEY MADELEINES

90g/3^{1}/$_{4}$oz unsalted butter, plus 30g/1oz melted butter for greasing the tins
2 teaspoons clear honey
2 medium eggs
75g/2^{3}/$_{4}$oz caster sugar
10g/^{1}/$_{4}$oz soft dark brown sugar
a pinch of salt
a few drops of vanilla extract
90g/3^{1}/$_{4}$oz plain flour
^{1}/$_{2}$ teaspoon baking powder

MAKES 14 LARGE OR 40 SMALL MADELEINES

These voluptuous little cakes are instantly recognisable by their scalloped shell shape and domed underside. The story goes that a girl named Madeleine from the town of Commercy in France made them for the Duke of Lorraine, who gave some to his daughter, Marie, the wife of Louis XV. From that point on they grew in favour, so much so that today they are popular all over the world. I love this passage from Marcel Proust's novel, Remembrance of Things Past: *'She sent out for one of those short, plump little cakes called* petites *Madeleines, which look as though they had been moulded in the fluted scallop of a pilgrim's shell ... And soon ... an exquisite pleasure had invaded my senses.'*

My thanks to Michel Roux, of The Waterside Inn at Bray, for this delightful, foolproof recipe.

Preheat the oven to 220°C/425°F/Gas Mark 7. Brush the madeleine moulds with the melted butter.

Put the 90g/3^{1}/$_{4}$oz butter in a small pan with the honey and melt it, then cool slightly. Put the eggs in a large bowl with both the sugars, the salt and vanilla. Whisk until pale and doubled in volume. Sift the flour and baking powder together, then sift a second time. Fold them into the egg mixture with a large metal spoon, being careful not to lose any volume.

Pour the melted butter and honey down the side of the bowl so it floods on top of the mixture. Fold in gently, still being careful not to lose any volume. Cover the bowl with cling film and leave to rest in a cool place for 30 minutes.

Put the mixture into a piping bag fitted with a plain 1cm/^{1}/$_{2}$ inch nozzle and pipe it into the prepared madeleine tins, piping a fat, even, solid line down the centre of each one. The mix will spread in the oven during baking, so there is no need for it to touch the sides of the mould. Place in the oven and bake for no more than 5 minutes for small madeleines, 10 minutes for large ones. Do not overcook them or they will be dry. As soon as they are done, flip over the moulds and turn them out on to a wire rack. Serve warm.

Claire's Notes
• If you are going to purchase madeleine moulds, I recommend you buy the metal ones. The flexible silicone moulds do not colour in quite the same fashion for this particular cake. I really like the crisp golden crumb the butter gives on the outside of the cake, in contrast to the light sponge centre. The metal moulds give perfect results.
• The madeleines are best eaten warm. If you do have any left over, they make wonderful crumbs for Apple, Cinnamon and Sultana Strudel (see page 85) instead of breadcrumbs. Just dry them in an oven preheated to 120°C/250°F/Gas Mark ^{1}/$_{2}$ until crisp, then crush to crumbs in a food processor.

VENUS NIPPLES

400g/14oz white chocolate
   (30–35 per cent cocoa butter),
   very finely chopped
200ml/7fl oz double cream
1 teaspoon instant coffee granules
25ml/1fl oz Tia Maria
1 tablespoon brandy
500g/1lb 2oz tempered white
   chocolate (see pages 212–213)
300g/10$^{1}/_{2}$oz tempered dark
   chocolate (see pages 212–213)

MAKES 50

This recipe is based on one from a very good friend of mine, Sara Jayne Stanes. Sara is not only the director of the Academy of Culinary Arts but a chocolate historian and author of Chocolate – the Definitive Guide. *One year I was lucky enough to be given the most delightful box of chocolates I have ever seen. Sara had made the aptly named Venus nipples, wrapped them in deep red tissue paper and placed them in a velvet black box tied up with the most decadently luxurious red ribbon. I was in heaven.*

Put the finely chopped white chocolate in a bowl. Bring the cream to the boil with the coffee granules, then pour it over the chopped chocolate. Mix well with a hand whisk to create a smooth, shiny ganache. Add the Tia Maria and brandy and mix well, then leave to cool.

Have ready a baking tray lined with baking parchment and a piping bag fitted with a 1cm/$^{1}/_{2}$ inch plain nozzle. Whisk the cooled ganache until it thickens to a soft piping consistency. Do not whisk past this stage, or the ganache will firm and set before you can pipe it. Quickly pipe the ganache into 2cm/$^{3}/_{4}$ inch bulbs on the lined tray, leaving a tip at the top of each bulb to create a nipple effect. The easiest way to do this is to lift the piping bag up as you pipe and then stop squeezing the bag but pull it up quickly. The chocolates are more interesting if they are not all exactly the same size and shape, so don't worry too much – as long as they are smaller at the top than at the bottom, you are on the right track.

Leave the tray of piped ganache in the fridge for an hour to firm (you can temper the chocolate in the meantime).

Dip each chocolate one at a time into the tempered white chocolate, using a dipping fork. Slide the chocolate off the flat dipping fork on to another tray lined with fresh baking parchment and leave to set. Then pick up each dipped white chocolate and dip just the top into the tempered dark chocolate. Leave to set once more. Store in a sealed plastic container in the fridge for up to 2 weeks. Make sure the container has a tight-fitting lid to prevent the chocolates sweating.

Claire's Notes
• If your ganache gets too firm before you can pipe it, heat it gently over a pan of simmering water or in a microwave. Make sure you do not melt it too much; there should be some solid ganache to whisk into the melted part to make a pipable consistency.
• If you do not have a dipping fork, wear a pair of tight-fitting thin, disposable latex gloves. Pick up the piped ganache from the top and dip the base part into the tempered white chocolate as far as you can without getting too messy. Once the white chocolate has set, dip the tip of the chocolate into the dark chocolate, making sure it completely covers the ganache.

VERJUS-PLUMPED RAISIN FINANCIERS

a little spray oil or melted butter
100ml/3^1/$_2$fl oz white verjus
100g/3^1/$_2$oz Californian raisins
125g/4^1/$_2$oz unsalted butter
4 medium egg whites
125g/4^1/$_2$oz caster sugar
50g/1^3/$_4$oz ground almonds
50g/1^3/$_4$oz plain flour

For the icing
100g/3^1/$_2$oz icing sugar
2–3 tablespoons verjus

MAKES ABOUT 40

Claire's Notes
• Verjus is the tart juice of unripe grapes. It is bottled and used extensively as a culinary ingredient here in California and many wine-growing regions of the world. I have found it in British supermarkets, so keep a look out for it in the vinegar section. If you cannot find it, use kirsch or white wine instead.

These moist little almond cakes are said to have become popular in the financial district of Paris, with the name, financier, *deriving from the traditional rectangular shape, which is supposed to resemble a bar of gold. They are made with beurre noisette (brown butter), which gives them a wonderful rich, nutty flavour. The aroma while they are in the oven is so tantalising that they never linger much past the warm stage, which is how I like to serve them. However, due to the high ratio of ground almonds, which keeps the cakes moist, they store well in an airtight tin and can be heated up successfully. If you don't have any rectangular moulds, make them in barquette moulds or small tartlet or petit four tins. The flexible silicone ones work particularly well here and come in various shapes and sizes. You can find them in any good kitchen shop.*

My recipe uses Californian raisins, which I plump up in warm verjus, but almost any dried or fresh fruit works well. If you are using fresh fruit, there is no need to soak it first. Figs, raspberries, dates, blueberries and cranberries are wonderful, as are stone fruits such as apricots, peaches, cherries and mangoes.

Preheat the oven to 170°C/325°F/Gas Mark 3. Lightly grease your moulds with spray oil or melted butter.

Bring the verjus to the boil, then lower the heat and add the raisins. Cook gently until all the liquid has been absorbed and the raisins have plumped up. Remove from the heat and leave to cool.

To make the beurre noisette, gently melt the butter in a small pan. Turn up the heat to medium and leave the butter on the stove until it starts to turn brown. Remove from the heat and pass through a sieve lined with a piece of muslin to remove the pieces of brown sediment. Keep the brown butter warm on the side of the stove. It should not be hot but you do not want it to start to cool so much that it begins to firm.

Put the egg whites and sugar in a large bowl and, using an electric beater, whisk to a stiff meringue. If you do this by hand, you will need to add the sugar in 3 stages, whisking well between each addition. Sift the ground almonds and flour together. Using a large metal spoon, carefully fold them into the meringue; do this as gently as possible so as not to lose any volume. Once all the dry ingredients are folded through the meringue, gently pour the beurre noisette down the side of the bowl so it flows on top of the mixture. Carefully fold this in, once again being careful not to lose any volume.

Pipe the mixture into the moulds, filling them no more than half way. Place a spoonful of the plumped raisins into the top of each cake, pushing them in slightly. Bake for 12–15 minutes, until they are well risen and golden brown and spring back when pressed lightly.

While they are baking, mix the icing sugar with enough verjus to make a transparent icing. Brush the icing over the cakes the minute you remove them from the oven. Place back in the oven for 2–3 minutes to set the glaze. Cool just enough to allow you to remove them from the tins, then serve immediately.

WALNUT AND PISTACHIO MARZIPAN

500g/1lb 2oz blanched almonds,
  roughly chopped
360g/12³/₄oz icing sugar, plus a
  little extra for rolling
50g/1³/₄oz shelled peeled
  pistachio nuts, finely chopped
3 medium egg whites
a little green food colouring

To finish
100g/3¹/₂oz baker's chocolate
  (cooking chocolate), chopped –
  or use a little dark tempered
  chocolate (see pages 212–213)
300g/10¹/₂oz walnut halves
500g/1lb 2oz tempered dark
  chocolate (optional)

MAKES 60

Claire's Notes
• You can make the marzipan in a
food processor but be careful not
to overmix or it will be oily. Using
the pulse setting, gently bring the
ingredients together until they
almost form a smooth ball, then
turn it out and work it by hand to
smooth completely.
• Try a selection of fancy cutters
for pretty shapes and designs.
• You could use hazelnuts and
pecans as well as walnuts.

These make an easy petit four to enjoy with coffee or prepare as a gift for anyone who loves marzipan. They are so simple to do and look very impressive. Making marzipan is not hard but you will need a coffee grinder or a food processor for the almonds. If you do not feel up to making your own marzipan from scratch, you can use ready-ground almonds, or you can simply use bought marzipan and mix the pistachios into it, then follow the procedure for shaping the petits fours.

Place the chopped almonds in a coffee grinder or food processor a little at a time and grind to a fine powder. Sift the icing sugar and ground almonds together on to a piece of baking parchment and add the finely chopped pistachio nuts.

Whisk the egg whites to a soft foam and add the nut and icing sugar mixture a little at a time, working the ingredients together to form a soft dough. Knead them together as they become firmer, adding more icing sugar if necessary to make the marzipan soft but not sticky. Add a few drops of food colouring and work it through the mixture, then shape the marzipan into a ball. Turn it out on to a work surface lightly dusted with icing sugar and knead to mix in the colour evenly. Dust the surface of the marzipan with a little icing sugar and then roll it out to 1cm/¹/₂ inch thick.

Using a plain round 4cm/1¹/₂ inch cutter, cut out discs of marzipan. Lay them on a baking tray lined with baking parchment so they are not touching. Re-roll the marzipan and cut out more discs until you have used up all the marzipan.

Melt the cooking chocolate in a bowl set over a pan of simmering water, making sure the water is not touching the base of the bowl. Fill a disposable plastic or paper piping bag with the chocolate. Cut a very small hole in the bottom and pipe a small bulb of chocolate on to 10 of the marzipan discs. Stick a walnut half on each of the discs, pressing them firmly into the melted chocolate. Do another 10 and keep repeating the procedure until all the discs have walnuts on them.

For a special finish, dip the discs into tempered dark chocolate. Before attempting to dip them, let them sit, uncovered, on the tray for 1 hour to firm up a little and form a skin. Then, holding them by the walnut, dip them up to the surface of the marzipan disc but not on to the walnut. Place them back on the tray, walnut-side up, for the chocolate to set before serving.

These keep really well in a sealed container for up to 4 weeks. If you do not want to make all the marzipan into petits fours, it will keep, tightly wrapped in a plastic bag in a sealed container, for up to 8 weeks.

STRAWBERRY, BLACK PEPPER AND BALSAMIC VINEGAR TRUFFLES

300g/10$\frac{1}{2}$oz white chocolate,
  finely chopped
150g/5$\frac{1}{2}$oz dark chocolate (55–60
  per cent cocoa solids), finely
  chopped
2 teaspoons balsamic vinegar
200ml/7fl oz double cream
1 teaspoon cracked black pepper
500g/1lb 2oz tempered white
  chocolate (see pages 212–213)

For the strawberry flakes
500g/1lb 2oz strawberries
2 teaspoons cracked black pepper

MAKES ABOUT 40

Claire's Notes
• Make the strawberry flakes the
day before and store them in an
airtight tin.
• Have the ganache made, piped
and in the fridge before you
temper the chocolate.
• I pick strawberries when they are
at their best in June and freeze
them. This way I can make the
truffles all year round with quality
fruit. Very ripe berries are perfect
for this recipe.

This recipe looks a little involved but it really is worth the effort. I love the days I get to make chocolates, which is nearly every day. I often think how lucky I am to start my day with a large pot of melted chocolate and finish it with bountiful amounts of beautifully crafted handmade chocolates!

Preheat the oven to 110°C/225°F/Gas Mark $\frac{1}{4}$. To make the strawberry flakes, blitz the strawberries to a purée in a blender until very smooth. Do not sieve it. Set aside a tablespoon of the purée for the truffles. Line two baking trays with nonstick baking mats and spread the purée out as thinly and evenly as possible, using an angled palette knife. Place the trays in the oven and leave the purée to dry and crisp for about 1$\frac{1}{2}$ hours. As the purée dries, it will change from light red to a darker shade. Be careful it does not become brown. If this does happen, reduce the oven temperature slightly. When the purée is done, remove the trays from the oven and let it cool completely. Once it is cold, it should be very firm and crisp

Meanwhile, make the ganache filling. Place the finely chopped white and dark chocolate in a bowl with the balsamic vinegar and the reserved tablespoon of strawberry purée. Bring the cream to the boil, pour it over the chocolate and whisk gently with a hand whisk to a smooth, shiny ganache. Mix in the cracked black pepper. Cover the bowl with cling film and let it cool completely at room temperature.

Line a baking tray with baking parchment and fit a piping bag with a 1cm/$\frac{1}{2}$ inch plain nozzle. When the ganache is cold, whisk it by hand for a minute or two until it thickens slightly, then quickly transfer it to the piping bag and pipe straight lines, about 2.5cm/1 inch apart, down the length of the lined baking tray. Place the tray in the fridge to chill for 2 hours, until the ganache is firm to the touch.

Turn the baking mats containing the dried strawberry purée over on to a piece of baking parchment and pull back each mat so the sheet of purée is on the paper. It should be very crisp and brittle and break into small flakes when crushed by hand. If it is not brittle, place it back in the oven to continue the drying process. Crush the brittle purée into small flakes and mix with the 2 teaspoons of cracked black pepper. Spread this mixture over a parchment-lined tray so it forms a thin, even layer, about 2mm/$\frac{1}{12}$ inch thick.

Take the tray from the fridge and cut across the piped ganache using a bread knife to make sticks about 4cm/1$\frac{1}{2}$ inches long. Warm the bread knife in a jug of hot water and dry it well before cutting the ganache. Do this each time you make a cut.

Take 10 pieces of ganache at a time, keeping the remaining ganache cool in the fridge, and dip them one at a time into the bowl of tempered white chocolate, using a dipping fork. Remove the chocolates with the fork and drop them on to the tray of strawberry flakes. After you have dipped 5 chocolates, before they set, sprinkle a little of the dried strawberry and black pepper over the top. Repeat the process until you have dipped all the cut ganache.

Once the truffles have set, you can lift them off the tray and on to a plate. Store in the fridge in an airtight container.

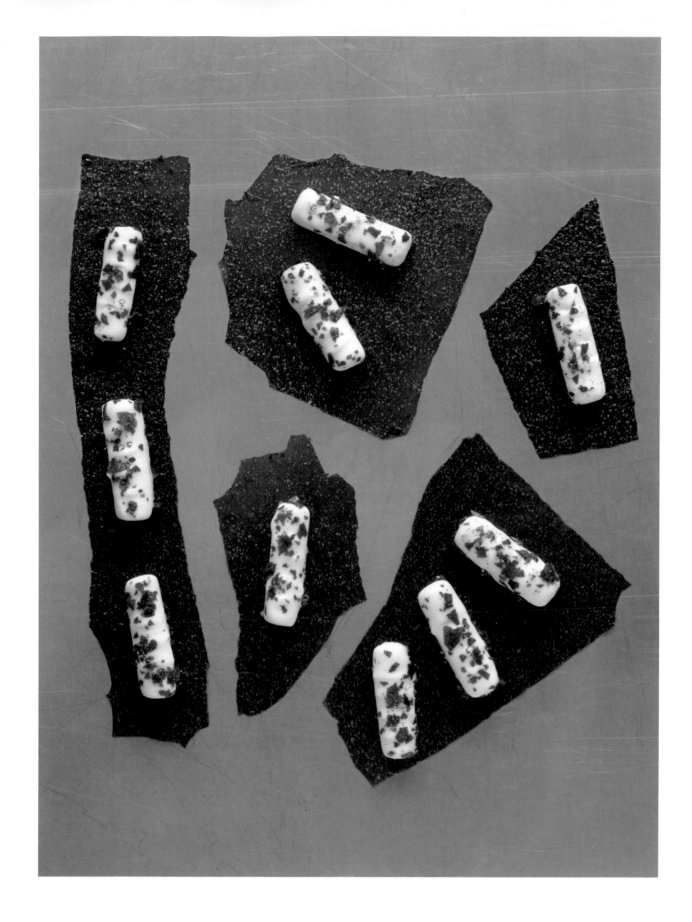

PINK CHAMPAGNE TRUFFLES

250g/9oz dark chocolate (70 per cent cocoa solids), finely chopped

200g/7oz milk chocolate (40 per cent cocoa solids), finely chopped

100ml/3^1/$_2$fl oz double cream

65g/2^1/$_4$oz unsalted butter

100ml/3^1/$_2$fl oz pink Champagne

4 teaspoons brandy

500g/1lb 2oz icing sugar

10g/^{1}/$_4$oz red berry powder, if available

750g/1lb 10oz tempered dark chocolate (see pages 212–213)

MAKES 40—50

Champagne truffles are one of life's little luxuries. Is there a woman out there who would not admit to having a penchant for the odd Champagne truffle from time to time? Well, this gem of a recipe combines dark and milk chocolate for an exquisite flavour. Too much dark chocolate does not balance with the delicate taste of the pink Champagne, while too much milk chocolate makes it too creamy. The proportions below give the perfect balance for the perfect pink Champagne truffle.

Put the chopped dark and milk chocolate in a bowl. Put the cream and butter in a pan and bring to the boil, then pour the mixture over the chocolate. Leave for 30 seconds, then add the Champagne and brandy. Mix gently with a fine whisk, whisking only enough to combine the ingredients into a smooth ganache.

Pour the mixture on to a plastic tray or into a large, wide bowl. The ganache needs to cool quickly and evenly, so a large surface area is best. Leave to cool at room temperature until it is firm enough to pipe. Using a piping bag fitted with a 1cm/^{1}/$_2$ inch plain nozzle, pipe blobs 2.5cm/1 inch in diameter on to a tray lined with baking parchment. Place in the fridge until they are set firm.

Remove the truffles from the fridge and, with your hands dipped and coated in icing sugar, roll them into even balls. Return them to the fridge to firm up again.

Sift the remaining icing sugar on to a tray with the red berry powder, if using. Put the tempered chocolate in a bowl. With a dipping fork, dip the truffles in the tempered chocolate and then roll them in the icing sugar mixture. Leave them in the tray of icing sugar until they are set – this will help them retain a good shape. Store in a sealed container in the fridge.

Claire's Notes
• If you cannot find red berry powder, use a spice grinder to grind down some of the freeze-dried red berries that are now available. It works a treat.
• If you do not have a dipping fork, dip the truffles into the chocolate with your hand. Dip them one at a time and keep the truffle at the side of the bowl, rolling it in the chocolate on the top. Do not immerse it in the middle of the pot where it will be difficult to retrieve. Rolling it on the side of the bowl helps remove the excess chocolate.

ALMOND ROCHES

500g/1lb 2oz strip or baton almonds (or whole blanched almonds, roughly chopped)
25ml/1fl oz Cointreau
100g/3^1/$_2$oz icing sugar, sifted
100g/3^1/$_2$oz cocoa butter (or good-quality hazelnut oil)
500g/1lb 2oz tempered milk chocolate (see pages 212–213)

MAKES ABOUT 40

Claire's Notes

• If the chocolate is setting too quickly and the roches do not look smooth, check the following points:
– Are you working in a draught?
– Is the room too cold?
– Is the cocoa butter warm enough?
– Is the milk chocolate below 28°C/82°F (see page 212)?

If your friends like almonds, these are the perfect solution to gifts or after-dinner petits fours. The important thing to remember is that although they look simple, simplicity is not always easy to achieve. There is a definite technique to making the roches look stunning. Follow the instructions below and I promise you your clusters will have the edge; you will be the envy of every roche maker. The secret is the ratio of cocoa butter to chocolate and a cool working environment – avoid draughts and hot kitchens.

Valrhona produces a great milk chocolate, with 40 per cent cocoa solids, and the Swiss make some of the best milk chocolate in the world, so you could try Lindt.

Preheat the oven to 180°C/350°F/Gas Mark 4.

Place the almonds in a bowl and toss them in the Cointreau until they are all coated. Add the icing sugar and mix well, making sure the nuts are well coated in the sugar too. Transfer the nuts to a baking sheet lined with baking parchment, place in the oven and bake for 10–15 minutes, until golden brown, turning them frequently with a spatula so they cook as evenly as possible. Remove from the oven and leave to cool completely.

For the next stage, you will need 3 small metal bowls, about 15–20cm/6–8 inches in diameter and not too deep. Melt the cocoa butter in a small pan, then transfer it to one of the bowls and keep warm (you may need to reheat it gently if it cools down too much, to prevent it solidifying). Place the cooled nuts in another of the bowls. Have the tempered chocolate to hand.

Using the remaining empty bowl, take a small handful of the toasted almonds, add a teaspoon of cocoa butter (or hazelnut oil) and mix well. Add enough milk chocolate to hold the nuts together. The purpose of the cocoa butter is to thin the chocolate so you can see the shape of the nuts through it. Too much chocolate will result in a pool of excess chocolate – or 'feet', as we call it – around the base of the roche once it has been spooned on to the tray; too much cocoa butter will make the chocolate too thin, so it won't adhere to the nuts. Play around with the quantities until you achieve perfect results.

Immediately spoon the nuts in small clumps on to trays lined with baking parchment or nonstick baking mats. Do this as quickly as you can, before the chocolate starts to set and the clusters lose the smoothness and shine that make them so attractive. Work with small handfuls of nuts at a time and keep repeating the process for perfect results. Store in a sealed container in the fridge to stop the chocolate sweating.

PÂTÉ DE FRUIT

a little spray oil or butter
700g/1lb 9oz fresh raspberries
500g/1lb 2oz preserving sugar
70ml/2$\frac{1}{4}$fl oz liquid glucose
150ml/5fl oz water
12g/$\frac{1}{2}$oz apple pectin (or ordinary
   pectin)
1 teaspoon lemon juice
100g/3$\frac{1}{2}$oz granulated sugar

MAKES 40—50

These lovely jellies are so fruity and look like little sparkling jewels. They keep for weeks and are a fantastic way of using up overripe fruit or berries that are soft and mushy. You can also use apple and grape juice instead of fruit purée. This recipe is for raspberry jellies, as fruits with a high pectin content work best. Besides raspberries, blackcurrants, apricots, plums and apples are all good choices. Hard fruits will need to be cored or pitted and chopped, then cooked until soft before use.

When I was pastry chef at the Portman Hotel in London, Frances Bissell, who was then The Times *food writer, came in with a huge basket of fresh damsons to show me how to make pâté de fruit. I really love the old English fruits, and damsons are among my favourites. Frances spent forever cooking the damsons and passing them through a large, flat sieve to obtain a smooth purée. When she had finished, her pâté de fruit proved to be stunning. Her recipes never fail to work.*

Lightly grease a 15cm/6 inch square baking tin, at least 2.5cm/1 inch deep, with a little spray oil or butter and line the base and sides with cling film. Make sure the cling film lies as flat as possible on the base.

Blitz the raspberries in a food processor or blender, then pass through a sieve to remove the pips. Weigh the purée – you will need 500g/1lb 2oz. Stir 50g/1$\frac{3}{4}$oz of the preserving sugar into the weighed purée.

In a large, heavy-based saucepan, mix the remaining preserving sugar with the glucose and water. Bring to the boil over a low heat, stirring until the sugar and glucose have dissolved. Place a sugar thermometer in the pan and turn up the heat to high. Boil, without stirring, until the mixture reaches 130°C/265°F on the sugar thermometer.

In a small bowl, mix the raspberry purée with the apple pectin. Once the syrup has reached the required temperature, add the purée and stir to combine. The temperature will drop. Bring the temperature up to 103°C/217°F. Do not stir the mix. Add the lemon juice and continue to cook to 106°C/223°F. Remove the sugar thermometer and place it in a jug of warm water. Stir the fruit mixture once or twice and then pour it immediately into the prepared tin. Place the tin on a wire rack and leave to cool and set overnight at room temperature, uncovered.

The next day, cut the mixture into cubes using a serrated bread knife. Place the granulated sugar on a plate and roll the cubes in the sugar until they are completely covered. Place them on a baking tray lined with baking parchment and leave to dry for an hour.

The pâté de fruit looks really pretty stacked on a small plate or gift wrapped in boxes lined with paper. Store in an airtight tin but not in the fridge, or the sugar on the outside of the pâté will dissolve. It will keep for 3–4 weeks.

TURKISH DELIGHT

450g/1lb caster sugar
1 teaspoon lemon juice
145g/5oz cornflour
1/2 teaspoon cream of tartar
2 teaspoons rosewater
red food colouring (optional)

To finish
250g/9oz icing sugar
50g/1³/₄oz cornflour

MAKES ABOUT 40 PIECES

This soft, tender sweet was invented 250 years ago by the Turkish confectioner, Bekir Effendi, for the Sultan to woo his many mistresses with. Effendi's shop – Ali Muhiddin Haci Bekir Confectioners – high up in the mountains of Anatolia, is still in existence today. I have not been there myself but I hear that it turns out the most sumptuous Turkish delight in the whole of Turkey. It is often flavoured with rosewater or lemon and rolled in icing sugar.

This recipe comes from my friend, Amanda Swallow. We used to make several huge 60 x 40cm/24 x 20 inch frames of it for the banqueting petits fours at Claridges in London. The whole department would be perfumed with the smell of rosewater during the endless hours it took for the Turkish delight to set and dry. I used to enjoy cutting the slabs into perfectly equal cubes, then rolling them in equally large trays of icing sugar. Mandy made many versions of this recipe – my favourite was vodka and lime.

Line a 15cm/6 inch square baking tin with cling film, then oil the film lightly. Make sure the sides of the pan are lined as well as the base.

Place the caster sugar, lemon juice and 250ml/9fl oz water in a large, heavy-based pan. Stir over a medium heat until the sugar has dissolved, then turn up the heat and bring to the boil. Put a sugar thermometer in the pan, reduce the heat and simmer without stirring until the sugar reaches soft-ball stage (118°C/245°F). Remove from the heat straight away.

While the sugar is boiling, combine the cornflour and cream of tartar, then mix to a smooth liquid with 250ml/9fl oz water. Place in a heavy-based saucepan and bring to the boil over a medium heat, whisking continuously (start to heat the cornflour mixture as soon as the sugar has reached 118°C/245°F and is resting; this allows the sugar to sit just long enough to cool but not so long that it gets too thick to pour). Pour the hot sugar syrup into the cornflour mixture and continue to simmer over a low heat for about 45 minutes to 1 hour, stirring frequently to prevent sticking. It will change to a very light golden colour. As it reaches the last 15 minutes of cooking time, you will need to stir it continuously to prevent it sticking to the bottom of the pan and burning.

Stir in the rosewater and add a few drops of red food colouring, if desired. Pour into the lined tray and spread evenly. Leave to cool in the tin, uncovered, overnight.

The next day, sift the icing sugar and cornflour for finishing on to a sheet of baking parchment on a tray. Cut the Turkish delight into cubes and roll them in the mixture on the tray.

Claire's Notes
• I like to leave my Turkish delight for a day once it has been coated in the icing sugar, so it firms up on the outside a little. Leave in a cupboard, uncovered, on a tray.

COFFEE AND WALNUT FUDGE

750g/1lb 10oz granulated sugar
250ml/9fl oz liquid glucose
315ml/10^1/$_2$fl oz double cream
375g/13oz milk chocolate
   (minimum 33 per cent cocoa
   solids), finely chopped
250g/9oz walnuts, chopped
75g/2^3/$_4$oz unsalted butter
1 teaspoon coffee extract, such as
   Camp coffee essence

This can be tricky to make, so use a sugar thermometer to eliminate the possibility of overcooking the fudge. It's an extremely versatile recipe and all sorts of variations are possible. Candied fruits, nuts, and oils such as sweet orange oil, almond oil or lemon oil work the best. Pastes such as chocolate hazelnut spread or peanut butter also work well, as does vanilla extract or seeds.

Fudge is one of those things that all age groups love, and it makes a wonderful gift, so why not box it with pretty tissue paper or wrap in cellophane bags and tie with ribbon as the perfect present for sweet-toothed friends?

Line the base and sides of a baking tray with baking parchment. Place the sugar, glucose and cream in a large, heavy-based saucepan and stir well to mix all the ingredients thoroughly. Cook over a medium heat, stirring until the sugar has completely dissolved, then raise the heat and bring to the boil, stirring all the time. Place a sugar thermometer in the pan and lower the temperature slightly. Cook, without stirring, until the fudge reaches 124°C/255°F. (If you are making the fudge in America, you will probably only have to take it to a temperature of 110°C/230°F because of the difference in the consistency of the cream; when it is ready it will turn light brown.) Remove from the heat immediately and mix in the chocolate, nuts, butter and coffee as quickly as possible.

Pour into the lined baking tray and leave to cool completely, preferably overnight. Do not place the tray in the fridge. Cut into pieces as desired.

Claire's Notes
• The fudge will boil up high in the pan, so make sure your saucepan is 3 or 4 times the size of the ingredients. Be careful when boiling the fudge, as it does not look as hot as it is and it burns very easily. Stir gently when adding the chocolate and other ingredients at the end, being careful not to splash. Keep the spoon away from your face.
• Have a jug of warm water by the stove; when the fudge reaches the correct temperature you can place the thermometer in the jug to help clean it immediately and keep the stove top clean.
• If you like your fudge to have a granular texture, stir it very well for 2–3 minutes once it reaches the required temperature. This starts the crystallisation process and makes the texture slightly grainy.
• If you prefer, you can replace the milk chocolate with white or dark chocolate. I like white chocolate with dried cranberries and blueberries or dark chocolate with orange oil and candied orange pieces.

MARSHMALLOWS AND HOT CHOCOLATE

For the marshmallows
350g/12oz caster sugar
150ml/5fl oz liquid glucose
7$\frac{1}{2}$ gelatine leaves
250ml/9fl oz water
2 medium egg whites
2 teaspoons vanilla extract
$\frac{1}{2}$ teaspoon salt
200g/7oz icing sugar

For the hot chocolate
700ml/25fl oz whole milk
600ml/20fl oz water
300g/10$\frac{1}{2}$oz Chuao chocolate or
   other dark 60–70 per cent
   chocolate of your choice, finely
   chopped

SERVES 6

Claire's Notes
• This is another recipe where the chocolate just has to be Chuao from Amadei (see page 148). Of course, we all have our favourites and if Chuao is not yours, then try the more earthy, robust Toscano Black 70%, also from Amedei.
• The marshmallow will be sticky until it is coated in the icing sugar. Keep a damp cloth nearby to keep your hands from getting sticky too.
• Marshmallows will keep for a few weeks. Store them at room temperature in a tin or plastic container with a little of the icing sugar to roll round in.
• For that moment of total all-out chocolate heaven, spoon a large dollop of whipped cream on top of the hot chocolate along with the floating marshmallows and then top with shavings of chocolate.

Ah, America, home of the marshmallow. This terrific recipe came to me from my chef de partie and co-worker at The French Laundry, Courtney Schmidig. Of course it was the Egyptians who first enjoyed the gooey marshmallow, which they made by mixing egg whites and sugar into a fluffy form with the mallow root sap, found in marshes – hence the name. Much later, the French modified the process to produce them commercially and keep up with demand. But it was the Americans who made marshmallows what they are today, adding gelatine and using a special machine to create the familiar shape.

Grease a 30 x 20cm/12 x 8 inch baking tray, then line the base and sides with baking parchment. Grease the parchment.

Put the sugar and glucose in a large, heavy-based pan and stir well. Place over a low heat and stir continuously until they both melt. Wash down the sides of the pan with a pastry brush dipped in cold water so they are free of any sugar or glucose. Turn the heat up high and bring to the boil. Put a sugar thermometer in the pan and boil, without stirring, until the mixture reaches soft-ball stage (118°C/245°F).

As soon as the sugar is boiling, prepare the other ingredients. Soak the gelatine in a large bowl of cold water for about 5 minutes, until completely softened. Remove and squeeze out excess water. Put the gelatine in a saucepan with the 250ml/9fl oz water and place over a low heat. Stir constantly until the gelatine has melted. Transfer the mixture to a freestanding electric mixer fitted with the whisk attachment. Add the egg whites and start the machine on a medium-high speed. Whisk until the egg whites form soft peaks.

When the sugar has reached the correct temperature, turn down the machine to a low speed and carefully pour the hot sugar into the whites near the edge of the bowl – don't pour directly on to the whisk or it will splash. Increase the speed to medium again and beat for 2 minutes, then increase to high and beat for about 10 minutes, until the mixture is full and glossy.

Lower the speed and add the vanilla and salt. Beat for a further minute, then spoon the mixture into the prepared tray. Leave to set, uncovered, overnight at room temperature.

Cut the mixture into whatever shape you like, using a knife dipped in warm water or a wet cutter. Sift the icing sugar into a bowl and toss the cut marshmallows in it to coat. Leave on a tray for a few hours so the outside of the marshmallow forms a skin.

To make the hot chocolate, put half the milk and all the water in a heavy-bottomed pan and bring to the boil. Pour this over the chopped chocolate in a bowl and whisk well to melt the chocolate. Add the remaining cold milk.

Carefully pour the hot mixture into a blender and blitz for 2–3 minutes, until frothy. Do this in batches, being careful not to overfill the blender, so there is room for the mix to froth up. Start the blender on a low speed and gradually work up to a medium to high speed to prevent spillages and burns. Check the temperature of the hot chocolate – it should be hot but not boiling, so reheat if necessary. Pour into 6 large mugs and serve with the marshmallows.

SUPPLIERS

All the companies listed below offer a mail-order service unless otherwise stated.

UNITED KINGDOM

CHOCOLATE

THE CHOCOLATE SOCIETY
Phone 0845 230 8899
www.chocolate.co.uk
Stocks the Valrhona chocolate range, including Manjari.

KEYLINK LTD
Green Lane
Ecclesfield
Sheffield S35 9WY
Phone 0114 245 5400
www.keylink.org
Chocolate products, including cocoa butter, baker's chocolate (listed as compound coating) and confectionery items.

KING'S
2 Mill Farm Business Park
Millfield Road
Hanworth
Middlesex TW4 5PY
Phone 020 8894 1111
www.kingsfinefood.co.uk
Stocks Amedei chocolate.

FREEZE-DRIED BERRIES

BODDINGTONS
The Ashes
Tregoney Hill
Mevagissey
Cornwall PL26 6RQ
Phone 01726 842346
www.boddingtonsberries.co.uk

COMMERCIAL FREEZE DRY
45 Roman Way
Longridge Road
Ribbleton, Preston
Lancashire PR2 5BD
Phone 01772 654441
www.commericalfreezedry.co.uk

POWDERED FOOD COLOURING AND GOLD LEAF

A PIECE OF CAKE
18-20 Upper High Street
Thame
Oxon OX9 3EX
Phone 01844 213428
www.apieceofcakethame.co.uk

VANILLA PODS

OAKLEAF EUROPEAN LTD
Oakleaf House
Station Approach
Ashley Road
Bournemouth BH1 4NB
Phone 01202 393311
www.oakleaf-european.co.uk

SPECIALIST PASTRY AND CAKE DECORATING EQUIPMENT

A PIECE OF CAKE
Contact details as above.

E. RUSSUM AND SONS LTD
Edward House
Tenter Street
Rotherham S60 1LB
Phone 01709 372345
www.russums-shop.co.uk
All speciality pastry equipment, including dipping forks, comb scrapers, cake crimpers, knives, moulds and tins.

CHOCOLATE BOXES, RIBBONS AND PACKAGING

KEYLINK LTD
Contact details as above.

GENERAL BAKING EQUIPMENT

ALAN SILVERWOOD LTD
Ledsam House
Ledsam Street
Birmingham B16 8DN
Phone 0121 454 3571
www.alansilverwood.co.uk
Manufactures a Battenburg cake tin. No mail order but the website has a list of stockists.

DIVERTIMENTI
Phone 0870 129 5026
www.divertimenti.co.uk

LAKELAND
Alexandra Buildings
Windermere
Cumbria LA23 1BQ
Phone 015394 88100
www.lakeland.co.uk

LÉON JAEGGI AND SONS LTD
77 Shaftsbury Avenue
London W1D 5DU
Phone 020 7580 1974
*Everything you could want for
baking, all under one roof. No
mail order.*

PAGES
121 Shaftsbury Avenue
London WC2H 8AD
Phone 0845 373 4017
*An Aladdin's cave of pastry equipment,
at trade prices. No mail order.*

SALAMANDER COOKSHOP
57 High Street
Wimborne
Dorset BH21 1HS
www.salamandercookshop.com
*Stocks Battenburg cake tins and
madeleine tins.*

CHOCOLATIER ELECTRONIQUE
10a Albert Court
London SW7 2LB
Phone 0800 783 2568
www.chocolatier-electro.com

AMEDEI US
www.amedei-us.com

CHOCOSPHERE
PO Box 2237
Tualatin
Oregon 97062
Phone 1-877-992-4626
www.chocosphere.com
*Sells Manjari chocolate and cocoa
butter.*

NUTS ONLINE
1201 E Linden Avenue
Linden
NJ 07036
Phone 800-558-6887
www.nutsonline.com

WILDERNESS FAMILY NATURALS
Box 538
Finland MM55603
Phone 1-800-945-3801
www.wildernessfamilynaturals.com

THE BAKER'S CATALOGUE
58 Billings Farm Road
White River Junction
Vermont 05001
Phone 800-343-3002
www.kingarthurflour.com

SUGARCRAFT
2715 Dixie Highway
Hamilton, Ohio 45015
www.sugarcraft.com

COOK FLAVORING COMPANY
200 Sherwood Road
Paso Robles,
California 93446
Phone 800-735-0545
www.cooksvanilla.com

SUGARCRAFT
Contact details as above.

J. B. PRINCE COMPANY
36 East 31st Street
New York, NY 10016-6821
Phone 800-473-0577
www.jbprince.com

WILLIAMS-SONOMA (AMERICA)
Phone 877-812-6235
Stores across America
www.william-sonoma.com

CHOCOVISION
Phone 800-324-6252
www.chocovision.com

INDEX

A

Adult lemon trifle 46
Almond roches 226
almonds
  Apricot and almond jalousie 88–9
  Four-nut Florentines 22
  Frascati biscuits 17
  Succès 108–9
  Amaretti 26
apples
  Apple and blackberry bande aux fruits 70–2
  Apple and cinnamon charlotte 186
  Apple and cinnamon steamed sponge pudding 176
  Apple and poppy seed cake 37
  Apple, cinnamon and sultana strudel 85
  Bramley apple and cinnamon risotto 189
  Tarte Tatin 73
Apricot and almond jalousie 88–9
Arlettes 29
assembling desserts 138

B

Baked chocolate mousse 144–6
Baked vanilla cheesecake 140
Bakewell tart 62
baking blind 61
bananas: Frosted banana cake 40
Battenburg cake 47–9
biscuits and cookies
  Amaretti 26
  Arlettes 29
  Chocolate chip cookies 16
  Chocolate-dipped gingernuts 21
  Four-nut Florentines 22
  Frascati biscuits 17
  French macaroons 25
  Goober cookies 15
  Langues de chat 216
  Oatmeal, pecan and raisin cookies 14
  Sablé biscuits 208
  Shortbread 12
  Wedding fingers 18
  Bitter chocolate, praline brûlée, espresso torte 156–7
  Black Forest trifle 142–3
blackberries
  Apple and blackberry bande aux fruits 70–2
  Blackberry compote 72
Blackcurrant spoom 198
Blood orange, cara cara and

mandarin jellies with pink grapefruit haché 170
blueberries: Fig and blueberry crème fraîche tarts 82–4
boiling sugar 136
Bramley apple and cinnamon risotto 189
bread and butter pudding, Marmalade 174
brownies, Chocolate fudge 53
buttermilk: Yoghurt and buttermilk panna cotta 132
butterscotch
  Butterscotch sauce 130
  White chocolate, butterscotch and macadamia nut whips 130

C

cakes
  all-in-one method 33
  creaming method 32
  lining tins 33
  whisked method 32–3
  Apple and poppy seed cake 37
  Battenburg cake 47–9
  Carrot cake 34
  Chocolate fudge brownies 53
  Chocolate red wine cake 50–2
  Frosted banana cake 40
  Fruitcake 41
  Gingerbread 42
  Lemon cake 46
  Orange pistachio cakes 38
  Sachertorte 45
Candied peanuts 78–9
caramel
  making caramel 136–7
  Caramel topping 93
  Caramelised salted pecan nuts 197
  Crème caramel 123
  Feuilletine caramel 147
  Rich chocolate ganache tart with salted caramel and candied peanuts 78–9
Carrot cake 34
champagne
  Pink champagne granité 205
  Pink champagne truffles 225
Chantilly cream 86, 192
Charlotte royal 162–4
cheesecake, Baked vanilla 140
cherries: Black Forest trifle 142–3
chestnut: Vacherin Mont Blanc 104
chocolate
  chocolate curls 213–14
  piping chocolate 215
  tempering chocolate 212–13
  Almond roches 226
  Baked chocolate mousse 144–6

Bitter chocolate, praline brûlée, espresso torte 156–7
Black Forest trifle 142–3
Chocolate and peanut cookies
Chocolate and pistachio semifreddo 200
Chocolate and raspberry dome 148–9
Chocolate chip cookies 16
Chocolate chip steamed sponge pudding 176
Chocolate éclairs 94–5
Chocolate fudge brownies 53
Chocolate red wine cake 50–2
Chocolate-dipped gingernuts 21
Feuilles d'automne 114–15
Feuilletine caramel 147
Four-nut Florentines 22
Frascati biscuits 17
French macaroons 25
Marshmallows and hot chocolate 233
Mint chocolate chip ice cream sandwiches 208
Opéra 158–9
Pink champagne truffles 225
Rich chocolate ganache tart with salted caramel and candied peanuts 78–9
Sachertorte 45
Strawberry, black pepper and balsamic vinegar truffles 222
Tia Maria and coffee délice 150–2
Venus nipples 218
Warm chocolate and raspberry tarts 66–7
Warm chocolate fondant 184
White chocolate, butterscotch and macadamia nut whips 130
choux pastry
  Chocolate éclairs 94–5
  Crème puffs 93
  technique 61
cinnamon
  Apple and cinnamon charlotte 186
  Apple and cinnamon steamed sponge pudding 176
  Apple, cinnamon and sultana strudel 85
  Bramley apple and cinnamon risotto 189
Citrus meringue quiffs 110–12
coffee
  Bitter chocolate, praline brûlée, espresso torte 156–7
  Coffee and walnut fudge 230
  Deluxe coffee ice cream 194
  Opéra 158–9
  Tia Maria and coffee délice 150–2

coloured sugar 127
compotes
  Blackberry compote 72
  Raspberry compote 201
cookies see **biscuits and cookies**
cream, whipping technique 138
Crème Anglaise 118–19
Crème brûlée 124
Crème caramel 123
crème fraîche: Fig and blueberry crème fraîche tarts 82–4
Crème puffs 93
Crystallised rose petals 42
custards and creams
  baked custard technique 119
  stirred custard technique 118
  Crème Anglaise 118–19
  Crème brûlée 124
  Crème caramel 123
  Fruit fool 127
  Lemon posset 120
  Spiced pumpkin custard with orange-infused granola 126
  Syllabub 131
  White chocolate, butterscotch and macadamia nut whips 130
  Yoghurt and buttermilk panna cotta 132

D

Deluxe coffee ice cream 194
desserts
  Baked chocolate mousse 144–6
  Baked vanilla cheesecake 140
  Bitter chocolate, praline brûlée, espresso torte 156–7
  Black Forest trifle 142–3
  Blood orange, cara cara and mandarin jellies with pink grapefruit haché 170
  Charlotte royal 162–4
  Chocolate and raspberry dome 148–9
  Feuilletine caramel 147
  Green tea and jasmine délice 153–5
  Hibiscus jellies with red berries 168
  Opéra 158–9
  Passionfruit and mango terrine with exotic fruits 165–7
  Tia Maria and coffee délice 150–2
dried fruit
  Fruitcake 41
  Old-fashioned Eccles cakes 81
Dumph noodle 179–80

E

Eccles cakes, Old-fashioned *81*
egg *whites, whisking 98*

F

Feuilles d'automne *114–15*
Feuilletine caramel *147*
Fig and blueberry crème fraîche
    tarts *82–4*
Four-nut Florentines *22*
Frascati biscuits *17*
French macaroons *25*
Frosted banana cake *40*
fruit
    Fruit fool *127*
    Hibiscus jellies with red
        berries *168*
    Passionfruit and mango
        terrine with exotic fruits
        165–7
    Red berry meringue heart to
        share *107*
    Summer berries steamed
        sponge pudding *176*
    Tropical fruit pavlova *100*
    Tutti frutti vol-au-vents *90–2*
    see also **dried fruit;**
        individual types of fruit
Fruitcake *41*
fudge, Coffee and walnut *230*

G

gelatine, *using 137–8*
ginger
    Chocolate-dipped gingernuts
        21
    Gingerbread *42*
    Gingerbread men *21*
    Lime and ginger sorbet *202*
golden syrup
    Steamed treacle sponge *176*
    Treacle tart *64*
Goober cookies *15*
Gooseberry, brown sugar and
    mascarpone tart *65*
granité, Pink champagne *205*
Granola *126*
grapefruit
    Blood orange, cara cara and
        mandarin jellies with pink
        grapefruit haché *170*
Citrus meringue quiffs *110–12*
Green tea and jasmine délice
    153–5

H

hazelnuts
    Feuilles d'automne *114–15*
    Four-nut Florentines *22*
    Succès *108–9*

Hibiscus jellies with red berries
    168
Honey madeleines *217*
Hot chocolate soufflés *181–3*

I

ice-cream machines 192
ices
    Blackcurrant spoom *198*
    Chocolate and pistachio
        semifreddo *200*
    Deluxe coffee ice cream *194*
    Lemon sorbet with raspberry
        compote *201*
    Mango, lime and ginger
        sorbets *202*
    Mint chocolate chip ice cream
        sandwiches *208*
    Orange and Grand Marnier
        soufflé glacé *206–7*
    Pink champagne granité *205*
    Popcorn sherbet *197*
    Quick strawberry ice cream
        193
    Salted pistachio ice cream *196*
    Vanilla ice cream with
        chantilly cream and hot
        chocolate sauce *192*
    Wimbledon knickerbocker
        glory *193*

L

Langues de chat *216*
lemon
    Adult lemon trifle *46*
    French macaroons *25*
    Lemon cake *46*
    Lemon meringue *101–3*
    Lemon posset *120*
    Lemon sorbet with raspberry
        compote *201*
    Lemon tart *74–6*
lime
    Citrus meringue quiffs
        110–12
    Lime and ginger sorbet *202*
    Mango and kaffir lime
        mirliton tart *77*
lining cake tins 33

M

macadamia nuts: White
    chocolate, butterscotch and
    macadamia nut whips *130*
macaroons, French *25*
madeleines, Honey *217*
mango
    Mango and kaffir lime
        mirliton tart *77*
    Mango, lime and ginger
        sorbets *202*

    Passionfruit and mango
        terrine with exotic fruits
        165–7
Marmalade bread and butter
    pudding *174*
Marshmallows and hot
    chocolate *233*
marzipan, Walnut and pistachio
    221
mascarpone: Gooseberry,
    brown sugar and mascarpone
    tart *65*
meringue
    techniques 98
    Blackcurrant spoom *198*
    Citrus meringue quiffs
        110–12
    Feuilles d'automne *114–15*
    Lemon meringue *101–3*
    Red berry meringue heart to
        share *107*
    Succès *108–9*
    Tropical fruit pavlova *100*
    Vacherin Mont Blanc *104*
mille-Feuilles, Strawberry *86*
Mincemeat steamed sponge
    pudding *176*
Mint chocolate chip ice cream
    sandwiches *208*
mousse, Baked chocolate *144–6*

N

Nougatine *108*

O

Oatmeal, pecan and raisin
    cookies *14*
Old-fashioned Eccles cakes *81*
Opéra *158–9*
orange
    Citrus meringue quiffs
        110–12
    Orange and Grand Marnier
        soufflé glacé *206–7*
    Orange pistachio cakes *38*
    Spiced pumpkin custard with
        orange-infused granola *126*

P

Pain de Gênes *101*
panna cotta, Yoghurt and
    buttermilk *132*
Passionfruit and mango terrine
    with exotic fruits *165–7*
pastry
    baking blind 61
    choux pastry 61
    puff pastry 58–9
    Quick puff pastry *60*
    rolling out and lining a tin
        60–1
    shortcrust pastry 58
    sweet pastry 58

Three-quarters puff pastry
    59–60
Apple and blackberry bande
    aux fruits *70–2*
Apple, cinnamon and sultana
    strudel *85*
Apricot and almond jalousie
    88–9
Arlettes *29*
Bakewell tart *62*
Chocolate éclairs *94–5*
Crème puffs *93*
Fig and blueberry crème
    fraîche tarts *82–4*
Gooseberry, brown sugar and
    mascarpone tart *65*
Lemon tart *74–6*
Mango and kaffir lime
    mirliton tart *77*
Old-fashioned Eccles cakes *81*
Rich chocolate ganache tart
    with salted caramel and
    candied peanuts *78–9*
Strawberry mille-feuilles *86*
Tarte Tatin *73*
Treacle tart *64*
Tutti frutti vol-au-vents *90–2*
Warm chocolate and
    raspberry tarts *66–7*
Pâté de fruit *228*
pavlova, Tropical fruit *100*
peanut butter: Goober cookies
    15
peanuts, Candied *78–9*
pecan nuts
    Caramelised salted pecan nuts
        197
    Oatmeal, pecan and raisin
        cookies *14*
petits fours
    Almond roches *226*
    Coffee and walnut fudge *230*
    Honey madeleines *217*
    Langues de chat *216*
    Marshmallows and hot
        chocolate *233*
    Pâté de fruit *228*
    Pink champagne truffles *225*
    Strawberry, black pepper and
        balsamic vinegar truffles
        222
    Turkish delight *229*
    Venus nipples *218*
    Verjus-plumped raisin
        financiers *220*
    Walnut and pistachio
        marzipan *221*
pistachio nuts
    Chocolate and pistachio
        semifreddo *200*
    Four-nut Florentines *22*
    Green tea and jasmine délice
        153–5
    Orange pistachio cakes *38*
    Salted pistachio ice cream *196*
    Walnut and pistachio
        marzipan *221*

Plum steamed sponge pudding
    176
Popcorn sherbet 197
poppy seeds: Apple and poppy
    seed cake 37
Praline brûlée 156
puddings
    Apple and cinnamon charlotte
        186
    Bramley apple and cinnamon
        risotto 189
    Dumph noodle 179–80
    Hot chocolate soufflés 181–3
    Marmalade bread and butter
        pudding 174
    Steamed treacle sponge 176
    Sticky toffee pudding 177
    Warm chocolate fondant 184
puff pastry technique
    puff pastry techniques 58–59
    Quick puff pastry 60
    Three-quarters puff pastry
        59–60
pumpkin: Spiced pumpkin
    custard with orange-infused
    granola 126

Q

Quick puff pastry 60
Quick strawberry ice cream 193

R

raisins
    Oatmeal, pecan and raisin
        cookies 14
    Verjus-plumped raisin
        financiers 220
raspberries
    Chocolate and raspberry
        dome 148–9
    French macaroons 25
    Lemon sorbet with raspberry
        compote 201
    Pâté de fruit 228
    Warm chocolate and
        raspberry tarts 66–7
Red berry meringue heart to
    share 107
rice: Bramley apple and
    cinnamon risotto 189
Rich chocolate ganache tart with
    salted caramel and candied
    peanuts 78–9
roches, Almond 226
rose petals, Crystallised 42

S

Sablé biscuits 208
Sachertorte 45
Salted pistachio ice cream 196
Scones 54
semifreddo, Chocolate and

pistachio 200
Shortbread 12
shortcrust pastry 58
sorbets
    Lemon sorbet with raspberry
        compote 201
    Lime and ginger sorbet 202
    Mango sorbet 202
soufflés
    Hot chocolate soufflés 181–3
    Orange and Grand Marnier
        soufflé glacé 206–7
Spiced pumpkin custard with
    orange-infused granola 126
spoom, Blackcurrant 198
Steamed treacle sponge 176
Sticky toffee pudding 177
strawberries
    Charlotte royal 162–4
    Quick strawberry ice cream
        193
    Strawberry, black pepper and
        balsamic vinegar truffles
        222
    Strawberry mille-feuilles 86
    Wimbledon knickerbocker
        glory 193
Succès 108–9
sugar techniques
    boiling sugar 136
    caramel 136–7
    coloured sugar 127
    sugar stages 136–7
    sugar syrup 136
sultanas: Apple, cinnamon and
    sultana strudel 85
sweet pastry 58
Syllabub 131

T

Tarte Tatin 73
tarts
    Bakewell tart 62
    Fig and blueberry crème
        fraîche tarts 82–4
    Gooseberry, brown sugar and
        mascarpone tart 65
    Mango and kaffir lime
        mirliton tart 77
    Rich chocolate ganache tart
        with salted caramel and
        candied peanuts 78–9
    Tarte Tatin 73
    Treacle tart 64
    Warm chocolate and
        raspberry tarts 66–7
Three-quarters puff pastry 59–60
Tia Maria and coffee délice
    150–2
Treacle tart 64
trifles
    Adult lemon trifle 46
    Black Forest trifle 142–3
Tropical fruit pavlova 100

truffles
    Pink champagne truffles 225
    Strawberry, black pepper and
        balsamic vinegar truffles
        222
Turkish delight 229
Tutti frutti vol-au-vents 90–2

V

Vacherin Mont Blanc 104
vanilla
    Baked vanilla cheesecake 140
    Vanilla ice cream with
        Chantilly cream and hot
        chocolate sauce 192
Venus nipples 218
Verjus-plumped raisin financiers
    220

W

walnuts
    Coffee and walnut fudge 230
    Walnut and pistachio
        marzipan 221
    Wedding Fingers 18
Warm chocolate and raspberry
    tarts 66–7
Warm chocolate fondant 184
Wedding fingers 18
White chocolate, butterscotch
    and macadamia nut whips
    130
Wimbledon knickerbocker glory
    193
wine
    Chocolate red wine cake 50–2
see also **champagne**

Y

Yoghurt and buttermilk panna
    cotta 132

ACKNOWLEDGEMENTS

Thank you to Fiona Beckett for introducing me to Absolute Press and having the confidence that I could write this book. Thanks also to everyone at Absolute Press: Jon Croft and Meg Avent, for believing I could write and giving me this wonderful opportunity; Matt Inwood, for the wonderful design; and especially to Jane Middleton, who has not only worked tirelessly on editing my drivel and making this book special but has done it from the other side of the pond. I cannot thank you enough. To Jean Cazals, for the truly amazing and stunningly beautiful photography; and to Sue Rowlands, for her inspired styling.

Enormous thanks to Amanda Swallow and Sarah Crouchman. Not only have they been my loyal and trusted friends since the Portman days, when they were my pastry team, but they have supported me through thick and thin. Amanda, thank you for the ten years plus as my sous-chef. I miss you in my kitchen, life is just not the same. Thank you for the endless hours of work making mise-en-place for the photo shoot for this book before I arrived in the UK, then getting up early and staying up late helping to cook and finish all the wonderful cakes, desserts etc. I could not have done it without you. Your love and friendship mean the world to me.

Thanks to Nigel Frost, executive head chef at the London Hilton Metropole, and Avner On, the general manager, for the use of the pastry kitchen to produce the items photographed in this book.

To my mentors, Ernest Bachmann, formerly head pastry chef at the Intercontinental Hotel, London, and Professor John Huber, formerly senior pastry lecturer at Thames Valley University, for all they taught me, for giving me belief in myself, for working me hard and making me the pastry chef I am today. I owe them everything. To Sara Jayne Stanes, director of the Academy of Culinary Arts, for sharing her love and knowledge of chocolate with me and for being a lovely woman and friend. And to all at the Academy of Culinary Arts, especially Brian Turner, David Dorricott, John Williams, Mike Nadell, Colin Martin and the late Ian Ironside, for nurturing me from the age of 21 all the way to the MOGB. To everyone on the committee of the Association of Pastry Chefs, which does such an amazing job for pastry chefs in the UK, especially Alan Whatley.

Thomas Keller, you are the most amazing person I have ever worked for. Thank you for your constant support and inspiration and for giving me the opportunity of a lifetime to share in the magic of The French Laundry. To Cory Lee, chef de cuisine, for your patience and creativity. Thank you to my present pastry team, Courtney Schmidig, Mimi M'bo, Janine Wiseman, Milton Able, Rob Stutts and Greg Mosko, for testing the recipes and holding the fort when I was sitting at the computer writing this book. Schmidig, you are a great pastry chef in the making. Thanks for the fun and happiness, and I won't mention the splinters in the chocolate from the wooden spoon! To Erin Tichy, Courtney Bone, Charles Bililies, Wendi Adamson, Molly Fleming in the office and Edward Keller, for helping me with just about everything under the sun, I do not know what I would have done without you, bless you all. Thanks, Larry, for letting me use your computer to write this book even if it did make you mad, especially on Thursdays and Fridays. You can have it back now, at least for a while! And to everyone else at The French Laundry who makes it such a wonderful place to be and work.

To Nadine and Andy Fricker and their beautiful family, Chloe, Julien and Fleur, for testing the recipes in a domestic setting.

Lastly and by no means least, to everyone who has worked for me, especially Mandy Swallow, Sarah Crouchman, Russell Chappell, Roz Batty, Mike Zietek, Lizzy Cooper, Charlie Church, Dagmar Pfeiffer, Andrea Ruff, Sarah Hartnett, Sharon O'Hare (née Mullins) and Melanie Ockwell. I am only as good as my team and you were my 'A Team'. Thank you.